SUCCESS AGAINST THE ODDS

Effective Schools in Disadvantaged Areas

National Commission on Education

London and New York

First published 1996
by Routledge
11 New Fetter Lane, London EC4P 4EE

Simultaneously published in the USA and Canada
by Routledge
29 West 35th Street, New York, NY 10001

© 1996 National Commission on Education

Typeset in Garamond by Keystroke, Jacaranda Lodge, Wolverhampton

Printed and bound in Great Britain by Clays Ltd, St Ives PLC

All rights reserved. No part of this book may be reprinted or
reproduced or utilized in any form or by any electronic,
mechanical, or other means, now known or hereafter
invented, including photocopying and recording, or in any
information storage or retrieval system, without permission in
writing from the publishers.

British Library Cataloguing in Publication Data
A catalogue record for this book is available from the British Library

Library of Congress Cataloguing in Publication Data
A catalogue record of this book has been requested

ISBN 0–415–13526–5

CONTENTS

CONTRIBUTORS

1 Fair Furlong Primary School

Agnes McMahon is a senior lecturer in the University of Bristol School of Education, teaching and researching in the field of education management and policy. She is currently researching on school effectiveness and the continuing professional development of teachers.

Jeff Bishop trained as an architect but his interests broadened to cover the human aspects of a range of environmental themes. After some years at the School for Advanced Urban Studies in Bristol, he formed with others an environmental consultancy, BDOR Ltd.

Roger Carrol is a chartered accountant employed by the Bristol and West Building Society in a senior managerial post. He has been active in parent–teacher associations and for the past ten years as parent governor of a large comprehensive school.

Brian McInally is Director of Hartcliffe Withywood Ventures, a not-for-profit training, community development and enterprise agency. He too is a parent governor, of an inner city primary school.

2 Crowcroft Park Primary School

Roy Jobson is Chief Education Officer of Manchester City Council. He is particularly interested in raising the aspirations and attainment of pupils in urban areas and sees his main task as promoting effective education for all.

Viv Bingham, OBE, retired after forty years of industrial experience, mainly in personnel, training and industrial relations. He is now a management consultant and governor of a school and a college in the locality.

Lesley Whitehouse is Chief Executive of Hulme Regeneration Ltd, set up in 1992 to coordinate the planning for the five-year Hulme City Challenge project. The initiative was designed to tackle the physical, economic and social problems of one of Western Europe's most distressed inner city areas.

Bill Rogers is Head of Inspection Services in Manchester Education Department. He is chair of the North West Consortium for the Study of Effectiveness in Urban Schools, and is also an OFSTED registered inspector.

3 Blaengwrach Primary School

Alan Evans is a lecturer in the School of Education at the University of Wales, Cardiff. He was for many years education secretary of the National Union of Teachers before returning to his homeland.

Peter Weavers is an accountant who previously worked in the open-cast mining division of the National Coal Board. Since 1995 he has been Development Director of Ryan Mining Ltd. He is a school governor.

Glyn John is an economist and a Quality Operations Manager of the Welsh Development Agency. He is a local historian with a deep interest in the Welsh valleys.

4 Columbia Primary School

Anne Sofer is Director of Education and Community Services, London Borough of Tower Hamlets. She was a member of the Inner London Education Authority (ILEA) until its dissolution into separate and smaller authorities.

Lesley Klein, at the time of writing, was Chief Executive, Bethnal Green City Challenge Company. Her background is in planning and inner city regeneration. Columbia School lies just outside the City Challenge area, though the community is very similar to that within it.

Judy Porter is Head of Community and Educational Affairs, BP Oil. Her background is in the corporate world of a multi-national company. Her department is engaged in promoting projects to raise aspirations in three London boroughs, including Tower Hamlets.

5 Lochgelly North Special School

John MacBeath is Director of the Quality in Education Centre and Professor at the University of Strathclyde, Glasgow. His research and development work with schools, parent bodies and school boards has had a significant influence on national policy in Scotland in the past decade.

Ron Cully formerly worked in the Chief Executive's department of Strathclyde Regional Council, specialising in policy development and urban programme delivery. For the past nine years he has been managing director of the local development company, Govan Initiative Ltd, Glasgow.

Ron Lander is chair and managing director of Scotlander plc, a business training consultancy. He is a member of the Glasgow Development Agency and the council of the Scottish CBI. He is Visiting Professor attached to the Department of Management Studies of the University of Glasgow.

6 Burntwood Secondary Girls' School

Peter Mortimore has since 1994 been Director of the Institute of Education, University of London, where, in 1990, he had been appointed Professor of Education and Deputy Director. His earlier career included service as a teacher in inner city secondary schools, school inspector, administrator and internationally renowned educational researcher, lecturer and writer.

Howard Davies is Deputy Governor of the Bank of England. He was previously Director General of the Confederation of British Industry (CBI) and Controller of the Audit Commission.

Sarah Portway is a former civil servant and special adviser to the Australian minister with responsibility for education and women's affairs. In 1987 she joined IBM Australia Ltd as a consultant on government relations and is currently Director of Corporate Affairs for IBM UK.

7 Haywood High School

Michael Barber is now at the Institute of Education, London University. Formerly Professor of Education at Keele University, he was also a secondary school teacher and then education officer of the National Union of Teachers.

David Carr is the Managing Partner of Hulme Upright and Partners, a firm of architects and town planners in Stoke-on-Trent employing more than seventy people. In 1994 he became Chair of the Stoke-on-Trent Community Partnership. He is a governor of the local Sixth Form College and a non-executive director of the Staffordshire Training and Enterprise Council.

Margaret Carter is Chief Executive of Stoke-on-Trent Community Partnership, an organisation seeking to develop partnership activities involving the public, private and voluntary sectors. She was previously General Secretary to Stoke-on-Trent Council of Voluntary Service.

8 Hazelwood Integrated College

Anthony Gallagher is lecturer in educational research in the School of Education, Queen's University, Belfast. He has published valuable research in the fields of equal opportunities and community relations and has a general research interest in the role of social policy in ethnically divided societies.

Robert Osborne is Professor of Applied Policy Research in the School of Public Policy, Economics and Law at the University of Ulster. He is currently engaged in a comparative study of higher education in the Republic of Ireland and the province of Northern Ireland.

Robert Cormack is Professor of Sociology in the School of Social Sciences and Dean of the Faculty of Economics and Social Sciences in Queen's University, Belfast. His research interests include participation in and access to higher education, and equal opportunities.

Irvine McKay is an independent consultant, a non-executive director, chartered accountant, stockbroker, and a member of the Belfast Education and Library Board. He is also chairman of the governors of the Jaffe School, and a governor of Ashfield Girls' School and Stanhope Nursery.

Stephen Peover is an Assistant Secretary in the Department of Education for Northern Ireland. He joined the Northern Ireland Civil Service in 1975 and served for thirteen years in the Department of Health and Social Services. He moved to the Department of Education in 1988 and currently heads its Policy Division.

9 St Michael's Roman Catholic Comprehensive School

Gerald Grace is Professor of Education in the University of Durham, School of Education. He was previously chair of the

Department of Education at Victoria University, Wellington, New Zealand. His major contributions have been to urban education studies and education policy.

Diane Bell is the Education and Business Manager for Teesside Training and Enterprise Council and is responsible for the development and implementation of the TEC's education strategy. She coordinates the activities of the COMPACT initiative, the Teacher Placement Programme, the School Associate Programme and Neighbourhood Engineers.

Bill Browne is Managing Director, W. A. Browne Building Services Ltd, a company that has been in Billingham since its inception sixteen years ago. The company is well known for the success of its endeavours to link schools with the world of business.

10 Sutton Centre

Jean Ruddock joined the staff of Homerton College in 1994 as Director of Research. She was previously a founder member of the Centre for Applied Research at the University of East Anglia, moving to a chair in education at Sheffield in 1984. Her research has focused on innovation and change in schools, careers and gender issues.

Kate Clarricoates is Director of the Cambridge Volunteer Centre and had previously been involved in research in the training and support needs of women from multi-ethnic communities.

Reg Norman was until his recent retirement Managing Director of the Agrochemical Division of CIBA-GEIGY UK. He has given distinguished service to a number of agrochemical and agricultural professional associations. He is a trustee of Homerton College.

11 Selly Park Girls' School

Tim Brighouse began as a teacher before entering the field of educational administration in 1967. For ten years from 1978 he was Chief Education Officer for Oxfordshire. In 1989 he was appointed Professor of Education at Keele University, but the lure of education administration proved too strong and in 1993 he was appointed Chief Education Officer for Birmingham.

Shirley Woolley is Director of Frederick Woolley Ltd. She is a member of the Birmingham Education and Business Partnership and of the Birmingham Chamber of Commerce.

Les Milner has for fifteen years been Director of St Basil's Centre Ltd, a charity with the remit of supporting homeless young people.

Lessons in success

Margaret Maden was, until recently, Chief Education Officer for Warwickshire County Council and has been a prominent member of the National Commission on Education since it was established. She spent many years in inner London as a teacher, headteacher, director of a sixth form centre, lecturer and adviser. She writes and speaks regularly on educational matters and is an O.E.C.D. consultant. She is now Professor of Education and Director of the Centre for Successful Schools at Keele University.

Josh Hillman was Research Officer at the National Commission on Education throughout its life. He also worked at the University of London Institute of Education and the then Department of Education and Science. He is now Research Fellow at the Institute for Public Policy Research.

ACKNOWLEDGEMENTS

The work which forms the subject of this book was commissioned by the National Commission on Education as part of the follow-up to its report *Learning to Succeed*. The follow-up project was generously funded by the Paul Hamlyn Foundation. The Commission is most grateful also to British Telecom, Lloyd's Bank and Midland Bank for providing further contributions which made possible this study of schools which have succeeded 'against the odds'.

The work was overseen by a steering group led by a Commissioner, Margaret Maden, who, together with Josh Hillman of the Commission's staff, is responsible for the final chapter reflecting on the conclusions to be drawn from the case studies. The other members of the steering group were Professor Michael Barber, Professor Peter Mortimore, Barry Wakefield, Josh Hillman and myself.

We are immensely grateful to the thirty-seven members of the research teams whose work on the case studies provides the core of the book. The project would not have been possible without the willing cooperation of the staff, pupils, parents and governors of the eleven schools, to whom we wish continuing success.

Especial thanks are due to Josh Hillman, who managed the whole exercise and contributed substantially to the drafting and editing of the volume. During these latter stages, Phil Williams of the Commission's staff also played an indispensable part, in assembling statistics, in preparing the manuscript for publication, and in contributing his own incisive comments. Finally, the support of staff at Routledge, in particular Helen Fairlie and Cyril Poster, has been much appreciated.

Sir John Cassels
Director
National Commission on Education
June 1995

Note: Any terminology which readers might find unfamiliar in this book will probably be found in Appendix B.

The locations of the case study schools
(numbers correspond to those given in the
chapter headings)

INTRODUCTION
The challenge of disadvantage
Josh Hillman

The National Commission on Education has identified educational under-achievement in deprived areas, particularly in inner cities but also in rural locations, as an acute problem. In *Learning to Succeed* it was argued that where multiple disadvantages combine, 'the dice are loaded' against educational success.[1] Despite this, remarkable work is done by many of the schools that face the most difficult challenges. This book is about eleven schools which have succeeded against the odds.

SCHOOLS IN DISADVANTAGED AREAS

The gap in educational performance between schools in advantaged and those in disadvantaged areas is wide and increasing. GCSE results have been improving fairly rapidly overall, but a gap is opening up; schools in the LEAs forming the top quarter in terms of advantage are now achieving results over 50 per cent better than those in the bottom quarter.[2] The gap between individual LEAs is, of course, much greater. What is even more significant is the fact that these gaps are widening over time. Meanwhile, variations between schools are even more striking: a school where nearly all pupils get five good grades at GCSE is often only just down the road from another where only one in ten achieves this.

There is a similar picture in the primary sector. Large discrep-
ancies exist between LEAs in the performance of their seven-year-
olds in Standard Assessment Tasks (SATs), but between a quarter
and a half of the differences are associated with the proportion of
households in social classes I and II.[3]

Examination and test results do not tell the whole story.
OFSTED's survey of schools in disadvantaged urban areas found
that across the system as a whole the residents of these areas are
'poorly served by the education system', and that 'pupils have only
a slim chance of receiving sufficiently challenging and rewarding
teaching throughout their educational career'.[4]

The clear message is that pupils in disadvantaged areas are less
likely to do well at school.

DISADVANTAGE

What are 'the odds' faced by schools in different areas? The term
'disadvantage', defined as 'unfavourable conditions or circumstances,
detriment or prejudice',[5] refers to social and material factors such
as income, unemployment, housing, health and environmental
conditions. In many senses, the term simply means 'poverty'.
Profound social and economic changes have resulted in increasing
disadvantage measured in a variety of ways:[6]

- after a slow and steady decrease between the war and 1977,
  inequality of income has risen rapidly;
- between 1979 and 1992, the poorest quarter of the population
  failed to benefit from economic growth, and the income of the
  poorest tenth after housing costs *fell* by between 9 and 17 per
  cent;
- between 1977 and 1991, the proportion of the population with
  incomes below half the national average rose from 6 to 20 per
  cent, with even higher figures for those with children;
- over a quarter of those in the poorest tenth of the population

are children, a large proportion of whom are in the younger age groups.

It is clear from these facts that the scale of disadvantage is larger now than it was in 1977, particularly for children.

EDUCATIONAL DISADVANTAGE

Educational disadvantage means the denial of equal access to educational opportunities, the tendency to leave education at the first opportunity, and the hindrance of achievement by social and environmental factors.[7] Despite the fact that there is an increasingly standardised school system, through pupils' entitlement to the National Curriculum and a national system of 'quality assurance' of schools through OFSTED inspections, educational disadvantage is as much of an issue as ever. By the age of five, children are already very differently placed in terms of the extent to which they are able to benefit from primary education.

The negative relationship between material and social disadvantage and educational attainment is well established in empirical national and international research findings.[8] Socio-economic and family background factors have been shown to be important influences upon pupils' educational achievements at all stages of their school careers. These factors are strongly related to measures of prior attainment at entry to school.

How does material and social disadvantage translate into lower attainment? Disadvantage both limits access to educational opportunities and reduces the ability of children to benefit from the schooling that they do get. A number of contributory factors are included in the following list.

- Poverty, resulting from unemployment or low incomes, results in stress; and reduces or precludes money being spent by families on learning resources such as books, or learning opportunities such as outings and holidays.

- Poverty also increases the need for teenagers to be in paid employment: in evenings and at weekends, reducing time for homework; in some cases, during the day, causing absenteeism; and at the first opportunity of leaving the education system.
- Health problems are more likely, with their associated effects on physical and intellectual development.
- Housing problems are more likely: for example, overcrowding, bed-sharing, lack of a quiet space for homework, and a greater chance of household accidents.
- Children's environment is less likely to be conducive to their development: for example, greater pollution, limited access to gardens and other places to play.
- There is a greater prevalence of crime and drugs.
- Racism 'stifles learning because children are distracted by it and spend time trying to cope with it'.[9]
- Family disruption is more likely, with increased incidence of depression and neurotic disorder.
- Parents are more likely to have lower levels of education and parenting and educating skills; and less likely to have knowledge about and confidence in the education service.
- Children are less likely to have a secure mastery and understanding of language, to have enough opportunities to read at home, to have high self-esteem, or to be subject to peer-group pressure to succeed at school.

The frequent inter-relation of these various disadvantages has been termed 'multiple deprivation'. Not only do they accumulate, but they also reinforce one another, so that their collective impact is even greater than the sum of the individual effects.

Disadvantage tends to exhibit obstinate survival over time, and between generations. This was recognised in a notable speech in 1972 by Lord Joseph, then Secretary of State for Social Services, in which he drew attention to the 'cycle of deprivation'.[10] Research both before and since then has indeed found considerable evidence of persistence in many of the individual social disadvantages, but also, as Michael Rutter put it: 'many opportunities to break the chain'.[11]

It remains the case that the odds are stacked against schools in poorer areas. The link between disadvantage and educational performance has so far proved too difficult for policy-makers at a national level to break. However, many individual schools in disadvantaged areas have been able to do so, through having vision, providing a challenge to all pupils whatever their perceived capabilities, and by pursuing particular policies and practices. It is this phenomenon that is described and analysed in these case studies of eleven schools 'succeeding against the odds'.

LOCATION OF DISADVANTAGE

In the view of the Policy Studies Institute: 'The decay at the heart of Britain's cities is one of the biggest challenges faced by its government'.[12] Combining factors available from 1991 census data to form indices of deprivation shows urban areas dominating the fifty worst-off districts in the country, in terms of both material deprivation and social deprivation.[13] For reasons already discussed, the performance of most schools in inner city districts is similarly unfavourable.[14] Although not on the scale of the United States, where schools are constantly blamed as a cause rather than a symptom of social and economic problems, the British media perennially run stories about crises in inner city schools.

Multiple disadvantage is not confined to the inner cities, but is also present in suburbs, outlying estates, smaller towns and rural areas.[15] Some of the circumstances are similar to those in inner cities: for example, declining or defunct industries, high unemployment and poor housing. In many rural areas there is a further form of deprivation which stems from the combination of a lack of a social infrastructure and the relative isolation of the communities. For example, rationalisation of services may lead to a village school, library or shop being closed down; if subsequently a local bus is withdrawn, those without access to private transport will suffer a further loss of opportunities.

POLICY DEVELOPMENTS

Individual schools are more than ever in the public eye, and as their responsibilities have increased so have expectations of what they can achieve. Schools have been profoundly affected by a number of policy developments since 1988:

- delegation of funding and responsibilities have made them much more autonomous institutions;
- their funding depends mostly on the number of pupils they can attract;
- the support that they receive from local government has been eroded and in some cases dispensed with altogether;
- parents are encouraged to exercise their consumer power in the new education marketplace through choosing schools for their children;
- the main source of quantitative data on school performance for informing this choice are the league tables of examination results now published in newspapers.

These arrangements can easily discriminate against schools serving disadvantaged communities.

Government attempts to address the problem of disadvantaged schools have been piecemeal. Arrangements for the distribution of resources for education have favoured some disadvantaged areas through the 'Additional Educational Needs' element of the formula for allocation of block grants to local authorities. However, significant anomalies arise from this system, which in practice favour some boroughs which have relatively good educational performance, and work against others which have much poorer results. Similarly, large variations in the local management of schools (LMS) formulas for allocating resources from LEAs to schools mean that, in some authorities, chronically disadvantaged schools receive hardly any extra money.

The government has also had specific initiatives to target resources to schools in disadvantaged areas. Section 11 grants are available for schools with higher proportions of pupils from Commonwealth or ex-Commonwealth countries, to be used for additional teachers for English as a second language. This scheme is now being substantially reduced in scale. For a short period in the early 1990s, there was a small allocation for 'raising standards in inner city schools' under the Grant for Education and Support and Training (GEST) programme of direct grants to LEAs from the DfE, the sort of initiative described by Tim Brighouse as 'time limited dollops – the equivalent of food parcels to the third world'.[16]

There have also been a number of initiatives either at the local level, or in the form of pilot schemes, often highly effective but not followed up.[17] These include LEA drives to direct funds to schools with high numbers of disadvantaged pupils; Reading Recovery for early intervention and intensive help for children with literacy problems; parental involvement schemes; and compacts between employers, schools and pupils.

In general, the attention of policy-makers, the media and the general public is shifting towards the performance of individual schools. There is evidence in particular that the DFEE is seeking to understand the issues at stake and to examine how external support can help schools in the improvement process.[18]

MEASURING SCHOOL PERFORMANCE

League tables of examination results do not tell us what the relative chances of success are for a particular pupil in each of the schools.[19] They tell us how the pupils that entered the schools five years ago fared. Intakes vary enormously, for example, in terms of the academic starting point of the pupils, and the educational background or material well-being of their parents. As has already been indicated, research shows that these advantages and disadvantages are powerful influences on academic achievement throughout a child's time at school, not least at the time when public examinations are sat.

However, taking account of these factors shows that there is plenty of scope for the individual school to make a difference. Schools with similar intakes do not promote the progress of their pupils at the same rate, and indeed there are schools that give such a boost to their pupils as to defy all expectations of a more mechanistic or social determinist kind. In other words, some schools are more effective than others in 'adding value' to pupils' life chances.

SCHOOL EFFECTIVENESS AND SCHOOL IMPROVEMENT

With the fact in mind that schools face different challenges, a large international body of research, with Britain, the United States and the Netherlands at the forefront, has examined the question of what makes a school effective.[20] In most studies, the definition of an effective school is on the lines of that given by Peter Mortimore: 'a school in which students progress further than might be expected from a consideration of its intake'.[21] From this work, a core of findings consistently emerges relating to school organisation and classroom practices which have a positive impact on pupils' progress;[22] and the findings are confirmed by teachers' own perceptions of effective management practice.[23] The important thing about these core characteristics and conditions is that they apply to those schools which are most effective in promoting progress, or those schools whose performance is continually improving over time, whether they be large or small, rural or urban, primary or secondary.

The findings of school effectiveness research do not provide an instant recipe to transform schools. They provide a 'vision of a more desirable place for schools to be but little insight as to how best to make the journey to that place'.[24] This is the central objective of 'school improvement', another international body of research with an associated approach to school development. School improvement is essentially about the strategies and underlying processes of change[25] by which a school can develop on a continuous basis. In the case of schools that face a range of problems, it is about those which recognise the need to improve, define success criteria, and move on to a long-term improvement path.

THE SUCCESS AGAINST THE ODDS PROJECT

As part of the follow-up to *Learning to Succeed*, the National Commission on Education embarked on a major new project on education in disadvantaged areas. It was felt that case studies in which the features, problems, strategies and initiatives of schools that are successful 'against the odds' are described and analysed could be a powerful mechanism for spreading good practice and thus helping others to lever up standards.[26]

The project involved eleven teams from around the United Kingdom, each undertaking to investigate a school which, on the basis of broadly comparable criteria, could be described as 'succeeding against the odds'. Each team included:

- a leading educationist, with knowledge about effective teaching and learning and expertise in school improvement;
- a person from the business world, able to offer fresh insight into the successful management of the school as an organisation and its interaction with the world of work;
- a person working towards the regeneration of disadvantaged areas, to give a perspective in which education is not seen in isolation but as a part of the life of a local community.

The schools were carefully selected by the research teams in close consultation with the National Commission. The selection was informed by academic outcomes adjusted for intake, inspection reports, and advice at the local level.

Collectively, the schools cover a broad spectrum. They include primary schools, with and without nursery classes; secondary schools, with and without sixth forms; and a special school. The locations comprise inner city, suburban, out-of-town estate, small township and rural areas. Type of governance includes local education authority maintained, voluntary and grant-maintained. The schools are scattered throughout all four countries of the United Kingdom (see the map on page xv). Two of the schools are girls' schools, the others are mixed. The pupils in two of the schools are almost exclusively Asian, whereas the catchment areas of other schools comprise predominantly white or ethnically mixed populations. One school is Roman Catholic, and another (in Belfast) 'integrates' Catholic and Protestant pupils. One school describes itself as a 'community school', sharing facilities with those in its neighbourhood. Despite all of these differences, what all the schools have in common is proven experience of overcoming difficult circumstances.

In each case, in-depth investigations of the life and work of the school took place, based on the guidelines which were provided by the Commission and are included as Appendix A. The programmes of each research team varied but generally included several visits to the school; interviews with senior managers, teachers, pupils, parents and governors, and in some cases members of the local community and LEA officers; observation of lessons, assemblies and extra-curricular activities; and examination of documents and statistics relating to the schools. Key facts and figures relating to the schools are included in the panels in each chapter.

The research teams were asked to make particular reference to the ten postulated features of success in *Learning to Succeed* which formed the basis for the proposals for raising achievement in schools. These are listed in the guidelines in Appendix A. They were also asked to examine all aspects of school policy including development planning, teaching methods, classroom organisation and the extent and nature of external support. The response of the school to various recent government reforms was to be probed; so also were issues of accountability arising in the school and how these are perceived by different people. Finally, the researchers were asked to analyse the process of improvement in the school, including its precise objectives, who was involved in setting these, what initiatives were taken and what is needed to maintain and improve present achievements.

The teams have attempted to explain the success of their schools in the accounts which follow. As might have been expected, they vary greatly. Some are detailed accounts of the life and work of the school, drawing on the views of pupils, parents and teachers to show what lies behind the effectiveness of the school. Others are stories of schools that were 'turned round' from being failing schools to being schools on a long-term improvement path. All are celebrations of schools that are transforming the life chances of their pupils.

REFERENCES

1 National Commission on Education (1993) *Learning to Succeed.* London: Heinemann.
2 Smith, T. and Noble, M. (1995) *Education Divides: Poverty and Schooling in the 1990s.* London: Child Poverty Action Group.
3 McCallum, I. (1993) *Testing Seven Year Olds: Performance and Context.* London Research Centre.
4 Office for Standards in Education (1993) *Access and Achievement in Urban Education.* London: HMSO.
5 Rutter, M. and Madge, N. (1976) *Cycles of Disadvantage.* London: Heinemann.
6 Joseph Rowntree Foundation (1995) *Inquiry into Income and Wealth.* York: JRF.
7 Mortimore, J. and Blackstone, T. (1982) *Disadvantage and Education.* London: Heinemann.

8 Douglas, J. (1964) *The Home and the School: the Study of Ability and Attainment in the Primary School.* London: MacGibbon & Kee; Wedge, P. and Prosser, H. (1972) *Born to Fail?* London: Arrow; Davie, R., Butler, N. and Goldstein, H. (1972) *From Birth to Seven.* London: Longman; Rutter and Madge (1976) *Cycles of Disadvantage;* Essen, J. and Wedge, P. (1982) *Continuities in Childhood Disadvantages.* London: Heinemann; Mortimore and Blackstone (1982) *Disadvantage and Education;* Wedge, P. and Essen, J. (1982) *Children in Adversity.* London: Pan; Pilling, D. (1990) *Escape from Disadvantage.* Lewes: Falmer Press.

9 Ranson, S., Martin, J., McKeown, P. and Nixon, J. (1995) *Encouraging Learning: Towards a Theory of the Learning School.* Open University (forthcoming).

10 Joseph, K. (1972) Speech to the Preschool Playgroups Association, 29 June 1972.

11 Rutter, M. (1984) *Continuities and Discontinuities in Socioemotional Development: Empirical and Conceptual Perspectives.* In Emde, R. and Harmon, R. (eds) *Continuities and Discontinuities in Development.* New York: Plenum.

12 Willmott, P. and Hutchison, R. (1992) *Urban Trends 1.* London: Policy Studies Institute.

13 Forrest, R. and Gordon, D. (1993) *People and Places: a 1991 Census Atlas of England.* University of Bristol.

14 Barber, M. (1993) *Raising Standards in Deprived Urban Areas.* In National Commission on Education (1993) *Briefings.* London: Heinemann.

15 Hudson, R. and Williams, A. (1995) *Divided Britain.* Chichester: Wiley.

16 Brighouse, T. (1994) 'Urban deserts or fine cities?' – Education: the alchemist's stone. Times Educational Supplement Greenwich Lecture.

17 Mortimore, P. (1993) *Teaching and Learning in England and Wales.* In Learmouth, J. (ed.) *Teaching and Learning in Cities.* London: Whitbread Education Partnership.

18 Barber, M. (1995) The dark side of the moon: imagining an end to failure in urban education. Times Educational Supplement Greenwich Lecture.

19 Institute of Education (1994) *Assessing School Effectiveness: Summary of a Research Study on Developing Measures to Put School Performance in Context.* London: Office for Standards in Education.

20 For example: Brookover, W., Beady, C., Flood, P., Schweitzer, J. and Wisenbaker, J. (1979) *School Social Systems and Student Achievement: Schools Can Make a Difference.* New York: Praeger; Rutter, J., Maughan, B., Mortimore, P. and Ouston, J. (1979) *Fifteen Thousand Hours: Secondary Schools and their Effects on Children.* London: Open Books; Wilson, B. and

Corcoran, T. (1988) *Successful Secondary Schools*. Lewes: Falmer Press; Mortimore, P., Sammons, P., Stoll, L., Lewis, D. and Ecob, R. (1988) *School Matters: the Junior Years*. Wells: Open Books; Teddlie, C. and Stringfield, S. (1993) *Schools Make a Difference: Lessons Learned from a Ten Year Study of School Effects*. New York: Teachers College Press; Dutch research reviewed in Scheerens, J. (1992) *Effective Schooling: Research, Theory and Practice*. London: Cassell.

21 Mortimore, P. (1991) *The Nature and Findings of Research on School Effectiveness in the Primary Sector*. In Riddell, S. and Brown, S. (eds) *School Effectiveness Research: Its Messages for School Improvement*. HMSO.

22 Sammons, P., Hillman, J. and Mortimore, P. (1995) *Key Characteristics of Effective Schools*. Office for Standards in Education.

23 Bolam, R., McMahon, A., Pocklington, K. and Weindling, D. (1993) *Effective Management in Schools*. London: HMSO.

24 Lezotte, L. (1989) 'School Improvement Based on Effective Schools Research.' *International Journal of Educational Research*, 13 (7).

25 Mortimore, P. (1995) *Effective Schools: Current Impact and Future Potential*. London: Institute of Education.

26 Her Majesty's Inspectorate (1977) *Ten Good Schools: a Secondary School Enquiry*. London: HMSO; Office for Standards in Education (1994) *Improving Schools*. London: HMSO; Louis, K. and Miles, M. (1990) *Improving the Urban High School*. New York: Teachers College Press.

1

FAIR FURLONG PRIMARY SCHOOL
South Bristol

Agnes McMahon, Jeff Bishop, Roger Carrol and
Brian McInally

Fair Furlong is in an area of considerable social and material deprivation, with a high crime rate, a very high proportion of single parents and very little prospect of the development of any industry which might lower the high unemployment rate: all of this might well have a devastating effect on the ethos of any school. At this school a devoted staff, effective leadership and the development of sound policies have done much to counter these adverse conditions. The work of the children, both academic and creative, generates an enthusiasm which communicates itself to parents and the wider community.

This is a study of a primary school in Bristol, a school which has a vibrant, exciting atmosphere, where pupils and teachers work hard and effectively. A school described by governors, parents and teachers as 'marvellous', 'absolutely brilliant', 'exciting', 'inviting' and about which the chair of governors said 'it's all buzzing in the school now'. The classrooms and corridors are filled with displays of children's work, there is a school choir which has sung in Bristol

Cathedral, children study the violin, participate in workshops with artists in residence, enter and win competitions, put on excellent, high-standard performances for their parents at Christmas, look after an area of woodland as part of an environmental project, enjoy and experience success with their academic work and above all are valued as individuals. The school prospectus states:

> 'We try to be a caring school where every child will feel secure, happy and valued and where purposeful learning can take place. We want the children to be happy at school and we want learning at school to be a positive experience . . . we aim at happy and hardworking children who are proud of their achievements.'

In the opinion of the research team, these aims are being achieved. Teachers in schools like this can be justifiably proud of their work, but the achievements here are greater, since this is a school that can accurately be described as one which is succeeding against the odds.

THE SCHOOL COMMUNITY

The data that follow are drawn from 1994 statistics supplied by Bristol City Council and from the bid for government funding by the Bristol City Challenge Steering Group (1992). The school is situated in one of the areas with the highest incidence of poverty in Bristol. Using six indicators – unemployment; free school meals; community charge rebates; children in households with no earners/in households with one lone parent working part-time; long-term illness; mortality rates for those under sixty-five – it is in the quintile of city areas with the highest incidence of poverty. The social characteristics of the area have been summarised as 'very high proportion of lone parents; clear evidence of poor health and premature death; poor community facilities; low educational expectations of young children; unemployment fifty per cent higher than the local average; long term unemployment worst in the city and remoteness from the areas of growth'. It is located about 5 miles from the centre of Bristol, a predominantly white area (98 per cent), in the middle of an outer city housing estate. The estate was built in the 1950s and 1960s with a mixture of semi-detached and terraced housing and flats, many of which are now beginning to deteriorate. About 45 per cent of the housing is owner-occupied; the remainder, owned by the local authority, is the more unpopular or poorer-quality accommodation – for example, high-rise flats. Unemployment in the area is 17.58 per cent; full-time employment is approximately 56 per cent and part-time 18.17 per cent (1991 figures). One of the key problems for the people who live here is that there have been few, if any, local employers since a major factory closed in 1992. The area is remote from the city's growth areas and road access to the city centre and the motorways are poor. This is judged to be one of the main reasons for the lack of private investment and commercial growth. Those people who have work have to travel into the city centre, many of them relying on expensive public transport, since 44.5 per cent of the households do not have cars. 'For a large number of the population, Bristol was regarded as being somewhere else: travelling to the city centre was seen as going into Bristol – a sign of the isolation felt in this area.'

A significant proportion of the families are headed by a single parent, often a young mother: a study completed by a local health centre in 1989 said that, in 70 per cent of families, one or both parents were under twenty-one at the birth of the first child. These families are frequently living in high-rise flats which are unsuitable for bringing up children. An estimated 50 per cent of families in the school catchment area are welfare-dependent. Money for housing, heating and food is in short supply and this can have a detrimental effect on physical health. Central heating in the homes is often absent altogether or too expensive to run, and washing and drying clothes can be a major problem, especially due to the dearth of local laundrettes. Shopping facilities are poor; the child-care facilities are inadequate given the potential demand and leisure provision is under-developed. A 1992 study concluded that about 30 per cent of young people in the area, mainly male, were drug users. Crime and fear of crime are major concerns in the locality.

How do these factors affect the families in the area and what impact do they have on the school? A local priest who ran a community project said that in his view the main problem was 'the lack of ambition, lack of self-worth' experienced by many people:

'There is a lot of hurt, pain, damage and it is very visible – children grow up trying to survive. There is no real feeling of security for the children; they are emotionally deprived. They experience verbal aggression/verbal assault; there is a lot of harshness verbally and physically in human relationships – it is hard to achieve some sense of stability and self-worth. For many children the school is the only area where there is consistency in adult relationships; they experience a sense of belonging and a sense of direction for the first time.'

A further problem that he identified was the lack of positive male role models; women are frequently the central figures in the community and there are many single-parent families headed by women:

> 'Men are often unemployed, at a loose end, not doing much for the community. Community activities are dominated by women. Men are seen in pubs, those who are working are outside the area, there are no jobs in the area to keep men here.'

Although these comments paint a bleak picture, it would be wrong to give the impression that every family is subject to these pressures. Certainly it would be wrong to imply that large numbers of children are neglected by their families. Though they recognise the problems in the community, the school teachers spoke very positively about the support that they received from the parents. One teacher commented:

> 'Historically the area has had a bad name. This is sad because we have some lovely families. They may have poor parenting skills but a lot of love.'

> (Deputy head)

Some of the factors mentioned by the teachers could be found in any area: for example, children spending time on their own because of a parent's unsocial working hours; children staying up late and watching TV and consequently being very tired next day at school. Many children learned to become independent at a very young age:

> 'A lot of children are on their own, parents don't have much time to give them. There isn't much to do after school and facilities in school are very much appreciated by the children.'

> (Class teacher)

> 'Some of my class (7 and 8 year olds) come to school on their own, go off to the shops, a lot are quite influenced, negatively, by an older sibling – it's difficult to get the pitch right.'

> (Class teacher)

One of the teachers echoed the community worker by identifying the problem of limited aspirations as a key issue:

> 'It's an estate, the boundaries are very limited. Families follow the same limited pattern and the aspirations of parents and children are low. I feel it's very important to try and widen their horizons and try and break the pattern.'

It seems that it is not uncommon for those involved in youth training schemes to find sixteen- and seventeen-year-olds who have never left the estate.

A major problem identified by teachers was that children entering the school could be as much as two years behind their peers in a middle-class area in terms of their experiences and skills; language skills were often poor, they might have lacked play experiences, some 'are not even toilet trained'. However, the key issue for the school, in the opinion of teachers, school governors and community workers was that the children's behaviour was difficult to manage. The community worker said that discipline was a major challenge for the teachers:

> 'We are dealing with children who outside the school are accustomed to clouts. Children expect a certain physical reaction to behaviour, there is a lack of conversation between parents and children. There is the difficulty of applying a new set of rules to children who were used to a different set of rules. Teachers have to apply a good deal more of their own personal influence – establish a rapport with kids who don't understand what is going on.'

He felt that poor communication skills led to problems: 'communication is a difficult area – they are used to swearing, no other way of expressing feelings'. He felt that some parents were themselves unable to manage their children's behaviour:

> 'Parents are unable to cope with their children's behaviour – so they collude with the child's behaviour and don't back up the

school. A number are frightened of their kids and have no control of them – parents are trying to survive against their kids and vice versa.'

WHAT IS THE SCHOOL LIKE?

The school is a large, mixed primary school, taking children from ages three to eleven. In September 1994 there were 382 pupils on roll including a forty-five-place nursery class. The nursery operates in two sessions and these children do not stay for lunch; 166 (49 per cent) of the children in the infant and junior classes are registered for free school meals. All the children are white and none of them has English as a second language. The average class size is twenty-seven. In the 1994 autumn term four pupils had statements of special educational needs though this number has since increased. There are twenty-two full-time and part-time teachers (16.2 full-time equivalents (fte)).

The school is predominantly a female environment. The head-teacher is a woman and there is only one male teacher; the caretaker and cleaners are all women. This gender balance is not the result of any deliberate policy; on the contrary, the headteacher said that she would like to have some more male teachers on the staff. However, the headteacher and the governors had developed a rigorous selection and appointment process and she said that the quality of male teachers who had come forward for interviews had been disappointing.

A visit to the school is a lively, stimulating and enjoyable experience. Children and their teachers appear busy and happy and there is a creative 'buzz' in the place; the classrooms are well resourced and organised, brightly painted and contain excellent displays of children's work. Noticeable also is the extensive security. The main school door is kept locked and there is an entry phone system for visitors. Despite having a noisy alarm system, the building has been broken into on several occasions and video recorders and other items of equipment have been stolen. Security is made especially difficult by the fact that there is an open playing field (some 65 acres) at the back of the school which largely belongs to the neighbouring secondary school. The school budget this year for repairs is £11,000, money which the staff would have preferred to spend on resources for learning. The staffroom has bars over two windows; a new CD ROM could not be installed in the library until security bars had been placed on the window. These are the realities of life in an area where the theft rate is high. The junior department in the school was destroyed by fire in August 1991 and arson was suspected. This section of the school has since been refurbished.

THE SCHOOL AS A WORKPLACE

The teaching and non-teaching staff all said that the culture and ethos of the school was positive and supportive, that it was a very good place in which to work and that they enjoyed being there:

'I enjoy it very much, lovely atmosphere, great support of each other – we help each other through good and bad times.'

(Deputy head)

'Exciting, never a dull moment, lots of visitors; the children are very rewarding; it's hard work – there isn't much time to relax. The staff here work really well together and that shows.'

(Class teacher)

'It is challenging, hard work, rewarding, fun; lovely team spirit; sometimes quite soul-destroying but generally quite positive – I love my job and I love working here.'

(Class teacher)

'Very demanding in lots of ways, but very well organised – lots of things planned and prepared. The standard expected here is the best I can do – there is no chance of coasting.'

(Newly qualified teacher)

The school governors were also all very positive about the school. Two parent governors said that the school was inviting and that more parents were now coming into the school, while previously they would have found it threatening. The whole atmosphere was 'brilliant', the children felt secure and valued. They particularly cited the fact that children were encouraged to take reading books home, as this was something that had not happened previously.

WHAT IS BEING ACHIEVED?

Is there any hard evidence that this is a successful school? The headteacher is clear that while pupil learning has improved across the board there is still progress to be made. Reading scores and pupil work are carefully monitored and show signs of improvement from year to year. The teachers are now assessing children on entry and intend to use these data as one means of measuring added value when matched against the SATs (standard attainment

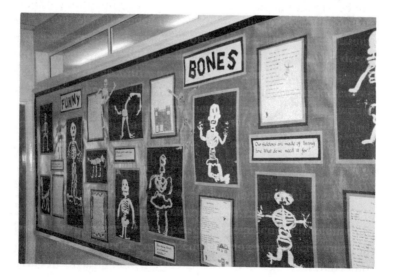

task) scores at Key Stages 1 and 2. For the last two years a reading audit has been conducted across the school and pupil reading scores have been carefully recorded; the staff are now considering also conducting a maths audit. These data, together with SATs scores, will give a broad indication of pupil progress, individually and as a group from year to year. The standard of pupil behaviour is very high and has improved immeasurably in the last four years. There are no unexplained pupil absences because the staff carefully implement the school policy on this issue. The staff provide a lot of extension and enrichment activities for the children: working with an artist in residence; a link scheme with a school in a very middle-class area of the authority; involvement in link projects with schools in Ghana and Malaysia; environmental projects. The children also participate in activities which in a middle-class school would be unremarkable but which in this community are unusual. For instance, the governors all commented upon the fact that pupils now take reading books home; that they can learn to play the violin; that there is a school choir which sings in public concerts; that the pupils enter and win art competitions at local and national level; and that they are polite and well behaved in school. Other indices of the school's effectiveness are that teacher turnover is low, that the staff absentee rate is very low and that the staff enjoy working in the school. The pupil roll has increased by approximately 100 in the last four years. Parental support for the school is strong, with approximately 98 per cent attending parents' evenings and excellent support for any activities – for example, concerts and fairs – organised by the school.

HAS THE SCHOOL ALWAYS BEEN SUCCESSFUL?

The present chair of governors has been a governor of the school for some twenty years and has experience of working with several headteachers. He has seen the school go through good and bad times but is open about the fact that before the appointment of the present headteacher, in June 1990, things were at a very low ebb. The difficulties were compounded by the fact that there were not one but two acting headteachers, the first acting headteacher having become ill, and an acting deputy headteacher put in post (for several months before the present headteacher was appointed). One of the staff who taught in the school at that time commented: 'We were getting lost and needed a strong leader.'

The most obvious and immediate problem was that the children's behaviour was very poor and this made teaching a difficult and stressful experience for the staff. A teacher who was appointed at that time was 'appalled originally by the children and the school'. One of the general assistants said that discipline was a key issue: 'kids did not know whom to relate to – they used to run everywhere'. The headteacher was worried about the amount of bullying by pupils that she found when she came into the school. However, although indiscipline was a matter of daily concern, a more serious problem that the new headteacher identified was the absence of whole-school policies and systems of management. Indeed, so worried was she by the overall condition of the school on her appointment that she wrote formally to the governing body to express her concern. The key issues that she highlighted were: the lack of a whole-school approach and a consistent philosophy and ethos; absence of effective administrative and procedural systems for teaching and non-teaching staff; the need for a school-wide curriculum policy and more detailed and systematic records of pupil progress; the need for strategies to improve pupil behaviour; the lack of adequate financial systems in place for local management of schools (LMS); the very poor condition of the building and the high level of vandalism. A further concern, in the second half of the 1990 summer term, was that there were several vacant posts, two of which carried incentive allowances. Filling the vacant posts required immediate action but, though this was stressful in the short term, the headteacher regarded it as a stroke of good luck in that it enabled her to bring some new people into the school. Her perception of the situation when she arrived was that:

> 'there was no structure in the staffing, no senior management team, no roles that people fulfilled in any way – no feeling of working as a team or to whom to go if you had problems. Staff in order to survive operated within the four walls of the classroom. What happened in the corridor and the playground they couldn't cope with.'

Some four and a half years later conditions in the school are very different: there is a sense of direction and purpose, clear evidence of team work on the part of the teaching and non-teaching staff and considerable evidence of pupil achievement. Yet the community has not changed, indeed some would argue that the social problems have worsened, and several of the original governors and teachers are still in post. What has brought about this transformation?

WHAT ARE THE FACTORS THAT ARE CONTRIBUTING TO THE SCHOOL'S SUCCESS?

The staff and governors who were interviewed were agreed that three factors had made a difference to the school. These were:

- the behaviour policy;
- the display policy;
- the leadership provided by the headteacher and the management systems that she has put in place.

The behaviour policy

The school has a 'good behaviour' policy, which is based on assertive discipline. The headteacher first came across this approach in the mid-1980s when she spent several months as a visiting principal in the United States. The behaviour policy was introduced over three years ago and now operates throughout the school, from the nursery to Year 6. There is one key rule for everyone, which is that everyone will act with courtesy and consideration to others at all times, and this is elaborated in seven supporting statements. The behaviour policy was developed collaboratively by the staff, and they now have a system in place which links the rules to a system of rewards and sanctions and which is clearly understood by the pupils and themselves. All the staff said that this policy has worked extremely well.

The headteacher said that, on taking up her post, she had immediately recognised the high level of stress that pupil behaviour caused the teachers and she was determined to do something about it:

'We needed to look at it as a shared responsibility: people were working in the classroom with different criteria. I came across assertive discipline – such a basic model. You decide on a basic form of acceptable behaviour, set few rules which must be understood by the children and implemented.'

The children are expected to behave as well with the non-teaching staff as with the teachers and these staff operate the same policy of rewards and sanctions. The LEA (local education authority) adviser, who had reviewed the implementation of the policy, said that he had been pleased that it was not crudely behaviourist but focused upon children's self-discipline; it was about children valuing themselves and raising their self-esteem and staff valuing them as people and forming relationships with them. Teachers spoke positively of the way the behaviour policy provided a framework for them:

'One of the best things was the introduction of assertive discipline. In my first year in this school the behaviour was very bad. We adapted the system to suit the school: firm rules and rewards. Children see the system as being very fair – I was amazed to see the change in the children's behaviour. The scheme is reviewed regularly and it really works for us. It does take a lot of the stress out of teaching in an area like this.'

(Class teacher)

The headteacher and the staff strive to create a calm and orderly atmosphere in which the children behave well because they are learning self-discipline rather than because they are constantly chided; the staff in turn model patterns of good behaviour for their pupils. Considerable emphasis is placed on praising and rewarding children for their work and general effort and for good behaviour. The school assembly every Friday morning is used as an opportunity publicly to praise pupils who have been identified by their teachers for good work and behaviour. They come to the front of the hall and receive a certificate from the headteacher which they can take home and keep. Whereas some are rewarded for merit in their work, the efforts of a child who comes to school on time every day after a period of late arrivals will also be recognised. The pupils in Year 6, the leaving class, are given special responsibilities around the school. Each child has a special task which changes every term; they help in the school office, photocopy material for the teachers, act as library monitors and they are also given a pastoral role in relation to the younger pupils, sitting with them at lunch and spending time with them in the classroom on wet playtimes. This pastoral role not only gives the older pupils a sense of responsibility but also reduces the likelihood that the infant pupils will be intimidated or bullied. The intention is that, rather than being intimidated by them, the younger children will see those in Year 6 as people who will take care of them.

The headteacher and the staff are very pro-active when any discipline problems arise. Every effort is made to sort the issue out immediately and parents are asked to come into the school to discuss the matter. The rationale for this is that the child will be helped to overcome the problem if the teacher and the parent are working together.

The display policy

The impression gained on entering the school is of a clean, bright and stimulating environment in which to work. The hall, corridors and classrooms contain brightly coloured displays of children's work which are changed on a regular basis; there are interesting and beautiful objects on show and, in so far as this has been possible, the furniture and fittings in the school have been chosen with an eye to their aesthetic qualities. All the space in the building is utilised and it is used well. It was not always like this. The quality of display was reported to be relatively poor before the appointment of the present headteacher, and teachers were sometimes reluctant to mount displays of work because they would be torn down or disfigured by the pupils. One of the governors said that there used to be mess and paper everywhere: 'going into the classrooms was like an obstacle course'. The changes have not occurred accidentally but are a result of a specific policy on display, developed by the art and craft coordinator and the headteacher, in consultation with the staff. Three aspects are worthy of mention. First, the policy itself sets out clear expectations about the way in which pupil work should be presented and how frequently displays should be changed. Individual teachers are responsible for their own classrooms and groups of teachers form 'corridor teams' and have responsibility for the displays outside their rooms. The meetings between teachers to discuss the display for their corridor area have made a significant contribution to school development. For the headteacher, the display policy was part of the inroad into the quality of learning; the children had a low self-concept and she felt they must be going for the best. She knew that three or four teachers could produce high-quality work and that when this work was displayed it would set a standard for everyone else.

A second aspect of the policy is that beautiful and interesting things should be seen around the school. For example, in the reception areas and corridors there are framed pictures and photographs, fish tanks, plants and flowers; albums of photographs of school events are available for parents and visitors to browse through. These high standards are maintained through the hard work, persistence and vigilance of the staff. Any broken windows are repaired immediately. Children are encouraged to keep the school clean and tidy so that it is a welcoming place and they clearly take pride in seeing their work on display. Initially, the teachers had to work hard, remounting work if it was torn down or defaced and immediately removing any graffiti found around the school, but these problems have decreased over the years. The chair of governors commented: 'the headteacher has made this school a palace for some of the children'.

Third, the headteacher has been concerned to make the school environment welcoming for staff as well as for pupils. The staffroom is a large, comfortable room in which the teachers can relax. Though these facilities are well appreciated, some of the teachers initially questioned whether improving the facilities should be a priority:

> 'When the head wanted to improve the staffroom, by painting the walls and recovering the chairs, I couldn't believe it – I thought we should spend the money on books. Now I see why she was doing it – it wasn't obvious then.'
>
> (Deputy headteacher)

> 'When the head said that she wanted new curtains and displays, I was uncertain, but the place looks smarter and the children behave better.'
>
> (Chair of governors)

In August 1991, when the present headteacher had been in post for little more than a year, there was a major catastrophe when one whole section of the school was destroyed by fire. This was a devastating experience for the staff. As one of the governors said, 'At the time we could all have cried.' Many of the practical improvements that had already been made to the building were destroyed. The headteacher spent the whole of her summer holiday that year supervising the clearing of the site and the installation of Portakabins so that the school could reopen in September. This was a crisis period for the school, but, nearly three years later, several people said that this terrible experience had had positive outcomes. The year spent working in Portakabins while the school was rebuilt had brought the staff together as a team and it had also given the headteacher the opportunity to put in place the high-quality learning environment that she wanted for the children. One of the staff said of the headteacher at this time: 'I would never have dreamt of asking for some of the things that she asked for – she paid constant attention to detail.' The LEA adviser's assessment was that the headteacher has been able to illustrate her philosophy of education in the building:

> 'It's in the internal organisation and the quality of the decoration. The music room, the drama room, the library, the corridor spaces and the public areas were able to reflect what she wanted which was a quality learning environment with quality illustration of children's success and achievement on show for people to see. The strong message it gives is, "we can do it".'

The leadership provided by the headteacher

The headteacher is highly experienced and is in her second headship. She had previously spent ten years as a very well-respected headteacher in a primary school in a middle-class suburb in Essex, a school which she had opened. On moving to Bristol, she deliberately chose to work in a different type of school. Her mission for the school is essentially very simple; she says that she was unhappy about the low level of expectations of the children when she first arrived and felt that they were not getting their entitlement:

'My vision was to offer these children the same quality of education that I had offered in my previous school – the same as they would have in a very middle class area.'

The interviews with teaching and non-teaching staff highlighted three sets of factors which have enabled her to make a big impact upon the school: she has clear ideas about what she wants to achieve; she is perceptive and caring and has abundant energy; she has excellent managerial skills.

Several people spoke about the headteacher's clear sense of direction. The staff recognised and welcomed the fact that she had clear aims and goals but they did not feel that these were being imposed upon them against their will. There were opportunities to talk things through, and if they disagreed with something they said so and the headteacher would listen. A teacher commented: 'She puts it over in a way that makes you want to do it.' One of the general assistants said of the headteacher: 'She wants the best – things as perfect as possible and she strives for that. She deals with problems and she doesn't lose her head. She can be sympathetic, she has to be tough.' The adviser's judgement of the headteacher was that she was 'A very focused leader, she knows where she is going, she knows what she wants, she takes action, she tries things – she doesn't always succeed but by that process she learns.'

Many people commented upon the headteacher's hard work and energy and her caring qualities. Staff said that they felt valued, that the headteacher recognised their contribution to the school and thanked them for their work. Her deputy commented:

'She is very committed and hardworking; we see her doing this. She is very knowledgeable and up to date, kind and caring to staff and willing to bring out the best in people.'

'She is very busy but always makes the time to talk to you.'

(Class teacher)

Her managerial skills are seen as being excellent:

'The head is an extremely organised person, a super manager, she seems to know what is going on everywhere. I have never known anyone who can juggle so many balls at once.'

(Class teacher)

'The head is an excellent manager, she is very aware of little things and has brought people together. The staff are hard-working and brilliant.'

(Class teacher)

'Everyone feels more confident, knowing where we are going. We have come to know what the head wants from us. When she started implementing new things then there was a bit of a rebellion, but we feel it will work out – it's all for the children's benefit.'

(General assistant)

The headteacher is conscious of the fact that she will be seen as a role model and tries always to demonstrate her philosophy of education through her practice. This can be seen in numerous ways – for instance, by the style of her conversations with and her behaviour towards the children, the staff and the parents; by her high personal standard of organisation and time-keeping; by the fact that her room is welcoming, tidy, decorated with pictures and flowers and that she is always well groomed and especially that she works extremely hard for long hours. She commented that she felt guilty if she was not the last one to leave the school although she realised that this was unnecessary. She said that she always tries to make time to talk to people when they want to see her and not to make them aware of the other pressures on her time.

SCHOOL MANAGEMENT IN PRACTICE

It is difficult in a short case study to convey a full picture of the school. Three key aspects of the organisation have been selected to illustrate the quality of work that takes place: the management of staff; teaching and learning; and the school's relationship with governors, parents and the wider community.

Staffing issues

When the headteacher took up the post she found that there were no effective management procedures for teaching and non-teaching staff. Teachers did not have job descriptions; the responsibilities of incentive post-holders were unclear; there was no senior management team; teachers did not work together and the infant and junior staff were somewhat divided; there was no tradition of staff participation in decision-making. One of her immediate goals was to get the staff to work together as a team and in this she has clearly been successful. During the first few weeks in the school, beginning in June 1990, weeks which were difficult and emotional ones for her because she found the situation worse than she had anticipated, the headteacher conducted a form of needs analysis, making out a check-list of what was good about the school and what needed attention. Her key decision was that she would establish a senior management team (SMT) and this was put in place the following September. She has said that she did not have time to consult about this but just told staff that was what was required. The SMT consists of the headteacher, the deputy and the four senior incentive post-holders, two of whom were new appointments that she was able to make in September 1990. The SMT meet weekly and the headteacher says that she sees it as one of the main levers in taking the school forward. There are set agenda for the meetings, and the minutes, which detail the action that will be taken, are published on the staff notice board. Full staff meetings also take place on a weekly basis, again with agenda and minutes. These meetings usually contain discussion about school policy issues and are often led by a teacher who has specific responsibility for a particular policy area. Discussion is actively encouraged; indeed initially the headteacher would deliberately ask people for their views, but this is now unnecessary as everyone participates. Her policy is to consult the staff as fully as possible, but to be aware of the demands consultation can make on staff time. On a procedural matter, for example, on how milk should be distributed to the classrooms, a suggested strategy might be presented to the staff just to check that they all agree with it. In contrast, a draft policy on language would be put forward for full discussion. The procedures adopted for these meetings act as a model for the staff about how they can conduct their small group meetings about curriculum matters and display. Staff regularly discuss issues about teaching and learning formally and informally; a newly qualified teacher commented that: 'the meetings are long enough for individuals to contribute – people don't say "don't bring that up it's time to go home"'.

A group of staff tended to meet informally in the staffroom for a coffee every morning at 8.10: 'often the best time for discussion because we are all awake – discussions tend to be quite deep, people are well up with what is happening in education'.

Each member of staff now has a clear job description and everyone, with the exception of new members of staff who are given a year to settle in, has a specific, school-wide responsibility. This process started with the headteacher conducting a professional development meeting with every member of staff, raising questions such as these. What skills have you got that the school is not using? What are your INSET (In-Service Education and Training) needs? What do you hope to do? From this initial meeting she negotiated a job description with that person. The practice of holding an annual professional development meeting with every member of staff has continued and these meetings enable the headteacher to keep in touch with staff needs and aspirations. The appraisal system is carried on independently and is used primarily as a means of identifying success and ways forward for development. All the job descriptions are published in the comprehensive staff handbook. A very simple strategy that she introduced as a means of breaking down barriers between infant and junior staff was to mix infant and junior classes on the same corridor. One of the rooms close to the staffroom has been turned into a resource and preparation room for the staff. As well as being generally useful, this has served a dual purpose in that resources are shared rather than being stored in individual classrooms and the informal exchange of teaching materials and ideas between teachers has been facilitated.

Teacher professional development is given a high priority. Many INSET activities are organised by the local federation of schools but individual teachers are given support to attend other programmes. For instance, four of the incentive post-holders have attended twenty-day courses in their specialist areas, maths, science and technology. Equally important is that staff feel confident to bring forward new ideas and to experiment in their teaching; they feel that they can take suggestions to the headteacher and will receive positive feedback and support. They are also mutually supportive, giving one another feedback and, where they have a specialist responsibility, acting as a resource person for their colleagues. An experienced teacher is appointed as mentor to a newly qualified member of staff in her first year so that she always has someone to turn to for advice.

Teaching and learning

The core purpose of the school is to provide high-quality learning experiences and opportunities for the children, and much is done to try to ensure that these are made available. Several strategies can be identified. First, priorities and targets are identified through the school development planning process and progress in achieving these is monitored over the year. Decisions about the allocation of resources, the selection of topics for discussion at staff meetings and the focus for professional development days are influenced by the priorities identified in the development plan. Second, priority is given to curriculum planning. Teachers meet in year groups to plan their work for the term, and each teacher has a file containing proformas on which they enter their individual lesson plans for the week; these files are then given to the headteacher weekly for comment and feedback. Third, there are detailed procedures for record-keeping and for monitoring the children's work. All children have portfolios which they build up as they progress through the school and which contain examples of their work; the teachers have recently instituted a system of moderating examples of pupils' work to try and ensure that they are operating a consistent standard. The children's work is valued and they receive positive feedback from their teachers; twice a day, at lunchtime and the end of the afternoon, pupils who have done a good piece of work are sent to show their work to the headteacher and receive her commendation. Fourth, the staff, as early as possible, try hard to identify any pupils, even in the nursery class, who have special educational needs, and to provide additional help and support where necessary. Several people praised the work done by the special needs teacher.

A fifth strategy that the headteacher has introduced is that, each Monday morning, she spends a couple of hours in a different class, observing the teacher and talking to the children about their work, and she follows this up with a feedback discussion with the teacher. Over the course of a school year she will observe each teacher on three occasions. Sixth, efforts are made to support the teachers in the classroom; every teacher has a period of release time each week which they can use for planning and they have the support of a general assistant for three half-sessions per week. In addition, curriculum coordinators get some limited time – for example, half a day every term – to work with their colleagues in the classroom, and also have one and a half days to attend subject specific INSET organised through the local federation of schools. This is an innovative strategy for a primary school since teachers in these schools frequently have no free time during teaching hours. A further distinguishing feature of the school is that the headteacher and staff are pro-active in seeking out opportunities to enrich the curriculum for the children. There are numerous extra-curricular activities, such as choir, recorder groups, football and rounders teams, swimming galas, art workshops and environmental projects, and the staff are prepared to enter competitions and take up initiatives that they feel will be valuable for the pupils. As one of the staff said:

'Anything that is offered – we will have a go.'

'The school fosters teaching and learning by the way it deals with individuals. The children know that everything they do is valued, this is shown in the display, the awards, this makes a difference – they bring work to show the head twice a day, this builds up their self-esteem which is very important.'

(Class teacher)

The school's relationship with governors, parents and the wider community

Several members of the governing body have been governors for many years. They are committed and very loyal to the school and very supportive of the developments that are taking place. The governors meet twice a term and there are a number of sub-committees (finance, personal, curriculum), which also usually meet twice a term. The headteacher attends practically all of the sub-committee meetings as well as the full meetings of the governing body. The chair of governors said that he feels that the government is currently expecting too much of school governors, that the role is becoming too demanding. He also pointed out that, because of the high rate of unemployment in the community, there are plenty of people who have time to devote to being a governor but many of them lack relevant experience: 'we don't have business people wanting to be governors'. Nevertheless, the governors are fully involved in decision-making about school policy and are active organisers and supporters of school initiatives. Recently, they have started the practice of formally visiting classrooms for a day, focusing on a specific area, so that they can be better informed about particular aspects of the school curriculum. For example, two governors will come into school to look at the implementation of the maths policy, and then report back to their colleagues at the next meeting.

Relationships with parents have improved immeasurably. The main indicator of this is that many more parents are now coming into the school to talk to the teachers and to see the work that their children have produced. The number of parents attending school productions has greatly increased:

> 'Now we have to send out tickets because so many want to come – we have to divide them up, it's lovely.'
>
> (Class teacher)

The teachers are in their classrooms from 8.45 a.m. and the parents are encouraged to bring any queries or concerns to them then or after school. The parent governors said that parents now found the school much more welcoming and felt comfortable about entering it. In return, the parents have learned how to help their children with reading and are very supportive of school activities. Over 98 per cent of parents attend parent evenings. There is a school association which organises social and fund-raising activities for the school and which is very successful. A group of parents run a toddlers' group in the school once a week. The high expectations that teachers have of the pupils is in turn influencing the parents: two parent governors said that they were thinking hard about the choice of secondary school for their children because they were anxious that the children should continue to make progress.

'When I first came here parents were only coming in to complain, often in a very aggressive way; most parents now are very positive, very appreciative, they are not afraid to come in for a chat.'

(Class teacher)

'Families on the estate are proud of the school – some walk a long way to get here, past two other schools. A good reputation has been built up.'

(General assistant who lives in the community)

'Parents do support and appreciate what the school has now achieved. It is a place where the children are safe, performing well, doing work. The school is demonstrating that there is a life beyond [the estate] and is providing examples of things that you can achieve.'

(Community worker)

CONCLUSION

This is a dynamic school which is moving forward and making progress. Neither the headteacher nor the staff feel that they have achieved their goals in relation to the quality teaching and learning experiences that they want to provide for the pupils. The headteacher's own assessment is that, though a great deal has been achieved, much still remains to be done. She feels that the necessary structures are now in place, that the school is well supported by the parents, that staff morale is high and that this has placed the school in a position where everyone can move forward on teaching and learning:

'The minute I feel the school has gone as far as it can, I should go. The minute we say we have achieved [our vision for the school] we should do some soul-searching.'

(Headteacher)

Several of the people interviewed had clear ideas about what were the school's future priorities: improving the external environment; developing the library; developing the use of information technology. Staff were agreed that the school was succeeding and was effective, citing as evidence the behaviour policy; the display policy; the fact that they set themselves targets and were able to meet them; the fact that they regularly reviewed and developed their policies and planning mechanisms; that they worked well together as a team; above all, that their expectations of the children were high. The community worker, explaining why he felt the school was effective, said:

> 'Because people do see things happening here that they can be proud of. If you do anything here parents turn up – willing and eager to take part. Children work and are encouraged to aim high in their work – things on the wall generate pride. The school has high expectations for the pupils, there is a sense in which teachers feel that there are standards to maintain for the children. They have a sense of belonging and owning what is going on; they are invited to do things and they do them well. There is no competitive snobbery – objective standards have been set. There is a sensitivity to children who don't or can't – no sense of writing children off and a genuine concern for families who can't perform well.'

None of the changes that have taken place in the school have occurred overnight. The present position of the school is the result of hard work by the headteacher, the staff and the governors over some four to five years. They hope to be able to sustain the momentum and to continue to make improvements in teaching and learning in the years ahead. In examining why this school is succeeding against the odds, this hard work over a number of years must be seen as a major explanatory variable. However, it is also important to note that this work and effort has had a clear focus and has been carefully planned by the headteacher in consultation with her staff.

All the features of the effective school referred to in the introduction can be identified in this Bristol school. The headteacher has been able to build her staff into a strong team, help them develop a clear sense of direction and purpose, and together they have turned the school around. It is for these reasons that the school is succeeding against the odds.

FAIR FURLONG PRIMARY SCHOOL

An LEA-maintained mixed school for 3–11-year-olds

The school

Headteacher appointed	1990
Number of pupils	382
Number of teachers (full-time equivalent)	16.2
Pupil/teacher ratio	23.6:1
Average class size	27
Annual school budget	£0.6 million

Pupils in the school

Registered for free school meals (%)	49
With statements of special educational needs (no.)	8
Ethnic background (%)	
White	100
Afro-Caribbean	0
Asian	0
Other	0
With home/community language other than English (%)	0

2

CROWCROFT PARK PRIMARY SCHOOL

Longsight, Manchester

Roy Jobson, Viv Bingham, Lesley Whitehouse and Bill Rogers

Located on the edge of the inner city, Crowcroft's local community is characterised by the key features normally associated with educational and social disadvantage: poor health, large families, a high unemployment rate. Additionally, there is a high inflow and outflow of recent immigrants, most of whom have English as a second language. Operating in less than satisfactory buildings, the school nevertheless demonstrates successful achievement and is building a sense of hope for the future and pride in the community.

Crowcroft Park is a county primary school in the Longsight ward of Manchester for girls and boys from five to eleven. There is also a nursery class which offers part-time and full-time education to children who are between three and a half and five.

The school has approximately 250 places with 210 children in infant and junior classes and a further twenty full-time and twenty part-time pupils in the nursery. There are three termly intakes annually into the reception class. The school is always over-subscribed, with children on a waiting list.

The average class size is twenty-nine. Including the headteacher, there are twelve teachers, one of whom is a temporary appointment. The deputy headteacher is currently working from the school but is seconded full-time to support the LEA (local education authority) Kickstart Reading Programme of which he is one of the two authors. The headteacher has been in post for eleven years; one teacher has been in post for twenty-three years, another for nineteen and one for nine years. Two teachers have been in post for eight years, one has been in post for five years, two have been in post for three years, and one has been in post for two years. For three of the staff who are in their first three years of teaching, Crowcroft Park was their first teaching post.

The urban characteristics of the school are self-evident. Sixty per cent of pupils qualify for free school meals. The school is multi-racial, with 55 per cent of its pupils coming from white families, and the remainder mainly Asian, predominantly Pakistani, and Afro-Caribbean. Seventy-eight pupils have a home or community language other than English. Half the 200 full-time pupils qualify for additional support under Section 11 of the 1966 Local Government Act. Many other pupils have similar language and learning needs but do not qualify for additional support. That only one pupil has a statement of special educational needs (SEN) is a reflection of the total resources made available to the LEA and the practice in the school of meeting individual needs from its own resources at an early stage.

ENVIRONMENT AND COMMUNITY

The school is situated on the edge of a park which lies on the main road between Manchester and Stockport and surrounded on the remaining three sides by narrow streets of terraced houses. The main buildings, which were completed in 1935, form an unusual continuous V-shape with a glass-roofed veranda along the inside. Leaking roofs and windy draughts are a feature of this particular

design, and Crowcroft Park is no exception. Several demountable classrooms – intended to be temporary but now a permanent feature – provide accommodation for Years 5 and 6 and for the Parents' Room which also supports a toddlers' group, parents' classes, and teacher INSET (In-Service Education and Training).

The Longsight ward has a significant number and degree of indicators of disadvantage. The statistics which follow are taken from the 1991 Census of Population.

- *Population*: the ward had the third largest proportion of nought- to fifteen-year-olds with limiting long-term illness. The proportion of residents born outside the United Kingdom was above the city average at 27.8 per cent.
- *Households*: the proportion of three- or more adult households with dependent children and the proportion of seven- or more person households were both the highest in the city. The proportion of households without a car was above the city average of 63.8 per cent.
- *Economic activity*: the unemployment rate and the youth unemployment rate – at 27.6 and 48.8 per cent respectively – were both above the city averages.
- *Housing*: the highest proportion of housing was in terraced property and the proportion of households in private rented property was twice the city average at 26.7 per cent. Longsight was one of only a few wards where owner-occupation fell between 1981 and 1991.
- *Socio-economic group*: the proportion of heads of households economically active in a manual socio-economic group was the city average at 65.3 per cent.
- *Qualifications*: the proportion of residents aged eighteen and over with a degree or diploma qualification was below the city average at 10.5 per cent.

According to a recent study conducted for the Office for Standards in Education (OFSTED) by the London Institute of Education, most of the features identified above figure among the eight most significant indicators of potential under-achievement.

CHALLENGES

Apart from the self-evident challenges facing the school, it had to contend with an additional and high-profile challenge from the Parental Alliance for Choice in Education (PACE). In 1987 formal complaints were made by two parents that the school was failing to meet its statutory requirements in relation to collective acts of worship and parental rights to withdraw their children from religious education. The Secretary of State found that there was no case to answer, but PACE then took advantage of the new complaints procedure introduced by the 1988 Education Act to renew the complaint and the whole process began again. The school became very much a test case and as a result received regular, unfair and adverse local and national media coverage. After a long legal process the Secretary of State, and finally the courts, found in favour of the school. The impact of such cases on a school and on its governors and headteacher in particular should not be under-estimated. Coming as it did at the point at which local management of schools (LMS) and open enrolment were being introduced, to overcome this challenge a great deal of stamina, mutual support and resolve was required.

ACHIEVEMENT

The school has consistently provided a good standard of education and has added significantly to the standard of pupils' achievement. Although there is a lack of base-line indicators in the British education system against which to measure progress, there is nevertheless a variety of sources which the team was able to use.

Regular visits and thematic inspections by the Manchester Inspection and Advisory Service and feedback from high schools to which the children transfer provided both objective and anecdotal evidence. The introduction of the standard attainment tasks (SATs), the results of which Manchester LEA commissioned the Manchester Victoria University to analyse for all of its schools, has provided a graphic basis for comparison with schools of a similar nature and against the school's own records for that particular cohort of pupils.

In 1992 there were a total of thirty-five pupils in the Year 2 class due to be tested using the national SATs. During the course of that year six of these pupils left and seven arrived, and three without any English. One child was admitted who had missed the previous six months' teaching. Of those children who had been in the class from the beginning of the year, one had been to five other schools and had long absences, one child had a serious hearing impairment, one child was identified by the educational psychologist as having specific language and learning difficulties, one had moderate learning difficulties, and two other pupils were affected by other difficult circumstances. In January of that year sixteen children were identified as having significant reading delays and were reading well below their chronological ages. Nineteen of the thirty-five pupils had transferred into the school during Reception, Year 1 or Year 2.

Despite the challenges to teaching and learning presented by this class the school achieved results in the SATs during the summer term of the same year which were close to the Manchester LEA average in English, science and technology and above the LEA average in maths – with almost twice the LEA percentage of pupils achieving level three in maths. These results were partly the result of specific strategies which the school used to support those pupils.

Although the school did not formally use and return the SATs test results in 1993 and 1994, the test material was used and supplemented the teacher assessments. These results, which are set out below alongside the national results for 1994, reflect two quite different cohorts of pupils to whom significant value has been added.

| | Teacher Assessment Year 2 (percentages) | | | | | | | |
| | Level 1 | | Level 2 | | Level 3 | | Level 4 | |
	1993	1994	1993	1994	1993	1994	1993	1994
Reading national results	18		51		28		0	
Crowcroft Park	14	13	43	60	29	13	14	13
Maths national results	17		70		11		0	
Crowcroft Park	11	0	50	39	70	30	0	0
Science national results	12		70		14		0	
Crowcroft Park	0		63		37		0	

One such strategy was an innovative approach to boost children's reading called Kickstart. The Kickstart Reading Programme is an integrated approach to reading for under-achieving readers in the early stages of their education and was developed by two teachers from Crowcroft Park; one was the deputy headteacher and the other soon to become the deputy headteacher at a neighbouring school. Their initial ideas and the related activities were refined and developed within the two schools. Rooms in each of the schools were adapted as training bases.

A pilot training project began in 1992 supported by the headteachers and governing bodies, together with Manchester City Council Education Department. Teachers, classroom assistants and parents from a small number of schools were trained in diagnostic assessment of reading, planning individual work programmes, organising resources and staff, and in developing the school-based strategy. During this period supportive computer software was commissioned and two complementary reading programmes, Early Start for parents and their pre-school children and Fresh Start for older pupils, were also developed. The positive results and enthusiasm generated by this pilot resulted in a successful LEA bid for a Grants for Education and Training (GEST) funded pilot under the Raising Standards in Inner Cities category. The pilot ran from April 1993 to March 1994 and was the focus of a very positive evaluation report.

That such a major initiative should have developed out of Crowcroft Park is a measure of the professionalism, dedication and management skills within the school. In addition to developments in literacy the school achieves excellence in music and musical performance, and has a programme of parental involvement in conjunction with the adult education service, which is of real benefit not only to its pupils but also to their parents, care-givers and other relatives.

SIGNIFICANT FEATURES OF THE LIFE AND WORK OF THE SCHOOL

From the outset of the investigation we felt that there were consistent features emerging which characterised the life of the school:

- clear, calm and effective leadership by the headteacher;
- committed staff working together as a team;
- clear roles for curriculum development;
- clarity of shared purpose;
- excellent communications;
- happy, industrious and achieving children.

The school has worked steadily over a period of years towards achieving a learning-focused culture, a positive atmosphere and effective systems. The changes which brought this about have been perceived as gradual even where they were not particularly so. This is undoubtedly due to the headteacher's careful and considered approach but may also be attributed to the effect of external factors, in particular the long-drawn-out court case against the school, bringing together staff, parents and governors to defend their school.

We felt the positive atmosphere in the school, evident in the behaviour of both the children and the adults. While the buildings and grounds are both inadequate in various respects, most notably in space and the condition of some parts of the ageing fabric, every effort has been made to make the very best possible use of them. We perceived a sense of community, a communal responsibility and pride in the activities of the school in the widest sense.

The school's culture is one of value, care and safety, not only in relation to the children, but also to care-givers, parents, volunteers and staff. Given the home situations of many of the children, this element of the schools value system is critically important in enabling effective learning, quite apart from offering models of behaviour. There are high and consistent expectations for each child. Both staff and children feel safe to make, admit to and learn from mistakes, and to share worries and concerns. The openness of this approach within the school community, moreover, is extended to visitors.

The overriding concern of the staff is the effective learning of the children. The headteacher noted that, when she first arrived at the school, talk in the staff room was about anything and every-thing but that. Now, there is a passionate interest throughout the staff team in how to improve learning, both in general and in respect of the needs, problems and abilities of individual children. Discussion of children's progress is extensive and runs alongside formal recording systems. The headteacher knows the names, home and family circumstances and progress of every child; staff also appear well informed not only about their own classes and areas but about the school as a whole. Children with special needs, whether physical or otherwise, are integrated and supported on an individual basis and in a calm and matter-of-fact manner. Teaching methods cannot be characterised as either traditional or progressive. A range of methods are used and elements of both of these stereotypical approaches are used as appropriate to the task or individual needs.

Each curriculum area is the responsibility of two members of staff, one from each Key Stage (KS). Each Key Stage, with KS1 incorporating the early years, is led by a curriculum coordinator. This devolution of responsibility is accompanied by regular whole-school discussion and monitoring by senior management. This monitoring takes a number of forms. Minutes of the weekly Key Stage meetings are given to the headteacher and used as a record of development. The headteacher or deputy attends selected Key Stage meetings. Curriculum coordinators and Key Stage groups report back on a regular basis to all staff, including senior management.

Parents are very much involved in the life of the school and a range of initiatives have been taken to extend and develop this involvement. A noticeboard in the entrance shows photos of all of the workers in the school so that parents know whom they are meeting. The school brochure, a newsletter, and daily face-to-face contact help to provide regular information. All parents have two formal opportunities each year to come and talk about their children's progress, and if the evening slots are inconvenient the school arranges for alternative times during the week. In between these formal parents' evenings parents are encouraged to ask about their children's progress and to raise any concerns they might have.

Volunteers wishing to work in classrooms with individual children or small groups are always welcome, although, as in many schools, they are difficult to find and keep as financial and social pressures create alternative priorities for single parents and families on low incomes. Nevertheless, the school is able to find volunteers to help with visits to museums, art galleries, concerts and the swimming pool, and to raise funds for incidental expenses. The Friends of Crowcroft Park is a group of such volunteers who work together to raise money and to arrange social events. None of this money is spent on basic provision of books and equipment or repairs and maintenance but is solely to subsidise extra-curricular activities and to purchase resources not normally available through the school budget. Recent initiatives supported in this way include improvements to the nursery garden and a computer for multi-media work.

The Parents' Room in a single demountable prefab in the playground is an important resource. On two mornings each week a parent-and-toddler group meets for a cover charge of 50 pence per session. On one afternoon each week a selection of children's books is on sale and on two afternoons a Family Shop sells a wide range of stationery items and some toys. Good-as-new uniform is on sale during the parent-and-toddler sessions and a library for parents lends books free of charge and has a supply of information leaflets on a range of relevant issues. These initiatives were introduced by staff but have gradually been handed over to parents who now run them themselves, with support from staff when requested. Coffee mornings which are jointly run by parents and staff provide a sociable way of linking parents into all of these other opportunities. A parents' and teachers' steel band rehearses weekly after school.

The school Parental Involvement Project, part of an LEA-funded project, has for some time been developing training courses for parents. These courses were particularly impressive, including subjects such as 'Peaceful Children and Happy Families' and a project on 'Bullying' to help parents and carers increase both skill and confidence. English as a second language classes are also provided.

We observed a general concern that parents understand the aims and activities of the school, know how their child is progressing, maximise their contribution to the learning process and both share in problem-solving and success. Channels of communication with parents are good. Not only do parents value and respect the head-teacher, her team and the work of the school, they also feel that they are valued and respected in turn. The parents shared with the team some very revealing views of the school:

'They are always consulting over the uniform and the meals. They consulted us about bullying and now we've set up a core group of parents to consult other parents through a question-naire.'

'They tell you about what is going on. They have information sessions for parents on the curriculum and other things.'

'They have two parents' evenings for every class every year. If you can't make it they will go out of their way to see you at any time during that week.'

'The headteacher has an open door. Parents can come in at any time to see her or other members of staff.'

'Sometimes you get a nice letter or a note. They will have a word with you when you come in to drop your children off or to collect them. There are parents' evenings and you also get reports.'

'Asked what aims and values they thought the school was trying to promote parents replied without hesitation: "respect; discipline; citizenship; understanding of other people and their cultures; respect of each other and for adults".'

The development of the whole child and life skills as well as covering the curriculum are notable ingredients in the mix that gives Crowcroft Park its particular flavour. It is very clear that every individual child is valued; whatever their progress or achievements this is unwavering. Recognition and reinforcement of good work or behaviour is regularly provided whether by verbal praise, a certificate or badge, or simply a smile and nod. Poor behaviour is dealt with calmly and quickly and, for the most part, this suffices. Only very rarely is the sanction of loss of playtime used, and only once in the last decade has a child been excluded from the school.

A wide range of extra-curricular activities are in evidence, not least at the school concert we attended at which the steel and wind bands and choirs performed with both gusto and pride. Drama, dance and movement were also in evidence and clearly enjoyed. Visits outside the school include a residential course for pupils in the junior classes at the LEA outdoor pursuits centre. Adults other than teachers who visit the school to work with the children include fire officers, police officers, charity workers, road safety officers and religious leaders.

Children take an active part in the running of the school, not only by being asked to undertake jobs, but also, very often, by using their own initiative. Every lunchtime pupils offer to carry out specific structured tasks which include first aid watch and tidying up or setting out materials. Children help one another as well as staff, and older children frequently play with nursery children in their playground. In classrooms one sees children thinking about, discussing and deciding what they want to do and how to go about it. Classrooms are organised in a way which enables children to be responsible as far as is possible, and to accommodate their own learning.

SCHOOL POLICY

We observed that the school's policies are well prepared and organised. Each policy area has been successfully developed, based on strong team work and effective leadership. The governing body believes that their role is supportive and encouraging, allowing the staff to develop effectively.

The whole-school approach has produced excellent relationships, based on mutual trust. This trust allows people not only to feel safe but also to be challenged. The staff are supportive of one another and there is a consistency in aims and expectations.

School policies are regularly revised and parents are involved in the processes. This is especially true of the parental involvement scheme, which was highly praised by parents. The staff are committed to this policy and there is clear coordination across the

school. It is a model example in terms of a whole-school policy being effective: every member of staff is involved and there is a great deal of hard work and dedication.

The school development plan has been produced on a cooperative basis, allowing a variety of people the opportunity to contribute to the establishment of priorities. Parents believe the aims and plans of the school have been well communicated and as a result problems are dealt with quickly and helpfully. There are whole-team staff meetings, as well as smaller groups, and there is an open spirit in which problems, opportunities, difficulties and success can be discussed in a friendly and helpful manner.

The school development plan has also been drawn up with appropriate attention to the needs of staff and children. There are clear references to the relationship of the priorities with INSET and the involvement of external agencies. The criteria have been established in order to make judgements about the quality of outcomes, and the resource implications have been identified. Reference is also made to methods of teaching, and more importantly learning, and there are criteria for making judgements about children's progress in relation to the plan.

Children with additional learning needs have been identified and resources have been allocated to meet these. In view of the high turnover of children in the school – some may move as many as three times in one year – the school has developed a record system which helps receiving schools to pick up where the children have left off and which, in the case of Kickstart, identifies the strategies which individual children are using in order to read.

Teaching standards in the school are high and senior management are clearly involved in reviewing teaching and learning, assessment and progress. There is a recognition that the role of the teacher is to allow each child to take full advantage of learning opportunities. Classes are well ordered, discipline is good, and there is clear evidence of support for learning and evidence of achievement. Children are happy, confident and well motivated. The headteacher, in particular, sets high standards as one of her main aims. She sees children's work on a regular basis and examines every child's work at least once a year. There is clear evidence that the school is not only trying to raise expectations, but also to assess the extent to which this is reflected in practice.

There are excellent examples of the actions which the school takes to raising expectations and hence motivation and parental involvement, and the Kickstart reading scheme has already been highlighted in this respect. The general ethos of the school is one in which there are high expectations of each and every child, whilst at the same time a realistic assessment of any learning needs and gaps, and how they can be met. In this respect the school policy on reading, and the Kickstart scheme in particular, is excellent. Care is taken with individual children to assess learning needs and there is a system in place to ensure effective use of resources. This is a whole-school policy which is consistent and clear. Class teachers are able to determine how individuals progress and when expectations are being set too low.

The school has good relationships with its community. There is a lack of commerce and industry in the locality but, in spite of that, continued attempts are made to involve a range of people with a variety of experiences and approaches in the life of the school and membership of the governing body.

There is a whole-school anti-bullying policy, soon to be set out in the school development plan. Parents and children are involved in a process of consultation, and when the policy has been produced it will be introduced to all children, staff and parents.

The school has consistent policies on attendance and punctuality, and they are seen as part of a positive approach within the parental partnership schemes. It is interesting that whilst there is a recognition and an understanding of parental problems, there is no lowering of expectation, either by teachers or parents, all of which contributes to a positive learning environment. This is reinforced by regular review by management of teaching and learning, assessment and progress.

The headteacher formally monitors individual teacher planning, recording and assessment and is a frequent visitor to all classrooms. Professional discussions are held with staff about the progress of individual children, and where necessary targets are set with individual children. Children are encouraged to show work which illustrates good progress to the headteacher and deputy head, and such work is recognised formally in both whole-school and class assemblies. The headteacher regards this valuing of work as a means not only of valuing pupils' achievements but also of valuing and reflecting the quality of teaching and learning.

There is good evidence that the school uses and is involved in the services and policies of the LEA. The headteacher plays a full part through her networks and is seen as a leader amongst her peers. Services such as Language and Learning Support (Section 11), Inspection and Advisory colleagues, the Adult Education Service and education officers are well used and involved in the life of the school.

HOW IMPROVEMENT HAS TAKEN PLACE OVER TIME

Crowcroft Park Primary was chosen as one of a number of schools across the city which are considered to be succeeding against the odds. In common with many of those schools its success has not been the result of sudden or momentous change but rather of a long and steady process of development.

Research which suggests that schools can 'drag themselves up by the bootstraps' at a particular point in time also observes that improvement gained in this way is often difficult to sustain. There may be many reasons for this, but one is that the challenges to improvement which schools such as Crowcroft face are not only deep-rooted but also shift their character over time. Dynamic and explosive change does not always result in the long-term structural and attitudinal improvement needed in these circumstances. Neither do change agents capable of sudden wholesale change necessarily have the qualities needed to sustain and continually renew development at a pace manageable by the school as a whole.

When the present headteacher arrived at the school eleven years ago, unemployment, already at a high level, had begun to rise significantly. New families had arrived from Pakistan and had yet to be fully accepted in the community. Within the school itself there was already a base on which to build, but there was a particular need to respond to the range of cultures, beliefs and languages represented by the children and to develop whole-school expectations, systems and behaviours with respect to classroom organisation, teaching and learning styles, pupils' attitudes and behaviours, and staff development.

In the middle of this process of development the school had to accommodate, along with all schools in England and Wales, the introduction of the National Curriculum and LMS together with the welter of statutory requirements which flowed not only from these two major changes but also from the Parents' Charter, the Children's Act and the 1992 Education (Schools) Act.

On top of all of this the headteacher and governors had the unique six-year challenge from PACE with which to contend. Their response to this particular challenge was to restate their belief that the school already met the statutory requirements but also to use the experience to improve the quality of planning, recording and delivery for both collective worship and religious education.

Eleven years on the main challenges outside the school, in addition to those faced by all schools, include the continually shifting ethnic composition of the community, and high levels of long-term unemployment. There is also an increasing rate of movement of children in and out of the school as parents and care-givers change their accommodation in response to financial pressures and changing family circumstances. A growing percentage of pupils arrive with or are seeking refugee status from countries and cultures as disparate as Iran, Ethiopia, Somalia and the former USSR.

The most distinctive feature about the change process at Crowcroft Park is that improvement has been steady and sustained throughout the eleven-year period. Every new obligation has been examined and woven into the fabric of the school system. Wherever possible, challenges have been regarded as opportunities, and problems have been tackled calmly and in partnership with staff, parents, governors or the LEA, as appropriate.

At Crowcroft Park the introduction of LMS has coincided with a reducing budget which has implications for long-term planning, staffing levels, class sizes and learning resources generally. The ageing building lacks the facilities for the delivery of a truly modern curriculum, and simply meeting the basic repair and maintenance requirements will leave no capacity for improvement to the fabric or facilities.

Many areas of development at Crowcroft Park would serve to illustrate how improvement has been achieved but three quite different, yet interrelated, initiatives have been selected for the purpose. When the headteacher assessed the needs of the school following her arrival she had concerns that teacher expectations and teaching and learning styles were far from consistent within the school; the school had general parental support but very little parental involvement; and levels of early literacy, particularly children's reading ability, needed to be raised. The recruitment of a deputy headteacher with a similar philosophy of education provided a firm base from which the headteacher began a gradual but consistent process of shifting the primary focus towards teaching, learning and achievement, and the role of assessment in that process.

Prior to any national expectation that schools should have development plans, Manchester LEA was encouraging schools to do just that. At Crowcroft Park the headteacher led the school in collaborative school development and ensured that issues of teaching and learning, assessment, and the recording of children's achievements, figured as continuing priorities within the overall plan. Staff were given responsibility for coordinating individual areas of the curriculum, but the headteacher and deputy both supported and monitored developments to ensure that consistent expectations and application were beginning to emerge. In-service training sessions for all staff, and where appropriate for staff as individuals, continued over time.

By the time that National Curriculum assessment requirements emerged the school had already made considerable progress and there is now a school-wide system of planning, assessment and reporting. All core subjects have continuous assessment during the year as well as summative assessment at the end of each year and Key Stage. During the dispute between teacher unions and the

Secretary of State for Education over the arrangements for the SATs the school carried on with teacher assessments for their own internal use. Assessment is used within the school not only to report on progress but crucially to adjust teachers' teaching and learning programmes to help individual pupils and groups of pupils to improve. This diagnostic use of assessment is particularly evident in reading, writing, speaking, listening, maths and science.

Many urban schools find it difficult to tap the initial hopes and expectations which parents have for their children's education and to engage parents as educators, or even as partners in the process, beyond the nursery and reception class. Crowcroft Park is an exception, despite the added dimension of the wide range of cultures and languages represented in the school community. The key features underpinning parental involvement are these:

- the level of respect for and the valuing of parents;
- the high level of information exchange and genuine consultation;
- shared decision-making; support and training of parents; and
- access for all parents and care-givers regardless of personal circumstance, culture or language.

From a level of involvement of parents based mainly on information-sharing the school has now developed a wide range of connections with parents. The Parents' Room, parents' notice board, parent-and-toddler group, coffee mornings and newsletter are in themselves examples of sound primary practice. Over the last two years the school has gone beyond this with a Parental Involvement project within the school development plan. This project has been strengthening the existing links while adding a Parents' Shop, the Friends of Crowcroft Park voluntary support group, and courses for parents tutored by the Adult Education Service on 'English as a Second or Other Language' and 'Peaceful Children, Happy Families', which is helping parents to prevent and to handle behavioural problems. The only financial cost of the project for the school has been an additional allowance for the teacher coordinating the project.

Kickstart, Early Start and Fresh Start have already been described earlier in the section which outlines the achievements of the school. The process by which these major reading projects developed from within the school, built on existing practice, tested out within the school itself and in partnership with a neighbouring school, before growing steadily and embracing other schools within an evaluative project is typical of the steady, systematic and thorough approach which helps to explain how improvement has been achieved at Crowcroft Park, and how it has been sustained.

There is a small number of key features common not only to the separate areas of improvement but also to the process of improvement as a whole within this school. There is a clear and unwavering philosophy of education shared by the headteacher and senior management which has consistently shaped the first principles from which all developments have flowed and against which all decisions are weighed. This philosophy is underpinned by a belief that all children can succeed; that education is a vehicle for the emancipation of working-class children; that equality of opportunity is an absolute entitlement; and that teaching and learning must be based on mutual respect and the raising of self-esteem.

Partnership based on professionalism characterises all planning and much decision-making. High and consistent expectations are continuously reinforced by formal monitoring and informal modelling of those expectations by the headteacher and deputy heads.

The curriculum management model operated by the Key Stage coordinators plays a key role. Staff are not only valued and supported but are also given the freedom and space to use their initiative. There have been and continue to be staff at all levels of responsibility and experience who have instigated and led innovative projects contributing to whole-school development.

Throughout the process there is an attention to detail which in itself serves to reinforce both the importance of and the standards expected by the mission of the school.

ACCOUNTABILITY

The school has a fairly typical vertical structure of accountability. The class teachers work with curriculum coordinators in each Key Stage; the coordinators report to the deputy headteacher; the deputy headteacher reports to the headteacher, who also has management oversight of the work of the administrator and lunch-time support staff. The headteacher is accountable to the governing body. The governing body is accountable to parents, the Department for Education and, in certain respects, to the LEA.

In practice, the headteacher is the managing director of the school and, whilst the structure identified above operates for most formal decision-making and planning purposes, the school is small enough for the headteacher to discuss work frequently with all staff directly on an individual basis. On paper, the spread of control may seem wide, but it works.

Under normal circumstances the management of the school is shared between the headteacher and deputy, and the role of the deputy headteacher is more evidently one of collaborative management than is seen in many primary schools. Time is made available for specific project management and development work and for monitoring progress against areas of the school development plan. For the past two years, however, the deputy head has been seconded to the LEA to joint manage the Kickstart Literacy programme. The decision was taken to appoint two acting deputies in order to spread the opportunity for professional development and the exercise of responsibility. The two acting deputies who are also coordinators for Key Stages 1 and 2 are used more on a project basis rather than in terms of deputising for the headteacher in overall control of the school.

Although each class teacher is in charge within the classroom of style, methods and curriculum development, there is no doubt each in turn feels responsible to the headteacher for the children's progress and frequently looks to her for guidance, encouragement and commitment of resources. Staff also look to other members of the management team and to one another for support in what is essentially a very open community. Similarly, the non-teaching support staff relate through a team leader with the management team and particularly the headteacher and the administrator. The support staff act as a very important part of the eyes and ears of the school and their contact with class teachers appears to be well developed.

Accountability outside the school is rather more sophisticated. In strictly legal terms, under the devolutionary powers of the 1988 Education Act the governing body has local accountability for the school, and its management through the headteacher and her staff. In practice, it appeared to us that all the major decisions about discretionary parts of the funding, curriculum development, approaches to statutory assessment, pressure for maintenance repairs and so on were generated by the headteacher. The major role of the governing body has been to support and endorse such action or proposals. The second function which this governing body fulfils is to act as a major consultative body for the headteacher and her senior staff to check ideas. This type of approach to a board is not unknown in the commercial world, where a strong chief executive will manage his or her board. Nevertheless, all policy decisions are ultimately taken by the governing body.

The governors played a major part during the difficult period when PACE was challenging the school's practice in relation to religious education and collective worship. The governors have recently formed sub-committees responsible for curriculum, staffing, finance and pay which are likely to strengthen their role in policy formation and decision-making.

The school is also well aware of its accountability to the parents of children attending the school, to the community of its immediate catchment area, to the LEA, and to statutory educational bodies such as the Department for Education.

Crowcroft Park Primary works very closely with its local education authority in terms of administrative support and a two-way involvement with the inspection and advisory service and various city-wide networks. These are seen by the school as supportive. In particular, the school is using this support to make best use of the quality standard setting potential of the OFSTED (Office for Standards in Education) framework for inspection and the external accountability of the four-year inspection cycle itself.

One of the most subtle and important relationships observed was that between the school and its immediate catchment area and the parents and potential parents of children attending the school. Despite the fact that none of the teachers lives in the immediate community served by the school there is a strong empathy with and understanding of social conditions, pressures and the problems and needs of individual children, parents and families. The classes for parents in English as a second language and involvement of parents and grandparents in support roles at the school are all appreciated. The parents with whom we talked directly made it clear that they valued the way in which their children's needs are sympathetically discussed, and the willingness of the school to discuss their own related problems and needs.

CONCLUSION

When the headteacher heard the results of our investigation she felt that we had captured the essence of the school but also felt, as she had done all along, that the school is unremarkable. She was concerned that readers would feel that this was an ordinary school doing the job it is expected to do.

This is perhaps the key to why this school is succeeding against the odds. Its progress has been steady rather than climactic, and yet there are some very special innovations and developments which have flourished on a secure and professional base.

Neither the headteacher, nor the rest of the staff, teaching and non-teaching, nor the parents, would regard the expectations of the school as unrealistically high or unsustainable, but other schools might, and do. Challenges have never been regarded at Crowcroft Park Primary School as excuses for low expectations or standards, but always as opportunities.

The headteacher also felt that her role as standard-setter, team leader and quality assurer was perhaps overstated and that of the other partners in the process less clearly acknowledged. We recognise very clearly that the success of this school comes from the unity of purpose and unflagging commitment of all of the teaching staff and non-teaching staff (including a caretaker who camps out in the school overnight when vandals or bad weather threatens!), of governors, and of a small but dedicated band of parents and friends. But this kind of loyalty and level of improvement is hard-won and equally hard to sustain.

Our view is that this is a school which in very difficult circumstances is providing a quality education and is adding significant value to the standard of the children's achievements. The features which are most likely to explain this include the clear and unambiguous mission of the school; the way in which the mission of the school is continuously reinforced so that it underpins the ethos of the school; the leadership provided by the headteacher which on one hand encourages participation and development and on the other ensures compliance; the fact that the school's attention to the social needs of the children and community in no way deflects it from a determined focus on teaching and learning; innovative approaches to teaching and learning which are not only tending to eliminate the long tail of low-attaining pupils which characterises urban schools but are also boosting the achievement of more able pupils; and the involvement of parents in policy formation and support for learning.

We had the strong impression of a school which sees itself as always working towards quality. Crowcroft Park is a school which under-estimates its own achievements but never its pupils, and for that reason alone it is likely to continue to succeed against the odds.

CROWCROFT PARK PRIMARY

An LEA-maintained mixed school for 3–11-year-olds

The school

Headteacher appointed	1984
Number of pupils	230
Number of teachers (full-time equivalent)	10
Pupil/teacher ratio	23:1
Average class size	29
Annual school budget	£0.81 million

Pupils in the school

Registered for free school meals (%)	60
With statements of special educational needs (no.)	1
Ethnic background (%)	
White	55
Afro-Caribbean	12
Asian	31
Other	2
With home/community language other than English (%)	34

3

BLAENGWRACH PRIMARY SCHOOL

West Glamorgan

Alan Evans, Peter Weavers and Glyn John

Blaengwrach is typical of many of the villages of South Wales. Once it was a thriving community almost entirely dependent on coal-mining and iron-smelting. Now, industry is much diversified, earnings are generally low and unemployment is in double figures. Many such villages no longer have the community spirit they once had, and their schools too have lost a sense of purpose. Blaengwrach is one that has not, as this invigorating account of this rural primary school demonstrates.

A PARTNERSHIP FOR CHANGE

Blaengwrach Primary School serves an isolated community in the upper part of the Vale of Neath at the north-eastern edge of the county of West Glamorgan. Blaengwrach itself is not a village that you come across accidentally. It is at the end of a no-through road, and only those who live in the village, who are visiting friends and relatives or who have business in the village come to Blaengwrach.

The present population of the village numbers 2,125, of whom 461 are below the age of eighteen. In the past, its livelihood depended upon the iron and coal industries. In recent years, however, Blaengwrach has experienced profound change and upheaval in its occupational patterns and its social and demographic structure. Metal manufacturing employs the largest number of the 760 people currently in employment and the coal industry is experiencing something of a revival, but the labour force also now straddles many other occupations in the construction and service industries, agriculture, forestry and fishing. Through all these changes, the village remains solidly working class in composition. The latest population survey shows that 46.5 per cent of the population are to be found in social classes IV and V – the highest proportion in West Glamorgan – and whilst the unemployment figure of 13.04 per cent among men in the village is not very much higher than the average for the county, it is still a cause for some concern. In addition, partly as a result of outward mobility, very few people who live in the village have higher educational qualifications (less than 3 per cent) and the age profile of the area indicates an ageing population (28.9 per cent of households were occupied by pensioners).

Given such geographical and social circumstances, it might have been expected that Blaengwrach School would be an average school which provided a reasonable education, but which made few demands on pupils, teachers and parents. In fact, this is not the case. Blaengwrach has a high reputation in the neighbouring Afan, Dulais and Neath valleys and at West Glamorgan's County Hall. It is known as a school with high standards and a distinctive educational philosophy, where the teachers have high expectations of the children and where parents and the community are welcomed as partners in an important educational compact. It is a school that is committed to dealing with the changes that take place, while nurturing in the children an awareness of history and a love of the community which is essential to their sense of identity and emotional well-being.

THE SCHOOL

The earliest record of a school in the area is that of a dissenting school which flourished from about 1712. There was mention of a works school in the area in the notorious inspectors' report ('The Blue Books') of 1847. This school was subsidised by the local coal and iron works. The present junior school opened in 1908, and in 1914 a separate infants' school was built. Although on the same site, these schools functioned separately until they were amalgamated in 1964.

From the outside, the school looks like many other traditional schools built in the South Wales valleys during the early part of this century. The nursery and infants' classes are still located in the former infants' school and the junior classes in the original 1908 building. These buildings are separated by a hard-surfaced play area. At present there are 143 children in the school, together with the equivalent of fifteen full-time nursery children. The teaching staff includes the headteacher, six full-time teachers, a 0.1 teacher and an NNEB nursery assistant. The classes are organised in the following way:

Blaengwrach	National Curriculum
nursery/reception	nursery/reception
reception/middle infants	reception/year 1
middle infants/top infants	year 1/2
junior year 1/2	year 3/4
junior year 2/3	year 4/5
junior year 3/4	year 5/6

Ideally, the school would prefer the children to be grouped in smaller, single-age classes, but resources do not permit this at the present time. Teachers do, however, attempt to minimise the difficulties presented by the mix of ages and are very aware of the need for differentiation in the work they give to the children.

Despite its age, the school is well cared for. The obvious care which all the staff and pupils invest in the buildings mirrors the caring ethos which characterises the relationship existing between members of staff and between staff and children. The character and work of the school is even more apparent on the inside. There is an abundance of display material, mostly emanating from children's work, attractively arranged, capturing in word and picture many of the experiences which the children have undergone themselves. Of particular note is the quality of the library books with their emphasis on the promotion of the aesthetic experience of the children. From an early age, the children are being encouraged to look at the work of artists at a level suited to their age and experience. In the nursery and infants' section the books *Art in Places* and *People in Art* are in the library corner. There is also a beautifully illustrated and engaging book on Picasso.

SHARING THE VISION

When David Davies was appointed to the headship in 1989, the school was doing the reasonable job that might have been expected of it. The infants' school had for some years had a reputation as a centre for progressive teaching methods, and an HMI report on the amalgamated school in 1987 described it as a school that 'is determined to keep abreast of new initiatives in education'. It also commented that the staff 'show commitment to their individual and collective responsibilities' and the pupils are described as 'lively, interested and polite . . . there are many indications that they feel happy and secure in school'. David Davies, however, believed that the school had the potential to do much more for the children in its care.

From the beginning, he wished to imbue the school with a particular vision and philosophy. He believes in the educability of all children. The kernel of the school's philosophy is that every child in the school is a special, unique individual and should be encouraged to achieve as much as possible, to develop an inquisitive mind and an interest in learning. A central building block in this philosophy is the importance attached to educating children to their full potential at the stage at which they find themselves, not only encouraging overt skills and competencies, but also seeking to identify and draw out latent talent – to help the children discover new possibilities. Providing a sensitive, caring and warm environment in which the children feel valued, respected and wanted is fundamental to the success of this approach.

From past experience and observation, David Davies understood that if such a philosophy were to stand any chance of being accepted and put into practice, all members of staff would need to understand and adopt for themselves its aims and objectives, both in the short and the longer term. It would also depend upon parents knowing what the school wanted to do and realising that they had a vital part to play in achieving its aims. Education of children was seen as a three-pronged effort to which the children, their parents and the school contributed. If any one of these failed the children suffered, and would not make progress to the level of which they were capable. For these reasons the headteacher has been careful to move gradually, taking all those involved in the life of the school along with him. His success in this might be gauged by the comment of one teacher:

'There is a collective expression, a collective commitment here. What goes on in this school isn't just down to personalities. There is a central ethos, a central driving force in us all – it isn't just down to one person.'

The way that David Davies has introduced his philosophy to the school is characteristic of his style of leadership. Although he is regarded by the governors as a good team leader and a strong character who likes working with other strong characters, his quality of leadership is not one which forces itself upon the staff. Rather, he is seen as an enthuser and enabler who has convinced those he works with by his example.

The imaginativeness of his approach in putting theory into practice is illustrated by the lizards that he keeps in his office. The children have been given the responsibility of caring for the lizards and are allowed to enter at any time for this purpose. Not only does this mean that the headteacher is totally accessible to the children, but it has also helped to break down barriers with parents and other members of the family who are brought in by the proud children to see the lizards. Another example of the trust that he has in the children, or '100 per cent belief' as one governor put it, is that if he is not in his office when the phone rings then the children are encouraged to answer, find out who or what is required and fetch the headteacher or an appropriate member of staff. The children are used to this responsibility and deal with telephone calls calmly and efficiently.

The isolated position of the village means that it has a very strong sense of community, and it was clear from early on that the approach which the school adopted would also have to relate to that community. The tightly knit nature of this village provided both an enrichment and a challenge. The community has given the school its very willing support. It has also provided children who have confidence in who they are: a confidence and pride that the school has been happy to foster. The chair of the governing body identified it in this way:

> 'Our children are robust children. Sometimes they are from low-achieving families but there is a confidence about who they are and where they are from and that they matter in this school.'

However, while parents are keen that the school should be a happy place for their children, they do not always have high expectations of what their children might achieve. The priority of the school has been to widen the horizons of the children through new experiences and awarenesses and to raise the expectations of all those involved with them about their capabilities and potential.

STAFF INVOLVEMENT: DEVELOPING A COMMON PHILOSOPHY

Members of staff show a remarkable degree of identity with the aims expressed by the headteacher. There is also an evident excitement amongst them about their teaching: they are open to new ideas and methods for enthusing children with a love of learning. The cooperation which exists between the teachers and the encouragement which the headteacher gives to new ideas and initiatives make it easy to share successes and easy to acknowledge failure.

The openness of the relationship that exists between the headteacher and the staff has been built up gradually over the years. David Davies recalls that shortly after he became headteacher he decided to improve display within the school. He began by developing the work himself but then asked for help with certain specific, practical tasks that he could not do, while at the same time encouraging suggestions for further improvements. The teachers responded to his requests for help and felt able to make suggestions and to name areas where they, in turn, needed help. Starting with a practical and relatively unthreatening area, this willingness to acknowledge where help is needed and to share expertise has now spread to other areas, such as teaching strategies.

All members of staff consider that the creation of a good atmosphere in which aims and values are shared is a necessary factor in the making of a good school. The deputy head expressed it in this way:

> 'We have developed together a similar philosophy about children and how they learn. We all have essentially the same values and beliefs, and those values and beliefs are communicated in our teaching: in how we assess, how we teach, how we praise, how we relate to the children, how we relate to the parents. This has evolved [over the last five years].'

They subscribe to the view that it is necessary to have high and consistent expectations of all pupils and to maintain a clear and continuing focus on teaching and learning. They are aware of the importance of caring for children because without that emphasis it would not be easy to stimulate and motivate them. One teacher commented:

> 'The aim is to get the most out of the children and we try and ensure that they are happy: happy children can learn, unhappy children can't.'

The caring is seen as an expression of the value which is placed on each child.

Staff development has taken place in the form of carefully planned INSET, both on and off site. Staff have also been encouraged to visit other schools, often hundreds of miles away, to observe good practice. Such visits were carefully planned so that what the teachers were observing was helpful at the particular stage they had reached. It was not considered helpful in the beginning for them to visit situations that were so far in advance of their own situation that they might become discouraged. Over time the visits have been extended and are still continuing because the teachers are constantly seeking to improve what they do. Those who have been on these visits have returned with new enthusiasm, eager to put the ideas into practice. A collaborative approach has been developed to the adaptation of new techniques and to their integration into the working practices of the school.

The school's commitment to making staff development effective is illustrated in a recent visit made to the conference on IT at Olympia. The school wished to acquire insights and technical knowledge of aspects of computer networks which could be incorporated into the staff's general teaching repertoire and used more specifically in the new computer laboratory that is about to become operational. Two of the teaching staff, along with the headteacher himself, attended the conference: full cover was found for them to do so. David Davies has a profound belief that innovation cannot be achieved effectively by one teacher attending a course, workshop or conference. From direct experience and observation he has an appreciation that if new techniques and ideas are to be transferred successfully into classroom practice then it is essential that a sufficient number of staff are involved in their development. He therefore challenges traditional orthodoxies and releases on occasions a third to two-thirds of his teaching staff for staff development activities which he considers are important for school development and, in particular, for the improvement of teaching and learning in the school. He has found money to do this from a number of different sources: the supply budget, GEST and sponsorship from industry. He also takes classes himself. In the last five years, only one parent has complained about the arrangements that have been made.

Close links have been developed between the teachers not only on a professional level but also a personal level. Such personal links have been encouraged to develop during activities such as canoeing, water-skiing and sub-aqua sports. The staff's strength as a team has been further reinforced by the very careful consideration given

to the new recruitments. Two staff were appointed only ten days after David Davies's own appointment, and one further appointment was made some three years later. In each case the headteacher and the deputy drew up first a long list and then a short list from the applications that were received and presented it to the governors for approval. On the day of the interviews, candidates were shown around the school together, and careful attention was paid to their responses to the children and their comments about what they saw. They each then had an informal interview with the headteacher and the deputy, followed by a formal interview with the governors. David Davies is convinced that this careful appointment procedure is vital to choosing the right person. One of the parent governors of the school observed, 'the staff get on well, and each appointment has added something'.

It is important that the efforts that have been made by the teachers to change their perceptions have been backed by positive resourcing. In order to provide them with the necessary funds to implement the new techniques and ideas, money has been raised through all kinds of initiatives from the PTA, the governors and industry. The school will shortly have two minibuses for use on its extra-curricular activities: a remarkable achievement for a school of its size, especially in a locality which has been particularly affected by recession. The most recent example of the school's achievement in this area is the new twelve-station computer laboratory, previously referred to, which will cost £36,000. It is being sponsored by British Coal Open Cast (now managed by Celtic Energy), and will give an added dimension to computer literacy for the children in the school.

CURRICULUM AND ASSESSMENT: MAXIMISING POTENTIAL

The school's statement on the curriculum makes clear that it is the duty of the headteacher and staff to shape the curriculum to meet the needs and requirements, both academic and other, of each child. The importance which the school places on the need for a precise statement on the curriculum is summed up as follows:

> 'If you're not sure where you're going, you're likely to end up some place else – and not even know it.'

The school aims to provide a balanced and integrated curriculum with an emphasis on literacy, numeracy and learning skills to meet these needs and requirements and to promote the whole development of the individual child. It seeks balance in the curriculum by providing learning situations which satisfy the spiritual, intellectual, physical, social, emotional and cultural needs of the child. The aim of an integrated curriculum is to provide greater interest for the children. An emphasis is placed on the children's acquiring discovery, interpretive and learning skills through first-hand experiences, with the school and its environment as the source from which the worlds of language, literature, art and natural science arise.

With a balanced and integrated curriculum it is hoped that attitudes to learning and living will be so firmly established as to provide each child with opportunities for growth through the secondary and further education sectors to a satisfying and responsible adult life. However, the educational journey is regarded not only as a means but also as an end in itself, and each step of the journey has intrinsic significance for personal fulfilment and growth. At this stage of the child's education the main emphasis is on fulfilling the primary child.

The curriculum statement stresses the importance of matching work to the ability, needs and readiness of children, of ensuring that the skills taught are both extended and applied, and of having expectations of pupils' performance which are realistically high. It sets out the following aims in order to help all children realise their potential:

- to ensure that each child has a command of language and the ability to communicate effectively and confidently in reading, writing, speaking and listening;

- to develop a knowledge and understanding of basic mathematical facts and concepts and of how to use them;
- to encourage scientific curiosity and to organise observational studies, particularly in the local environment;
- to awaken children's awareness to their heritage, both local and national, and to give some understanding of their place in the world;
- to give an understanding of moral and ethical codes, religious beliefs and ideas and of how to live with others;
- to teach skills and the appreciation of aesthetic qualities in the creative arts: art, craft, music and drama;
- to develop and maintain a healthy body by providing enjoyment in physical activities;
- to create a happy school environment;
- to help children learn that courtesy, good manners and consideration for others are very important qualities, and to make each child a responsible member of the school community and also of the wider community;
- to encourage children to develop a habit of learning and to develop a lively enquiring mind and a cooperative attitude towards all the people who are working for the successful achievement of these aims.

The teachers recognise that the translation of ideas and principles into the practical day-to-day task of teaching demands extensive curriculum planning. As with other aspects of school life, this process involves the whole staff, although curriculum leaders take responsibility for introducing developments in specific areas. It is interesting, however, that although much time and careful thought have gone into the process of curriculum planning, the school is only now producing documentation in respect of its schemes of work. Such documentation had been left until 'the philosophy was up and running' and the staff had been able to identify the approaches which were most effective. Whilst recognising that this order is controversial, the headteacher, the staff, governors and parents are united in choosing to do it this way. Their policy has also been explained to inspectors and advisers visiting the school.

Teachers are provided with clear guidance for assessment. A significant element in carrying it out is the use of portfolios of children's work. These portfolios are kept for a number of purposes and reasons. They are to benefit children by giving them a sense of progress and achievement in the work done. They support the judgement of the teachers in their assessment and in recording and reporting achievement. They monitor entitlement and promote continuity and progression.

The portfolios contain samples of work done by the children in mathematics, in language, both English and Welsh, and in science. Some of the artwork done by children is also included because it is considered that artwork gives an insight into the development of children. Accompanying these samples is a record of the date on which particular pieces of work were completed, a note on the process describing the stimulus, the degree of collaboration and the planning and drafting stages. Areas identified for development or improvement are also noted, and there are comments by the teachers and by the children. These give information about the significance of the pieces of work and about the progress or development of the children in particular areas of the curriculum.

As they grow older, and in accordance with their stage of development, children are given increasing responsibility for keeping their portfolios up to date. This is to ensure that they will be of maximum benefit to the children in promoting both an awareness of their own progress and achievement and also a sense of worth and pride in what they have achieved.

Members of staff are aware that the nature of assessment will vary according to the needs of each child. It may be necessary in the case of children at an early stage of development, or where a child is experiencing particular learning difficulties, to record assessment in greater detail.

The only quantitative data that the school has to date to confirm its assessment of the pupils' progress are their 1992 SATs results. The school questions the value of SATs and so supported the boycott of these tests in 1993 and 1994. The 1992 tests demonstrated that the pupils achieved average or above average scores in all curriculum areas except information technology. However, these tests were carried out at a relatively early stage in the development of the school's approach. One way in which the school responded to the results was by affording the development of IT high priority: an initiative which led to the visit to Olympia and the new computer laboratory. In this area at least there are very clear signs of progress.

RAISING THE CHILDREN'S EXPECTATIONS

The school has a number of generally accepted strategies by which the children's expectations are raised. The creation of a good learning environment is seen as a partnership involving the extensive planning of the programme for children. In this school, the close links between members of staff allow this to be done not only formally but also informally. Cooperative planning allows for a flexibility of approach and enables teachers to provide stimulating and 'hands-on' experience for the children.

Teachers are constantly aware of the need to stimulate and motivate their pupils in order to maintain the sense of excitement in learning. The stimulation and motivation take various forms, such as changing the learning environment by organising visits to places connected with particular themes and encouraging children to learn independently. The school is responsible for an extensive range of activities, from organised visits to museums, theatres and concerts to adventure activities and residential visits. Places such as Borfa House and Knelston Camp Craft Centre on the Gower,

Abercregan Field Study Centre in the Afan Valley and Dan-y-Coed near Swansea are regularly used by the school.

One visit provides a good example of the way in which such activities are used by the school. The culmination of a study on Victorian Britain was a trip to the National Folk Museum where the children, dressed in Victorian costume, were taught as children in Victorian times. The experience allowed them to compare methods of teaching in their own school with those in Victorian schools. The children were keen to point out the dreary reading books used at that time. The enforcement of rigid discipline by the teacher (their own in Victorian dress) was also a matter for comment. The visit gave the children a vivid insight into the education of children at the time of Queen Victoria and it allowed them to look perceptively at the methods used in their own school.

Visits such as these amply demonstrate that the excitement which the teachers bring to their work, and the professionalism which they show in carrying it out, are not restricted to the classroom. The teachers are concerned for the whole child, and for that reason they become involved in every kind of out-of-school activity which might broaden the children's perceptions about their ability to achieve and so raise their expectations. All the teachers take part in these activities and they recognise that their participation is one element in the establishment of the close links between them.

Teachers also involve children in the assessment of their own work by discussing with them how improvements may be made. They encourage critical self-analysis and discussion of work in peer groups with the aim of building greater self-discipline and an element of self-assessment into the general approach of the child to his or her work. There is an awareness that having an intimate knowledge of each child and being able to use that child's strengths to encourage progress are crucial to the task of motivating and stimulating children. From the nursery class right throughout the school, good work and effort are constantly acknowledged.

Children receive praise in various ways. Their work is shown to be valued by not only being displayed in their own classroom, but also by being shared with staff and pupils in all parts of the school. Reward stickers are given, which the children can choose to display either on their person or in their books, alongside the work which has merited praise.

AN 'OPEN DOOR' POLICY: THE INVOLVEMENT OF PARENTS AND THE COMMUNITY

The headteacher and staff of the school consider that their efforts to raise the expectations of children need the active support of parents. They are aware that among parents and the community there is support for the school as an institution which provides a warm and caring atmosphere for their children. However, few parents seem to have high expectations. In order to counter this the headteacher and staff realise that the education programme must extend to parents, and a strategy is being developed to encourage the greater involvement of parents in the education of their children. From our interviews with parents and governors it is apparent that what the school is aiming to do, to involve parents in the work of the school and in this way to heighten expectations for their children, is being met with some measure of success. The headteacher is the first to admit that it calls for a strategy which requires time, patience and sustained effort.

The process begins in the nursery. At this stage it is easy to exploit the natural concern of parents for what their children are doing. Most parents bring their children to school at this age. It is, therefore, the deliberate policy of the school to involve as many parents as possible in the learning which takes place in the nursery class. Parents are invited to stay with their children to observe how they learn. The practice has developed of meeting parents in groups to discuss issues such as reading involving the education of nursery-aged children. There is a parents' notice board which informs the parents of ways in which they are able to help with their children's learning. A new scheme is also being developed for nursery staff to meet with parents in their homes before the children come into the school. It is hoped that such initiatives might make parents aware of the need to have appropriate expectations for their children: to increase their awareness of what is possible in the long term, while at the same time being realistic about what can be achieved at each particular stage.

At the lower end of the school, attempts to involve parents in the classroom have met with success. One teacher was even led to remark, 'Sometimes in the morning I can't get in for the parents!' This particular teacher positively welcomed the situation, and always found specific and, if possible, interesting tasks for the parents to do. In some cases such involvement has led to parents seeking greater involvement by pursuing courses as care or nursery nurse assistants. However, the school is realistic about the extent to which parents of older children can become involved in the classroom. In a predominantly working-class community it is realised that as children grow older it is more than likely that both parents will be employed either full- or part-time. Although fewer parents then are involved in their children's activities in the classroom, the school's open door policy and the ready availability of teachers to meet parents enables them to continue expressing interest in their children's progress.

A significant part of the strategy to involve parents in their children's education has been the encouragement of their participation in out-of-school activities. This strategy has been particularly successful in involving fathers, who appear to be rather more reluctant than the mothers to enter the classroom. In a village in which playing for the local Rugby team is considered to satisfy the highest expectations, parents are beginning to see that there are other activities in which children can succeed and in which they themselves can achieve. The encouragement of parents' participation in these activities is viewed by the headteacher and staff as part of the process of extending horizons and heightening expectations. Parents are now taking part in canoeing and snorkeling expeditions as well as being involved with the school's sports teams. In our interviews with parents and governors it was acknowledged that the profile of the school had been raised by the involvement of parents, and their awareness of what their children are capable of in very many different spheres was having an effect on their perceptions of what should be expected of children. Parents and governors are beginning to see the school as a good school, not only because of its obvious caring atmosphere, but also because it sets challenging standards for pupils in all that they do. Governors who have played a large part in appointments to the staff are increasingly aware that the school is staffed by highly professional people whose aim is to provide high-quality educational opportunities for all children.

As the school's new computer laboratory demonstrates, local industry is beginning to note the high standards which the school is setting and is responding to an appeal for a responsible partnership between community, industry and the school. The laboratory is seen by one governor as part of the process of 'developing the school as a tool for the community' and of bringing people of the community into the school. The remark of this governor that school should not finish at 4 p.m. is significant in relation to the growing perception of the place of the school in the community.

THE NEXT STAGE

After the children leave Blaengwrach School, most of them travel 9 miles down the valley to Llangatwg Comprehensive School – a journey of about 15–20 minutes. David Davies acknowledges that the transfer to Llangatwg can be difficult for some children, but says that the school tries to make the transition as smooth as possible. There is very close liaison between the two schools, and during the summer term Year 6 children, along with their peers from the other feeder schools, make daily visits to Llangatwg to go through their timetable for the following year. Particularly good relations have been established with the PE and science departments at the school. The headteacher of the lower school in Llangatwg also visits Blaengwrach to speak to the children on their own ground. David Davies considers that the comprehensive school shares many of the primary school's general aims, but has different constraints in the way it works. However, he does not believe that the differences in the way the schools operate should prevent his school from carrying out its work in the way that it considers to be best for the children at the primary stage.

COMMITMENT TO EXCELLENCE

In Blaengwrach school there is a commitment to excellence, to high expectations and to partnerships with parents, the community and local industry. This commitment is consistent with government aims to raise standards in schools and to increase parental choice and influence as provided for in the education legislation enacted between 1980 and 1993, which brought into being national frameworks for the curriculum, assessment, inspection and appraisal. However, Blaengwrach School expresses that commitment in the form of its own particular educational alchemy.

The headteacher and the staff have a contagious enthusiasm for learning, a sense of mission and a commitment to raising standards, enhancing quality and using the school's resources efficiently and effectively. They are committed 'school improvers' who realise that without the help and support of the parents, community and local industry they would, at best, succeed only partially. They also appreciate that there is much to be gained from this approach. The pupils receive a challenging and enriching education. The teachers benefit from increased motivation and job satisfaction. Parents and governors become increasingly involved and gain greater confidence in the school.

The headteacher has taken professional risks to invest in the vision he has for Blaengwrach School. He shares with Bruner the sentiment that 'we have yet to discover the treasures of the minds of young children' and is deeply committed to that educational odyssey. Nothing will detract him from this enthralling prospect. Quite properly, all those interested in and committed to Blaengwrach School have their own sense of why it is such a happy and successful school. It is above all a school where the children are treasured and cherished, where quality learning is given primacy but is also fun, and where the contributions of teachers, parents, governors and friends of the school are recognised and celebrated. It is a school where all those involved, in whatever way, work together for its development and enrichment.

BLAENGWRACH PRIMARY SCHOOL

An LEA-maintained mixed school for 3–11-year-olds

The school

Headteacher appointed	1989
Number of pupils	159
Number of teachers (full-time equivalent)	7
Pupil/teacher ratio	22.7:1
Average class size	26.5
Annual school budget	£0.23 million

Pupils in the school

Registered for free school meals (%)	18.2
With statements of special educational needs (no.)	2
Ethnic background (%)	
White	100
Afro-Caribbean	0
Asian	0
Other	0
With home/community language other than English (%)	0

4

COLUMBIA PRIMARY SCHOOL
Tower Hamlets, London
Anne Sofer, Lesley Klein and Judy Porter

Columbia School is in Bethnal Green, an area that for over a century has known successive waves of immigrants. The school itself is nearly as old, and is built in a style well known in inner city areas where space is at a premium: classrooms originally designed for sixty pupils seated at bench-type desks and playground space at a minimum. The pupils are predominantly of Bangladeshi origin, and there are inevitably language and cultural barriers with the parent community when the home language is not English. From these inauspicious circumstances comes an account of considerable success.

Columbia, like almost half the primary schools in Tower Hamlets, is an old London School Board three-decker: a red brick galleon moored beside the famous Columbia Sunday flower market. It is surrounded by the remains of the warren of streets of two-up, two-down houses built for the artisans of Bethnal Green in Dickens' time; most of them were cleared away in the 1950s to make way for tower blocks. On Sundays the area is flooded with market customers from far and wide, including tourists and wealthier Londoners from north and east. During the week, it reverts to reality: a neighbourhood which has never, since it was absorbed into London in the early nineteenth century, known affluence or economic security. In the immediate post-war years, aspiring working-class families, third-generation Jewish families and members of the thriving East End criminal sub-culture lived here cheek by jowl. Now the same space is shared by first-generation families from rural Sylhet, the poorest district of Bangladesh, a beleaguered and ageing working-class white community and a paper-thin layer of middle-class gentrification.

The school building has the strengths and weaknesses of its kind. It is draughty, with confusing staircases, too much hall space and too high ceilings. The classrooms were built for sixty children in tiered seating but now barely manage to accommodate a class of thirty, with their book corner and technology display and science gear and paintings. It is permeated by the smell of school dinner, yesterday's boiled vegetables on one of the team's visits, but on the next, a wet January morning, a heavenly welcome of baking shortbread biscuits.

The building is hemmed in by an inadequate asphalt play-ground, teeming at break times with ball-throwing, rope-skipping, hop-scotching, gossiping, chasing children: the imagination baulks at what it must have been like a hundred years ago with two or three times the number.

On the other hand it is a solid and self-confident edifice, which has a history and has lasted. The boiler, the wiring, the pipe work, the door and window frames are a perpetual problem both to the governors and to the local education authority, but the building has given scope for some extremely imaginative remodelling. A dark hall on the first floor has been transformed by a large glass panel in one wall. And the Early Years' Unit, integrating the reception and nursery classrooms with arches and mezzanines and unexpected comfortable nooks and crannies, is as enticing as any purpose-built example.

In preparation for writing this chapter the three of us attended a whole-school assembly at Columbia. The theme for the term was animals, and this assembly focused on the story of Noah's Ark. The headteacher, Penny Bently, describing God's instructions to Noah to build the Ark on three storeys, added in parentheses, 'just like Columbia School'.

I am sure it was a throw-away remark, or perhaps a result of that compulsive habit of good primary teachers to 'make links', but it started a fanciful train of thought. Perhaps Columbia, and schools like it, are a sort of Noah's Ark. They represent a self-directedness, a moral aloofness, a determination to survive and a respect for diversity that are at the heart of the Noah story. And maybe the building itself represents these characteristics to those who work in it. So who does work in it?

THE CHILDREN

In January 1994 there were 464 pupils on roll. This had increased from 394 in 1990, in line with the local increase in the child population. In the statistics which follow, figures in parentheses show the comparison for the borough of Tower Hamlets as a whole. Eighty-four per cent (as against 50 per cent) of those pupils are of Bangladeshi origin; 6.8 per cent (as against 31.6 per cent) of English, Welsh or Scottish origin; 2.9 per cent (as against 5 per cent) of Afro-Caribbean origin.

Seventy-one per cent of these children were entitled to free school meals, compared to 64 per cent for Tower Hamlets as a whole, and 16 per cent nationally. School-level data on parental occupation are no longer collected, but in 1988 seventy-two of the children had no parental wage-earner. That proportion has almost certainly risen since then.

The statistics all shriek 'deprived'. And none of us, neither the school nor the LEA (local education authority), ever try and hide them. Indeed, we collect them assiduously in order to support the argument for resources based on our needs. But ever present, particularly in this school, is the bracing consciousness that harping on about deprivation can do terrible things to expectations and self-esteem. Like other children, these children have great gifts and strengths and hopes.

The school population is not entirely representative of the immediate area. White children living nearby walk past the school to attend other schools, often church schools, where their parents feel more comfortable with the racial balance. The school may have exacerbated this trend by taking an uncompromising and up-front stand on the issue of racism. The headteacher tells a story about some white parents who took her to task on the issue. Maybe, she suggested after a long discussion in which she had apparently failed to convince them, they should send their children elsewhere if they felt so opposed to the school's philosophy. 'But we don't want to – it's a good school!' they exclaimed.

She tells another story about the staff. At the time of her arrival eight years ago she interviewed every member of staff. Many of them expressed to her the view that 'standards had fallen', but, oddly, these were the ones who appeared to be most strongly in support of the retiring headteacher. It became clear to her that the blame for falling standards was being attributed not to the leadership but to the children, specifically to the Bangladeshi children then entering the school in greater numbers.

There has been a complete turnover of teachers since then. Most are white female graduates with more than five years' teaching experience, selected with great care for their commitment and actual or potential quality as teachers.

The pupil–teacher ratio, excluding Section 11 teachers, is 25.7:1. Including section 11 teachers, of whom there are now 4.7 full-time equivalents, down from the original allocation of 7.5, the pupil–teacher ratio is 17.9 to 1. This is average for Tower Hamlets, though clearly more generous than the national average of 22.7:1. Given the circumstances of the school, however, it is by no means positive discrimination run riot.

The support staff represent a different profile and one that connects the school more strongly with its history and locality. The secretaries, senior helpers and meals supervisors are local white women from the surrounding area. The younger primary helpers are first-generation young Bangladeshi women who may, typically, have had three or four years of their education in this country. Some of the helpers are 'volunteers', who came in to find out if there was a job and stayed to work for nothing, or at least for no money: the return in terms of English acquisition, understanding of child development and career advice will be considerable. There are two young white nursery nurses and a Bangladeshi bilingual instructor.

This three-layered staffing profile is typical of Tower Hamlets primary schools, and can make for difficult and often unspoken tensions of age, gender, class and race. In Columbia the tensions appear to be, if not resolved, at least greatly reduced by a policy of including and giving value to the contributions of all members of staff.

The governors of the school consist of the elected teachers, the elected parents, the LEA appointees and co-opted governors. The parents are, mostly, from the white minority: a not unusual situation in schools like this, since language and cultural barriers are difficult for the Bangladeshi parents to overcome. There are, however, governing bodies in Tower Hamlets where Bangladeshis are well represented and active. The co-opted governors are high-powered: they include a senior employee of the Stock Exchange who was coincidentally visiting the school on the same day as ourselves. The chair is an architect and a parent, one of the tiny handful of white middle-class families who live locally and strongly support the school.

The two parent governors we spoke to had the highest regard for the teachers' standards, planning, hard work and sensitivity to individual pupils' needs. They worried about the social segregation of the parent communities, and recognised that, huge problem though this was, it was something the governors themselves should turn their minds to. There was a recognition that a lot of effort had gone into trying to make the school more welcoming: the mosaic mural along the front wall was mentioned, and the parents' room and toy library.

The governors as a whole are strongly supportive and non-interventionist. The recent inspectors' review suggested that this was a potential weakness: 'their role should be further developed so that they take up fully their responsibilities in relation to the curriculum and administration of the school'. Efforts were clearly being made in this direction: there is now a governors' development committee and an active, effective finance committee.

SUCCEEDING AGAINST THE ODDS?

So in what way is Columbia School succeeding against the odds? Why was this school selected for a case study? For a Director of Education this is a sensitive issue. It is important to say straight away that Columbia is not the only good school in Tower Hamlets. On the criteria I used there were several others that could as easily have been chosen.

The criteria themselves were both quantitative and qualitative. In terms of the quantitative, the LEA has developed measures for putting in context what test results we have. In secondary schools we track individual pupils and compare GCSE results with their reading attainment on the London Reading Test taken five and a half years previously. In primary schools, where we have no comparable base line, we give each school a 'predicted' London Reading Test score on the basis of averages scored across the borough by children with particular backgrounds and experiences: with English as first or second language; entitled, or not, to free school meals; and with varying lengths of time in the UK education system. This is then compared with the actual score in each school.

This is fairly crude: a single test, for a single year group, in a single, albeit key, subject area, where the marks are in many cases so close together that 'league tables' are pretty meaningless. However, pending the full introduction of Standard Attainment Tasks (SATs) it is all we have. And what it does identify, and what we take seriously, is the handful of schools that are, year on year, scoring significantly above or below their predicted level, as well as those which are consistently moving up or down.

For qualitative judgement I rely on the inspectorate: both the LEA inspectorate's regular monitoring and reviews, and OFSTED (Office for Standards in Education) inspections or informal HMI (Her Majesty's Inspectorate) feedback where we have it. For all of our schools we have a mixture of these different types of evidence.

I was looking for a school that had scored twenty or more places above its predicted rank order on the London Reading Test for the last three years and which had received a highly favourable review or inspection report within the last two years. There are currently four such schools and I predict that next year there will be up to a dozen. For a number of practical reasons I chose Columbia out of this four.

Columbia's tested reading levels are well above the average for our borough and around the average for inner London as a whole, which means only slightly below the average nationally. Interestingly, when the Columbia figures are computed solely for those pupils with English as a second language, the scores are significantly higher. Given that this average includes many children who have been in the country only a short time and have not attained English fluency, this points to a significant proportion of confident, competent first-generation English speakers capable by eleven years of age of taking on their peers nationally.

The same impression is given by the review of the school carried out by inspectors in June 1994. This was reported in the new standardised OFSTED format, but none the less managed to convey a sense of unusual quality: eighty-eight per cent of lessons 'good or very good', relationships between staff, pupils and parents 'very good', the standards of oracy 'impressive', a 'consistently high pace of work' in technology, 'excellent examples of creative writing' in English, 'evidence of high quality investigative work' in science, 'particularly high standards in close observational drawing' in art. The following comment is particularly relevant to the ethos of Columbia: 'It is impressive to observe the mature way pupils of all ages approach morally and spiritually challenging stimulus material and are able to communicate their responses in visual form.' Comments such as these are by no means the norm in inspectorate reports in this new OFSTED era, where 'satisfactory' or 'sound' are the prevailing adjectives for schools not causing concern.

So what are the secrets of success in this case? The characteristics listed in the research literature fit like a glove: purposeful, curriculum-focused leadership; staff consultation and team work; an agreed and commonly understood purpose and values; regular feedback on performance; high expectations of both staff and pupils; concern for the physical environment of the school. But rather than merely describe the practices of the school against this check-list, it may be more interesting to describe the school as seen by the two 'non-educationists'.

LEADERSHIP AND ETHOS

Lesley Klein describes her impression of the school in the context of her preoccupation with the regeneration of the area. It is significant that she sees a strong stand on ethical issues and community self-confidence as key issues. This is what she writes:

> 'One of the elements that makes Columbia very special is that it has chosen to tackle the issue of racial division, but with an extraordinary lightness of touch and innate respect for people that belie the difficulty and emotional intensity involved.
>
> For a primary school to develop and promote a strong anti-racist ethos in the East End of London is a courageous step. In the locality it provides one focal point where everybody is clear about what is and what is not acceptable behaviour. It creates a moral high ground that is empowering for those who are usually the most disempowered. This ethical stance is as critical to regeneration as tackling the housing and employment rises, since race goes straight to the heart of the problems of this community.
>
> The creation and implementation of the equal opportunities policy is one plank in a cohesive and broad-based strategy adopted by the headteacher. The leadership and vision she has provided and the thoughtful tactics she has employed to tackle

improvements to all aspects of school life have after eight years of hard work created a robust structure for high-quality learning. Her vision of a place where involved adults and children are all motivated and purposeful around achieving an agreed common aim is a daily reality in a school where there are high expectations, exemplary behaviour, self-discipline, powerful educational standards, but all in an atmosphere of kindness and mutual respect.'

STAFF TEAMWORK

All of us were struck by the strength of the senior team and the consistent quality of the rest of the staff. Not many headteachers are in the fortunate position of having been able to hand-pick their entire staff. The headteacher herself describes this as 'mostly luck'. This is only half the picture. The high levels of turnover of teachers typical of Tower Hamlets up to about three years ago have in this school been confronted by the headteacher's uncompromising attitude towards quality. The ethos and structures of the school also tend to bring out the best in the adults who work in it: we heard more than one anecdote of a teacher who had decided to give up, changing her mind after a few weeks' supply work at Columbia.

However high the quality of individuals, it is the added ability that derives from getting them to work as a team that really matters. Judy Porter, who from her position within BP was taking a particular interest in the transferability of business management processes, describes the practice within Columbia as follows:

'The staff have a daily fifteen-minute staff meeting which all teaching staff attend to discuss immediate matters of the day and take the opportunity to share each other's plans. Points are also raised for discussion at greater length at the full staff meeting. This is proven good practice. It enables matters to be dealt with as they arise and ensures that everyone knows what is going on. Staff are made aware of visitors to the school, events and activities, availability of resources, and so on. Each term the headteacher and/or deputy set aside time in their diaries to consult individually on termly plans and monitor the quality of planning.

The staff meet fortnightly after school for curriculum development. This meeting alternates with a fortnightly meeting for each age group separately. In addition, the senior management team of five meets weekly. The helpers have a weekly meeting led by the deputy headteacher. These are seen as a valuable opportunity for sharing skills and experiences and tend to be activity-based, for example, art and technology techniques to be used in the classroom. The content of the five annual INSET (In-Service Education and Training) days, in which helpers also participate, are carefully planned by the senior management team, the appropriate curriculum leader and individual members of staff who volunteer to join planning groups.

The quality of teaching is monitored by the assessment of pupils' work and by regular attendance in classes by members of the senior management team and curriculum leaders, to observe and then give feedback.

There is an appraisal system in place, active long before the statutory system. Reviews are formally completed twice yearly. Results of the observation sessions are fed into the appraisal process. Self-development and self-appraisal are encouraged.

All of these are indicative of the strength of the team at the school. There is no fear, only benefit, to be gained from the process. Informal reviews introduced by the senior team not only identify development opportunities as they arise but also ensure that a continuous assessment is completed, and there is a 'no surprises' approach to the formal appraisal, a practice preached but often not practised in industry!

The helpers find that not only do they participate in the life of the school by helping the teachers and the pupils, but that they too are learning. Their sense of self-development makes for a more enjoyable and rewarding partnership.

One of the key early initiatives that the headteacher believes has led to the successful development of the school was to bring in an external consultant, a common business practice which often tells you what you already know, but helping to reinforce the message. Following an initial review the consultant then acts as a facilitator for the development of outcomes. In this case the school engaged the Grubb Institute, to work initially with the headteacher and deputy and then the whole staff to look at the role of the institution and the roles within it. This resulted in the production of the school's development plan. Every year the development plan is evaluated, reviewed and developed for the next year by the whole staff. The school has retained one of the original team as consultant to the senior management team.'

One important characteristic of the staff, in particular the teaching staff, is their perfectionism. Few I spoke to were satisfied with what they were achieving. There was even a wariness about the idea that the school had been chosen as an exemplar of a 'successful' school. They could see that there were shortcomings: after all, the children were not yet achieving up to the level of their peers in other areas. Whilst they would probably have been angry at outsiders making crude league-table comparisons, for all the obvious reasons, they are still setting those standards for themselves.

BEHAVIOUR AND DISCIPLINE

The development of a behaviour policy with the participation of all adults and children in the school was seen by everyone we spoke to as a milestone in the school's development. Catering staff commented, when asked why they thought the school was identified as particularly successful: 'The biggest change we have seen is in the children's behaviour.'

The process of developing the behaviour policy was as significant as its final content. Everyone, children and adults, was asked to describe behaviour they liked and did not like. The results were discussed and consolidated into a simple booklet listing responsibilities for children, for teachers and helpers, and for parents. Examples of misbehaviour, with appropriate sanctions, are listed under 'minor incidents', 'more serious incidents' and 'very serious incidents'. Simple conflict resolution techniques are taught to all children and used regularly to diffuse conflict and teach children to listen to one another and express their feelings.

Here is Judy Porter's description of the school council:

'Opportunity is given for all the school to participate in the issues relating to school life. This may either be through raising issues of concern to the pupils themselves, each class having the opportunity to raise one item for discussion at the council, or by responding to a whole school issue on which the council may be asked by the headteacher for its input.

Each class, from Year 3 upwards, elects a representative to stand for a term. The class has to understand the criteria for election and the election process and fairly select their item for discussion, including the expected outcome.

The meetings are held in a formal manner, with one child as chair, guided by the headteacher, and all questions passing through the chair. Minutes are produced and passed back to the classes. Control and communication are all managed by the young people, not the teachers.

It is evident that this is teaching the young people both communication and meeting management techniques normally not experienced at this age, giving young people a sense of responsibility, and a feeling of ownership of both the issues and solutions relating to school life. The type of issues raised and discussed at this meeting demonstrates the strong ethos of the school: the emphasis on caring and consideration for others. For example, a decision was taken against opening a tuck shop because it would differentiate those who had money from those who were less fortunate. Another recommendation was that a drinking fountain located in the infants' playground should be mended so as to prevent them getting hurt crossing through the junior playground area.'

We saw another recommendation of the school council in action. This was that indoor play should be available for the youngest pupils at lunch playtime, in order to relieve overcrowding in the playground and minimise pressures on the smallest children. Fleetingly as we left the school at the end of a visit we witnessed a hall full of five-year-olds sitting in small groups playing with Lego, puzzles and construction toys, each group supervised by a Year 6 pupil who had volunteered on a rota.

COMMENTARY

The above has been a sketchy description, based on statistics, documented inspectorate assessments and the impressions gleaned from the visits of the team. They cannot do justice to such a complex organisation as a primary school. To flesh out the picture I want to try and discuss three difficult issues which relate to this and other schools in Tower Hamlets and where they fit into the developing national education scene. These are: the 'political' climate of the school; minorities within the school; and the nature of 'good' teaching. All three interrelate.

The 'political' climate

I have used both a small 'p' and inverted commas in introducing the political dimension. But the big and small p's do not exist in watertight categories, and quotes do not protect any of us from the rawness of the situation. Politics in Tower Hamlets is complicated and intense, and is inextricably tied up with issues of race. When I first met the headteacher in 1989, the school was under the ILEA (Inner London Education Authority) and she had been an active campaigner for it to remain so, not least because of the perceived position on race of some of the borough's political leaders at the time. She wholly identified with the ILEA commitment to the 'progressive' platform: child-centred primary education, comprehensive secondary education, anti-racism, a heavy emphasis on equal opportunities. In her own philosophy none of these is inconsistent with high standards; indeed, they are an essential concomitant.

Her strategy, however, is to colonise whatever structures present themselves in pursuit of these aims. She played a leading role within the community of headteachers in moulding a mutually supportive relationship with the new education authority, despite all the misgivings about the end of the ILEA; seized on the National Curriculum as a way of helping her team to raise standards; and qualified as an OFSTED inspector to find out about and influence its workings. Externally she and the teachers appear to have embraced the 'reform' of the last ten years. Yet in reality they are profoundly antipathetic to much of its thrust. In many of their attitudes they might seem to conform to the 'trendy teacher' stereotype, and yet this would be a very superficial judgement.

One example is the fact that this school, unlike many others in Tower Hamlets, has not taken advantage of the menu of activities offered by the thriving local Education Business Partnership. Given that we had Judy Porter on our team specifically to ensure that the perception of the 'world of work' was included in our assessment, this was a mild embarrassment. In fact the school has a multitude of visitors, but mostly, as the headteacher explained, from the world of the arts or from other educational institutions of all kinds. There is an air of slightly sixties-ish distance from 'business'.

We discussed among ourselves whether this was a weakness, and decided that, in any case, if it was, it was marginal and was probably in the process of being rectified. After all, the new governor who just happened to be visiting the school that day was from the Stock Exchange! And Judy herself will now be following up an offer to provide some curriculum materials to support Year 6 study of the properties of oil.

This issue is important because of the current tendency to equate certain political and educational philosophies with poor teaching. 'We have to challenge teachers to abandon the "progressive" ideas some still cling to,' says Her Majesty's Chief Inspector. He typifies 'bad schools' as demonstrating 'a collective solidarity in the face of perceived political interference or inadequate funding'. That, at moments like the cut in Section 11 funding in 1993, was a good description of the Columbia teachers. On the other hand he describes a 'good school' as one where there is 'a questioning culture which allows everyone to contribute to a continuous review of what works and what does not work'. And that describes Columbia too.

Minorities within the school

My thoughts about minorities in the school are inconclusive. But because I do not believe the issue can be swept under the carpet, I will record them here. There are two obvious minorities: among the children, non-Bangladeshis; and among the adults, men.

Again it is not unusual to have only three men on the staff of a large primary school. This school is in fact lucky in that the early years coordinator, a member of the senior management team, is a man. But there is a very strongly female culture, particularly relevant perhaps in the context of the traditional attitudes in the parent community. Last year a whole school topic on gender roles culminated in a lively exhibition, with plenty of stories and illustrations of achieving women and caring men.

The fact that all of us writing this chapter, the head and the visiting governor from the Stock Exchange, are women would hardly raise an eyebrow in the world we all live in. In the inner city 'tough' areas top management in the public sector is now as often female as male. But have we done enough thinking about what this means for the self-image of boys, both those growing up within the traditional patriarchal values of the local Muslim community, and those from white working-class families where the tradition was until recently of physically demanding 'men's jobs' dominating the local economy?

A global futurist might say that the social climate of Columbia is dominated by the two groups whose energies, recently released, will be of huge significance to the world of the twenty-first century: well-educated women and migrant Asian communities. But what of the others? Fortunately, both the headteacher and the parent governors, some of whom themselves represent the 'others', are keenly aware of the 'minorities' issue, although it has perhaps not yet been fully discussed.

The nature of 'good' teaching

The impression gained by all three of us, none of whom was a primary education specialist, was that a great range of styles and groupings was being used: whole-school, where the assembly was a sustained educational experience which commanded the total attention of over 400 children for half an hour; whole-class; group work, both pupil-led and teacher-led; and individual activity, both self-selected and teacher-directed. Usually it was working. Sometimes it wasn't, but that was inherent in a philosophy of teaching which was open to new techniques. As long as there is constant evaluation and revision, as it appears there is, this diversity of method is a considerable strength.

Most classes in the school have thirty pupils. With Section 11 teachers, primary helpers and volunteers, there are often two or more adults in the classroom, and therefore frequent decisions to be taken by the teacher both about the deployment of the team and in relation to grouping. Some groupings are based on ability, some not; the latter often deliberately mixing ability for social reasons or to give an able child the opportunity to reinforce learning by helping others less advanced.

The success of such flexibility and such a repertoire of techniques obviously depends on detailed planning and skilled evaluation. Whether it could be replicated in schools with a less experienced and committed team is a difficult question. This conclusion is not helpful to anyone seeking a definitive description of the nature of good teaching; but clearly the issue is more complex than tabloid headlines and categorisations such as 'traditional' and 'progressive' would imply.

One possible model that is helpful is the concept of the 'learning company', or in this case the 'learning institution'. In most organisations and groups of workers, there is a mixture of more and less experienced, and more or less gifted, practitioners. If the organisation fully recognises this reality and arranges its affairs so that teaching and learning is taking place all the time for everyone, then practice is likely to improve. Ironically, since schools are so focused on the importance of children learning, the equally important adult needs tend to be overlooked. Columbia does not make this mistake; and it is perhaps this focus, rather than any particular methodology, that makes the difference.

Finally, there is one essential ingredient of successful teaching which needs emphasising. This is something which seems to have been in danger of getting lost in recent years: that is, the element of infectious enjoyment. Columbia teachers seem to know this. The headteacher reports that she sometimes has to send a teacher home when she is clearly too ill to be working, but does not want to miss the excitement of an experience she had planned for her class.

To illustrate this sense of delight, this chapter concludes with a contribution from one of the pupils. Speaking to a national

conference on inner city education last year, the headteacher finished by saying that however important all the diagnostic and summative assessment and recording, the statements of attainment and level descriptors, the programmes of study and value-added statistics, it was 'particularly important for teachers to give themselves a treat from time to time'.

And this was the treat – a poem written by a girl in Year 6 – to celebrate the birth of a friend's baby.

Lullaby for a new-born baby

High up in the sky a baby is born
With eyes like a shining sea.
His nose is like a sweet river
Lips are lovely like a flower
Like a moon he will grow
Dancing like apples

That grow on the trees.
His first touch is like the sky
He will be helpful like mother nature
Who made trees and flowers and gave us life.
He will have a lovely nature
And have love from his friends
And from his mother and father
And from us, who give him best luck
As he begins his life.
We want him to be a good boy
When he is going to school,
To be good at everything,
And to have a heart like a prince.

Sultana Begum

COLUMBIA PRIMARY SCHOOL

An LEA-maintained school for 2–10-year-olds

The school

Headteacher appointed	1986
Number of pupils	445
Number of teachers (full-time equivalent)	24.8
Pupil/teacher ratio	16.8:1
Average class size	26.5
Annual school budget	£0.78 million

Pupils in the school

Registered for free school meals (%)	71
With statements of special educational needs (no.)	2
Ethnic background (%)	
White	6.8
Afro-Caribbean	2.9
Asian	84.2
Other	6.1
With home/community language other than English (%)	71

5

LOCHGELLY NORTH SPECIAL SCHOOL

Fife, Scotland

John MacBeath, Ron Cully and Ron Lander

The research team describes this as 'a very special school'. The case study makes inspiring reading. Children and young people up to the age of eighteen who were for the most part rejected by mainstream schools as ineducable or incurably anti-social are nurtured to as high a level of success as they are capable of attaining. The school will never appear in league tables of examination performance, but, if there were such measures for staff dedication and parental support and satisfaction, it would rank among the best in the United Kingdom.

Success can be looked at in two different ways. One way is to measure and compare people against a gold standard such as examination achievement; another is to define success in terms of individual potential and progress. There are also two ways of looking at schools. We can see the school as a kind of 'black box', discounting the particular individuals who may happen to occupy it at any given time, defining it in terms of the structural features which make it a more or less effective school. Alternatively, we can see the school as an organism which is created and re-created by the particular people who inhabit it and give it its identity. So, in defining the success, or effectiveness, of a school we are offered two possible starting points – one with the school as an institution, the other with individual pupils, with their lives at home and in the community.

Schools have been studied from both of these perspectives ever since the mid-1960s, and research has produced an often savage critique of schools' failure to meet the needs and expectations of the disenfranchised groups for whom no promise of success was offered against the cumulative odds. Yet the two streams of research, which we might call ethnographic and 'school effects' research, have never come together in a common mainstream. That is in part because of the difficulty in reaching consensus on the key success criteria for schools, in part because of the difficulties in finding reliable and valid measures of those things which teachers, parents and pupils themselves value as 'education'.

A CASE STUDY

A small and successful special school provides a useful focus for exploring these issues because it illuminates both the complexities of the task and the value of undertaking it. Historically, special schools have moved progressively across the spectrum from an institution-centred view to a more organic and dynamic way of seeing learners and the learning–teaching relationship. They have offered challenge after challenge to conventional expectations and to our collective understanding of success.

The case study can be approached from both a 'top-down' and 'bottom-up' perspective. That is, we can study those aspects of the school's existence and identity which precede the particular pupils who enter it, and we can also track ways in which its character and ethos are actually shaped by children's individual needs and inter-relationships. We can, pursuing both these routes, address the essential question, 'what is it about this school that makes it especially successful?' or, from a parent's point of view, 'what will my child gain here that he or she would not gain elsewhere?' We might call this a 'value-added' way of seeing things because it is concerned with gains, and with the extra gains that can be expected in one school as against another.

So how might we go about assessing that added value? We will try to answer that question by reference to a small special school in Scotland and to the eighteen young people who comprise it, examining it in terms of the National Commission's ten salient features of an effective school. Evidence for its success against the odds, derived primarily from interviews and questionnaires, will be offered from the point of view of parents, teachers, auxiliaries, administrative staff, pupils, the education authority and HMI (Her Majesty's Inspectorate).

Questionnaires were given to all staff and parents. They contained twenty questions related to the ten National Commission criteria. Ten items asked for a 'strongly agree/agree' and 'disagree/

strongly disagree' response to statements such as 'the headteacher is a good leader'. Ten statements about staff, pupils and parents asked for a response in one of four categories 'true of all, true of most, true of a few, true of none'. Questionnaires were not used with pupils but discussions were held with older pupils about their attitudes to school.

This, together with visits, observation and participation in school, classroom and playground activities provides the basis for the following appraisal of Lochgelly North School.

THE CONTEXT

For Scottish people the name 'Lochgelly' has immediate and unhappy associations because it was in this town that the manufacturers of the 'tawse' (or belt) did a thriving trade up until the early 1980s when corporal punishment was finally abolished in Scottish schools. For the present generation 'the Lochgelly' is a quaint but symbolic museum piece.

The school sits on the edge of the town, its north-facing classroom windows looking across fertile valley and farmland to the kingdom of Fife. The southern aspect is less picturesque – a 1960s council housing scheme. The only tourist to see this part of the town, or indeed the town itself, would be one who had lost their way *en route* to a more celebrated destination.

It is, in fact, a more typical Scottish town than those on the tourist route, geographically and culturally adrift from the mainstream, its economic base diminished by the loss of coal-mining and other local industries. The unemployment rate among the economically active in the town as a whole is about 11 per cent, but in the immediate area of the school 12.5 per cent.

Nearly a quarter of the 4,000 people who live in the immediate area of the school are of pensionable age. Only 2 per cent are aged between five and fifteen and 7 per cent are of pre-school age. Twenty per cent of all children are living with a lone parent, in nine out of ten cases the mother; 99.8 per cent of the population is described as 'white'.

The immediate area of the school consists of 61 per cent council-owned housing and 35 per cent owner-occupier. About 4 per cent rent privately or from a housing association. Of the council-owned households, 72 per cent have no car.

The statistics are in many respects inadequate because they do not provide the more fine-grained detail of the quality of life, nor do they describe the social background of many of the school's pupils who come from further afield, from other towns and villages. Nor do they describe the nature of disadvantage which, for some, is compounded by socio-economic deprivation but for all derives from an accident of birth. All eighteen children have some form of learning difficulty which would make it hard for them to survive in the educational mainstream. All eighteen will face difficulties in living independent lives and finding employment. For most, neither of these expressions of success are realistic goals.

Local employers are themselves in an economic squeeze and are unwilling to take on young people whose contribution to the essential activity of money-making is likely to be outweighed by the amount of supervision they require. For the dwindling number of employers prepared to offer such opportunities it is an act of good will rather than a calculated business decision.

Opportunities for continuing education are few. The local adult centre offers little in the way of continuing education and a regular five-day placement is an exception, not the rule. Its principle of voluntary attendance means that young adults can take the line of least resistance and stay at home, throwing a burden back on their parents. Colleges of further education in the locality have minimal provision for this level of special educational needs.

To be accepted by others in your community, to be treated fairly, to continue your education after school, to live independently as an adult and to have a job are not rights but achievements. These have to be hard won and are beyond the grasp of many in Lochgelly North.

THE ALTERNATIVES

The alternatives to the school are local nursery, primary and secondary schools. The nearest schools which cater for pupils with similar learning difficulties are within a 10- to 15-mile radius. Most pupils come from the immediate area and have been in the school from an early age. In some cases parents who live at a considerable distance from the school have decided that Lochgelly will be most likely to meet their child's needs. Some pupils have joined more recently as a result of unsuccessful experiences elsewhere.

Mainstream primary and secondary schools are not an option for most of Lochgelly North's pupils although some have come through that route unsuccessfully and unhappily. One father compares this school with his son's previous experience in a mainstream school:

> 'The teachers there didn't have time for him. It was too big. He was a lost soul and unhappy. Here he's come a long way in his reading, talking and behaviour. He can learn a lot up here. There's a big, big, big improvement.'

A mother makes a similar point by comparing Lochgelly North with a mainstream primary school:

> 'The difference between here and the primary school is that kids are individuals and are treated as such, and the targets set are set for them as individuals. To be quite honest I don't even know if they know what a target is up there.'

A parent whose daughter had experience of special provision in another town made this comparison:

> 'There it was all doom and gloom, problems, difficulties, hassles, what he can't do, won't do. Here it is all positive, optimistic, giving you hope for the future.'

THE SCHOOL

The eighteen pupils of Lochgelly North range in age from two to nineteen. Two are of nursery age, six of primary school age, eight of secondary school age and two are over eighteen. All have learning difficulties, in most cases compounded by physical disability. Ten of the eighteen pupils have severe motor and mobility problems (three are non-ambulant). Seven suffer from epilepsy and four from cerebral palsy. Two are microcephalic and one is macrocephalic. One boy has Down's Syndrome. Nine of the eighteen have socio-emotional and behavioural difficulties, two of whom are autistic.

There are three full-time and one half-time teachers, three instructors and three auxiliaries. There is also a part-time administrative auxiliary. The staff divide more or less evenly between long-serving (eight to ten years) and those appointed within the last year or two. The present headteacher was appointed in 1992 but came to the school as a teacher in 1987. The school has three classrooms housing the three age levels – the juniors, the middle years and the seniors. There is also a newly equipped Snoezeln room, a sensory wonderland of lights and sound and textures. This has been designed to help stimulate normally passive children to explore their environment and discover the effect they can have on things around them. This room is also used for relaxation, massage and aromatherapy.

There are two histories of the school. The official one describes its metamorphosis from an occupational centre to a school in 1974. In 1980 it appointed a qualified teacher for the first time and brought in a second, the present headteacher, four years later. Only at that point, less than eight years ago, did teachers begin to teach in classrooms as opposed to extracting pupils for 'education' in a separate part of the building.

The other history of the school is a less dispassionate story told from the perspective of parents whose association with the school has spanned those years. One mother who brought her four-year-old Down's child to the school in 1982 described it in these terms:

'It was a dumping ground for weans that nobody else wanted.'

This was perhaps as much a reflection of social attitudes in the early 1980s as of the school. This same mother 'threw the health visitor out the door' after she had dismissed Daniel, at the age of three, as 'a waste of energy'. Daniel would, added the visitor, 'patently never make anything of himself'.

The school in 1995 is described by that parent as 'literally a different place'. Actually it is the same place, the same building and set of classrooms (and in a few cases the same staff) but the day-to-day quality of life is immeasurably different. But perhaps 'immeasurable' is the wrong word because its success can be quite specifically delineated.

The fact that the school's own success criteria accord closely with the ten features described in *Learning to Succeed* is not co-incidental. It reminds us that however individual in character and organic in growth a school may be, there are still some key principles of effective learning, effective teaching and effective school management.

STRONG, POSITIVE LEADERSHIP OF THE HEADTEACHER AND SENIOR STAFF

The current success of Lochgelly North School is attributable in large part to the leadership of two headteachers, the present head-teacher and her predecessor. Although they were different in style they shared some common convictions which now permeate the whole school. Its aims reflect a commitment to a view of learning which is shared by staff, school board governors and parents. The first of its aims is:

'to recognise learning as a continuous process taking place within the context of home, school and community and to forge strong links between those environments'.

It is not by accident that in this formulation of aims home learning precedes school learning. Staff and parents share the conviction that what is learned in school is only effective to the extent to which it builds on and strengthens what is learned at home.

Conviction and commitment to a robust educational philosophy are important qualities of the headteacher, but her strengths also lie in an openness and willingness to learn from the youngest member of staff or from the newest of parents. Staff describe her as 'informal and approachable', 'listening', 'flexible', 'willing to learn and to change', 'learning-focused'. This, in their view, is a difficult combination to achieve.

In the words of one parent, 'she doesn't carry her professionalism in front of her'. Her professionalism is so deeply rooted that she can meet parents on their ground and talk to them in their language. She is confident enough in her own authority to be genuinely open to learning from parents, and willing to adapt accordingly. As another parent put it:

'The school never stands still because the head and her staff always want to do better, and that means doing better for the weans.'

The questionnaire to parents and teachers asked for agreement/disagreement to the statement that the 'headteacher is a good leader'. There was a 100 per cent positive response to this from both parents and staff.

School management is described in the following way by an HMI report:

'It is firmly grounded in learning and teaching, supporting and enhancing good practice through a planned approach, setting clear goals and targets agreed by all as reflecting the essential purposes and priorities of the school.'

The headteacher herself, reflecting on management style, gives credit to staff as a whole:

'It's all about valuing people, staff and pupils, and it's about a management style that pulls it all together. We have a totally committed strong team who are interested in what they do and committed to working together to achieve their goals.'

Table 5.1 compares responses from parents and teachers on staff collaboration. It is one of the questionnaire items couched in negative terms but is unanimously rejected as a valid proposition.

Table 5.1 Staff don't work well together

	Strongly agree	Agree	Disagree	Strongly disagree
Parents	0	0	5	9
Staff	0	0	6	7

Note: Parents n = 14; staff n = 13

Visitors to the school do have difficulty in knowing who are teachers, instructors, auxiliaries or who is the headteacher, because the staff work closely as a team and because leadership is genuinely shared.

A GOOD ATMOSPHERE OR SPIRIT – SHARED AIMS AND VALUES AND THE PHYSICAL ENVIRONMENT

School ethos is often described in physical terms, pot plants and pictures, carpets and colours, welcoming notices and the display of children's work. On these measures the school is perhaps no more than above average, but in terms of a sense of shared values it is exceptional. To describe shared values as tangible may seem extravagant, but from the moment of entry to the school the visitor cannot but be aware of a community of purpose. It is positive and optimistic, expressed in smiles, in touch and gesture, in a constant stream of encouragement and praise which never seems to be dutiful or hollow.

That visible behaviour is not simply the expression of nice or friendly individuals. It comes in part from the appointment of staff who have that personal and professional capacity, but it is also a product of sustained staff development. It comes from talking and planning, challenging and learning from one another.

Their shared commitment to the essential mission of the school is reflected in the current development plan. It arose out of an exercise in which the staff worked in small groups, first brain-storming school priorities, working these down from twenty-five to fifteen to ten and then to the final five key priorities.

'The fact that the four groups all came up with the same five priorities showed how much in tune all the staff are with the whole school and all the pupils.'

(Headteacher)

The following two tables (Tables 5.2–5.3) provide supporting evidence for the assertion that school's ethos is less a product of its physical features than of a shared commitment.

Table 5.2 Inside the school is attractive

	Strongly agree	Agree	Disagree	Strongly disagree
Parents	3	11	O	O
Staff	2	11	O	O

Note: Parents $n = 14$; staff $n = 13$

Table 5.3 I am in favour of everything the school is trying to do

	Strongly agree	Agree	Disagree	Strongly disagree
Parents	11	3	O	O
Staff	8	5	O	O

Note: Parents $n = 14$; staff $n = 13$

HIGH AND CONSISTENT EXPECTATIONS OF ALL PUPILS

An effective school might be described as one that meets and exceeds expectations. High expectations are created both corporately and individually. They are created, first and foremost, through the ethos of the school as a whole – what HMI in Scotland have referred to as 'an ethos of achievement'. One parent's description encapsulates that well:

> 'This is a school that does not understand failure.'

Within that whole-school ethos high expectations are conveyed on an individual basis to pupils and to their parents. One parent whose expectations of her autistic son had been greatly exceeded said that she had 'come to realise the power of what could be possible'. The words of another parent, the mother of a Down's Syndrome boy, remind us of what has come to be known as the self-fulfilling prophecy:

> 'If we don't believe in what could be, it never will be.'

One avenue to raising of parents' expectations is by providing opportunities for parents to come in, to observe and to work with their children. Linda's mother describes the value of coming in twice a week for one school term:

> 'I learned not just what I could do to help her in the house and that is important, mind, but it made me want to do more for her and push her to do more for herself.'

Expectations are high but they are consistent too, at least in the sense that they are not arbitrary and shifting. They are not consistent, however, in the sense that they apply uniformly to all. Pupils have very different levels of latitude and tolerance, and it is part of the 'curriculum' that all members of the school community come to understand and accommodate these differences. It is seen as part of their preparation for the inconsistencies of life in the wider community beyond school. For the seniors it is particularly important, because in their role as befrienders of the younger ones they have to learn how to adjust to those expectations and demands as members of the school community.

A CLEAR AND CONTINUING FOCUS ON TEACHING AND LEARNING

The statements that pupils are 'given the fullest opportunities to learn' and 'make good progress' in their learning are unanimously endorsed by parents and staff (Tables 5.4–5.5):

Table 5.4 Pupils are given the fullest opportunities to learn

	Strongly agree	Agree	Disagree	Strongly disagree
Parents	12	2	0	0
Staff	7	6	0	0

Note: Parents *n* = 14; staff *n* = 13

Table 5.5 Pupils make good progress in learning

	True of all	True of most	True of a few	True of none
Parents	11	3	0	0
Staff	8	5	0	0

Note: Parents *n* = 14; staff *n* = 13

The emphasis in Lochgelly North is on learning. Teaching is all the more effective because of that consistent focus on learning and because in the process teachers themselves are learning and growing professionally. The goals and starting points for learning are so individualised that it means treating each child as unique and trying to find a key to their learning. To push five-year-old Fiona more towards exploring her environment and her own senses has presented her teachers with a daily challenge. Helping Fiona to learn is a constant process of invention and adaptation on their part. The objective of getting her to put her hands into a bowl of water was, after a series of ploys, eventually achieved by colouring the water blue.

At the same time staff are alert and responsive to any initiative made by the child, so when Fiona eventually took the initiative to go outside and stand for five minutes in the pouring rain, her teacher joined her, less through a sense of duty than to savour and celebrate that breakthrough with her.

Staff have discovered that for Gavin to learn to raise his head of his own accord the most effective strategy is to record his favourite TV programmes and replay them with Gavin lying on the floor, having to raise his head in order to follow the action.

Lack of suitable reading material for senior pupils led the teacher to use a tabloid newspaper, the *Daily Record*, as the stimulus for reading. The weather, the TV page, the sports pages offered an easy and engaging starting point for the group. Stimulated by pictures of people they recognised, pupils were spurred on to read the text and, where the text was too difficult, they made up their own stories from the headlines and the photographs. The group have just produced the first edition of their own newspaper.

This process of constant invention does not mean that there is no repository of expertise or curricular framework. In fact there are clear and specific learning targets in line with the national 5–14 guidelines but geared to addressing each individual need. The translation of these targets into learning and teaching strategies comes about by trying out and sharing good ideas. Skills of measuring and timing are learned through boiling eggs for different lengths of time, or making jelly with hot and cold water, and comparing the differences in texture and taste. Trips to the seashore and woodlands are a part of the science curriculum, exploiting every opportunity to develop a whole range of skills. Pupils explore the environment through observation, touch, taste and smell, developing motor coordination by netting in sea pools and putting bugs in matchboxes.

The science of survival is also an important aspect of that curriculum. It set out to develop life skills such as 'learning to anticipate', 'experimenting with cause and effect relationships', 'recognising potential hazards', 'judging speed of movement', 'detection of poisonous substances'. For some children learning is a dangerous business because they have not developed an awareness of the hazards of their environment and they have learned neither to generalise nor to differentiate; each new situation is met as if it were unique and unpredictable.

Opportunities to learn and to practise generic skills present themselves in a variety of situations, in the school, in the local community and beyond. Going to the swimming baths, for example, offers many opportunities for learning in a well-defined social setting, in some ways predictable, in some unpredictable and life-threatening. For pupils it is recreational; for the staff it means monitoring and developing social and life skills such as:

- learning to use a community facility;
- dressing and undressing;
- showering;
- adopting appropriate social behaviours – for example, voice volume;
- judging levels of familiarity with strangers;
- spotting potential hazards;
- anticipating cause and effect;
- exercising personal choice;
- negotiating obstacles;
- sharing experiences.

The success of what is learned in Lochgelly North is always tested by its value in the 'real world'. Children have to learn to fit into that real world. But the school also has to help the real world to accommodate these children, and it has to persuade people that they share some responsibility for the children's welfare too. The wider the variety of social settings the greater the opportunities for learning by pupils, teachers and the local community.

WELL-DEVELOPED PROCEDURES FOR ASSESSING HOW CHILDREN ARE PROGRESSING

Measurement of progress is an ongoing part of school life and an integral part of staff consciousness. A high level of alertness and interest in progress means that every gain is noticed. Because even the smallest gain is significant, it is celebrated, shared and recorded.

For example, a member of staff has kept a careful note of the length of eye contact which Fiona is able to sustain, and each increase is recorded as a significant step forward from her autistic world into the social world of other people. In interactive play she now waits for you to head the balloon back to her rather than just walking off.

Staff awareness of each individual child's needs is seen unanimously by parents and staff as a positive feature of the school. In interpreting the responses in Table 5.6 it must be borne in mind that the question assumes a very high standard for all staff in relation to every individual child.

Table 5.6 Staff know the needs of each individual child

	True of all	True of most	True of a few	True of none
Parents	13	1	0	0
Staff	8	5	0	0

Note: Parents n = 14; staff n = 13

Every pupil has targets which are set in consultation with parents, and progress towards those targets is carefully noted and monitored. A video recording of specific skills in action also allows these to be tracked and monitored over time. Parents find this a valuable form of record-keeping:

> 'I can look back at where Alice was last year. When I see how much progress she has made in that time it makes me more optimistic in what she might be in the year to come.'

Record-keeping is primarily there to support learning but it also has an accountability function. One member of staff, describing working with an autistic five-year-old, says:

> 'It would be very easy to just give a little less time, put in a little less effort with a child because you do put in so much energy at times to get so little back. It can at times seem such a waste of time. If you do give up and give time to someone more rewarding no one will blame you, no one will even know.'

The child is a silent witness. She will never tell on you, never hold you accountable. Tomorrow she may not even remember.

RESPONSIBILITY FOR LEARNING SHARED BY PUPILS THEMSELVES

For many of the eighteen pupils what is learned is highly structured and highly directed by teachers and parents. For some, the responsibility for their own learning seems impossible or a long way off in the future. Encouraging pupils to take responsibility for themselves is, however, a cardinal principle because it is the key to that future.

The emphasis on encouraging independence and initiative is confirmed by the responses in Table 5.7:

Table 5.7 Pupils are encouraged to be independent as much as possible

	Strongly agree	Agree	Disagree	Strongly disagree
Parents	12	2	0	0
Staff	10	3	0	0

Note: Parents n = 14; staff n = 13

Teachers, always willing to raise their sights, have devised ways of getting senior pupils to record and talk about their own progress and achievement. Self-evaluation is difficult for many and impossible for some, but as the teacher of the seniors believes:

> 'The pupil has got a valid opinion. A lot of people don't appreciate how much they can contribute to their own learning. Self-assessment gives them the opportunity to say how they are feeling . . . they can identify strengths and it gives them a sense of self-worth. They get a lot out of it.'

This principle is gradually filtering its way down to younger pupils and is accepted as an essential element of the assessment process. Staff talk about constantly trying to 'throw responsibility back on to pupils', but at times that can conflict with the actions taken by parents. Some parents find it difficult to challenge dependent behaviour and can often be over-protective and afraid of risk-taking. Perhaps teachers might be accused of taking risks which go beyond their status of *in loco parentis*. Allowing Fiona to stand in the rain and get a soaking might have gone against a parent's natural instinct. William's mother would not allow him to make toast or boil a kettle at home and was at first shocked to find that he was allowed to do this in school. Pushing back the boundaries of risk has, from parents' own accounts, been important learning for them. They have learned to shelter their children less and to help their children be more independent. As one parent notes:

> 'He will be dependent on me all his life. I would like him one day to be independent, to live on his own but it will be difficult for me to cope with because that will also be walking a line for him, a difficult and sometimes dangerous line. I must welcome every effort to take him in that direction even if it is a little heart-stopping at times.'

PARTICIPATION BY PUPILS IN THE LIFE OF THE SCHOOL

There are not many opportunities in Lochgelly North for young people to be involved in consultation and decision-making on matters of school policy, but that does not prevent staff from listening to their views and encouraging their involvement in every aspect of school life.

Participation in the life of the school is made much easier when distinctions between classroom and school, curriculum and extra-curriculum, work and leisure, learning and living are blurred. Learning in this school is not viewed in discrete segments. Playtimes, snack-times and lunch-times are 'quality time' for developing and practising skills. Senior pupils go out to the shops, choose and buy food, make the lunch, set the tables, serve the food and clear up afterwards. That sequence crosses the boundaries of classroom and school and school and community, and benefits the school at the same time as it develops initiative, decision-making and essential survival skills.

One senior pupil, comparing his previous school with this one, described Lochgelly North as a place where he could be happy because he knew that his ideas would be listened to and taken into account. As his teacher put it:

'They do have things to say. They think about things. They have opinions. They feel, like everybody else, but they cannot articulate those feelings, so we have to work harder at tuning in to what they expect of us and ways in which they want us to do better as a school.'

The weekly assembly which brings the whole school together in an act of corporate celebration is an opportunity to recognise and reward all kinds of achievements and to give more and more responsibility to pupils themselves in that particular expression of the school's life and values.

REWARDS AND INCENTIVES TO ENCOURAGE PUPILS TO SUCCEED

There is a large measure of agreement from parents and staff that encouragement and reward are the essential ingredients for success. The responses in Tables 5.8–5.9 suggest that those principles are, in fact, carried through into practice.

Table 5.8 Staff praise children when they have done well

	True of all	True of most	True of a few	True of none
Parents	13	1	0	0
Staff	11	2	0	0

Note: Parents *n* = 14; staff *n* = 13

Table 5.9 Staff don't encourage pupils enough

	Strongly agree	Agree	Disagree	Strongly disagree
Parents	0	0	2	12
Staff	0	0	6	7

Note: Parents *n* = 14; staff *n* = 13

Learning in Lochgelly North is built on success. The experience of failure is minimised by setting appropriate and realistic targets, with every small incremental gain recognised and rewarded. Where failure occurs it is important that children learn how to cope with it. A leap forward for Andrea was to be able to feed herself. It was preceded by a sequence of small steps, each one reinforcing the last and encouraging her, until she made that final breakthrough, a moment to be shared by staff and pupils together. Andrea's parents came into school and were surprised and delighted at this progress. Unfortunately they could not get her to reproduce this behaviour at home. A little diagnostic probing revealed that at home she was being given a spoon rather than a fork and could neither make the conceptual shift nor master the different technical skills which a spoon and fork required. Learning for Andrea is, in common with many children, context-bound.

Interactive play which is used as a key learning strategy with younger children exemplifies the approach to learning and teaching throughout the school. The pupil is encouraged to take control of the situation, whether throwing a ball or acting out a fantasy, to which staff respond by mirroring and reinforcing the action and moving it on to a higher stage. It is what behavioural psychologists would describe as 'reinforcement of learning' rather than reinforcement in the sense used commonly by teachers to refer to reinforcement of teaching.

In order for learning to be transferred from one context to another, parents and teachers have to share a common understanding of how learning occurs, how it is shaped and reinforced.

It means becoming more aware of some of the subtle factors at work in the school and home environment in relation to expectations, support and reward. Believing it can be done, encouraging the child to try it out and then celebrating success is, in a sense, a simple and common-sense sequence but it is embedded in a relationship and a past history. For parents to help their children to succeed means rewriting some of that past history.

William is now sixteen. He came into the school at four, hyperactive, manipulative, anti-social in behaviour and largely written off by the professionals with whom he came into contact. His mother's description of that four-year-old was: 'A pair of horns stuck on his head and he would have fitted the part.' William, at sixteen, is personable and responsible. He takes a weekly shopping expedition on a Thursday morning to choose and buy food for the following day's lunch which he makes in school. At home, much to his mother's continual surprise, he vacuums, does the dishes, makes his bed, and entirely on his own initiative will decide to clear out and tidy cupboards. The ability to manipulate is still there and will be used on the unwary, but it is one of the successes of the school that they have known how to handle it, made William aware of it and helped his parents to recognise and deal with it. Their systematic approach to monitoring and evaluating, rewarding and reinforcing good behaviour is now used by his parents at home. The skills of the reflective professional have been applied to the reflective parent.

> 'I have learned to step back. I have learned how to see what his behaviour is like and what he is learning and break it down into small bits and help him string the bits together.'

PARENTAL INVOLVEMENT IN CHILDREN'S EDUCATION AND SUPPORTING THE AIMS OF THE SCHOOL

Parents give the school their full support. In the view of staff and parents this is true of most, rather than all, parents (Tables 5.10–5.11).

Table 5.10 Parents give the school their full support

	True of all	True of most	True of a few	True of none
Parents	6	8	0	0
Staff	3	10	0	0

Note: Parents n = 14; staff n = 13

From the school side, keeping all parents in constant touch is a high priority.

Table 5.11 Parents (we) are kept in touch regularly with how their (our) children are getting on

	Strongly agree	Agree	Disagree	Strongly disagree
Parents	12	2	0	0
Staff	8	5	0	0

Note: Parents n = 14; staff n = 13

Every pupil takes home a daily diary. It contains a brief description of what he or she did that day, how he or she has been, successes and problems. The parent reads this and replies, describing how he or she has been at home, also noting any achievement or problems. It is seen by parents, pupils and teachers alike as an important and effective communication link. It is one that is systematically used and helped by pupils' own enthusiasm for it.

> 'It is the first thing she does when she comes through the door. Gives us her diary and we read it together. She creates merry hell if anyone forgets to give her her diary at the end of the day.'

There is a video version of the diary. Short sequences of pupils doing different things are videoed and sent home on cassettes supplied by the parents. They show short sequences of the child or young person engaged in tasks such as making lunch, reading, swimming, or demonstrating a newly learned skill. Although there is no formal reciprocal video of what children do at home, some pupils bring in videos of themselves – on holiday, for example.

The diary and the video are not just informational, however. They are a focus for dialogue between parent and child.

> 'It is difficult to get a word out of them about school. But the diary, and the video especially, are triggers. They give you a whole lot to talk about between you.'

The diaries also reward and reinforce progress by drawing attention to what has been achieved and give parents opportunities to praise their children's efforts and achievements. This is further enhanced by visits of parents to watch and participate in their children's classroom activities. One parent describes the home–school relationship as 'keeping the finger on the button'. She describes the constant vigilance which does not allow any small success to slip by. It is for her a transparently obvious educational philosophy:

> 'I can't see much sense in not building on what they are doing right. That would be a crazy way!'

EXTRA-CURRICULAR ACTIVITIES

There are no regular after-school activities in Lochgelly North School. This is seen by staff and parents as an area in which the school could do better (Table 5.12):

Table 5.12 There isn't enough in the way of activities after school (extra-curricular activities)

	Strongly agree	Agree	Disagree	Strongly disagree
Parents	4	7	1	2
Staff	0	9	3	1

Note: Parents n = 14; staff n = 13

This is the only item on which parents express a more negative response than staff. Perhaps it reveals a specific unmet need. The more guarded response of staff to the statement is moderated by their knowledge of logistical constraints and an awareness that there are a number of initiatives under way which do not neatly fit the extra-curricular category but which are important complements to the daily work of the school.

Parents have, for example, organised a Monday night youth club which all children attend. On Thursday nights senior pupils attend an activities night in the local high school. There is also a one-week summer school every year which consists mainly of games, sports and trips and is anticipated eagerly months ahead.

The once-weekly assembly is a time for celebrating success, for handing out certificates and trophies for achievements, both curricular and extra-curricular. The hand-chimes group visits sheltered housing and homes for the elderly, plays in local churches on special occasions and, according to one mother's (perhaps partial) account, 'stole the show at the High School's Christmas concert'.

There might, perhaps, be still greater scope for these if the transport and logistical difficulties could be overcome and appropriate resources and expertise identified. The willingness of most staff to be involved is not in doubt from either a parent or staff perspective (Table 5.13):

Table 5.13 Staff are willing to work extra hours if necessary

	True of all	True of most	True of a few	True of none
Parents	10	4	0	0
Staff	6	7	0	0

Note: Parents *n* = 14; staff *n* = 13

A PLANNED APPROACH

If the school can be judged to be doing well in terms of all ten features of an effective school, it rests firmly on its approach to whole-school planning and staff development and the support of the education authority for that process. It is described by the authority's senior adviser in the following terms:

'I think the school is one of the best examples I have seen of staff involved in development planning. They knew what they wanted of the school and they had a keen sense of where they wanted the school to be and what they wanted for their pupils. The documentation is clear and sophisticated, a good example of what a development plan should be but it was the richness of the discussion which led up to it which will be the real long-term benefit to the school.'

The acid test of the plan was during the prolonged absence of the headteacher through illness. In that time the plan gave a sense of continuity and confidence for the staff. Success criteria are depicted in the form of a series of pie charts on which segments are filled in as the school progresses towards its targets. The senior adviser commends the school's use of such 'simple ideas':

'The school is outstanding in using simple ideas ... for example, the pie chart on the wall where everyone can see it when they come to the school. The staff gain satisfaction and confidence from it and visitors to the school can see it.'

ADDING VALUE – SUCCESS AGAINST THE ODDS

Success is measured intuitively and impressionistically by staff in terms of the difference between a child on entry and on exit. The school secretary, whose office faces the front door, watches pupils come and go. She sees children who come into the school lacking in social skills and social awareness, often aggressive and frustrated because their efforts to communicate have been misunderstood or misinterpreted, go out as 'different children':

'Watching them go out the door you wouldn't recognise them as the same kids. A complete personality change like that ... you wouldn't ever have believed it was possible.'

Parents' observations of their own children's progress echo that:

'She just ticked over, passing time till she came here. Then she just took off. Well, it took a few weeks but then she was just a different wee girl. Honest, you wouldn't have recognised her.'

Another parent comments on the speed of change:

> 'We still cannot believe the change in him even in a month or two. He's happy, confident. He just loves the school. He doesn't want to take his holidays. He has just come away in leaps and bounds.'

Such gains in self-confidence and social competence are highly significant in their own right but they are also a necessary prerequisite for development of technical skills in reading, writing and mathematics. As one member of staff put it:

> 'Confident happy children are able to learn. They are less likely to run away from the challenge.'

For each of eighteen individuals in Lochgelly North School there is unambiguous evidence of success in both a relative and absolute sense: relative to achievements in other contexts, and absolute in terms of knowledge acquired, skills gained and behaviour learned. The 'added value' which lies between entrance and exit may be illustrated by one pupil. His progress shows how success is achieved against the odds and offers some salutary lessons to other schools.

MARK

Mark came to the school at the age of fourteen. He brought with him a report from his previous establishment which was uncompromisingly negative. It described him as showing little interest, aggressive and unresponsive, unable and unwilling to share or take turns, 'living life on his own terms'.

His most recent report from Lochgelly North is overwhelmingly positive. Among its comprehensive and detailed list of success criteria it includes the following:

> 'We are delighted with his progress particularly in terms of his self-control, confidence and relationships.'

'He has responded well to consistent behaviour management and an individualised programme which allows him to experience success on a daily basis.'

'He has good concentration skills. He can understand fairly complex text. Sight vocabulary is good and he can glean information from a daily paper.'

'He is confident in number up to one hundred and can do simple adding in his head. His money work is progressing and he has mastered calculator skills for more complicated work.'

'Aggression towards peers and staff is almost non-existent. He is now aware if his behaviour is unacceptable and he has recently shown remorse following an incident.'

'Although displaying immature behaviour during sex education lessons (giggling) he is now beginning to participate by expressing opinions.'

'He is very fond of younger children and is pleased when asked to take some responsibility for them.'

The key to what lay between the first and second reports illustrates ways in which the school helps every individual in its care to surmount the historical legacy which they bring with them. The single most important element in dealing with Mark was less by focusing on his behaviour than by addressing the factors which set the context for that behaviour: relationships in the home, the peer group, and with the school staff. Focusing on those contexts it was possible to provide opportunities for him to experience the success which had previously eluded him. One of the key factors to be addressed was his home background and his close, volatile relationship with his mother, a single parent who at times had difficulty in coping with his frustration and aggression. With support she was able to focus on positive aspects of his, and her own, behaviour instead of control and confrontation.

Success was achieved by encouraging his mother to treat him as a young adult, broadening his scope for choice, noticing and rewarding his good behaviour, picking up less on attention-seeking bad behaviour, taking time to look at his school work and keeping in touch with teachers through the home/school diary and telephone.

The second area of focus was through the peer group. Introducing a volatile teenager with anti-social behaviour into a small group which is beginning to gel and work together collaboratively presented a potential setback for everyone. Teachers had to work hard with the group to help them accommodate this new person into their lives.

The third focus was with the staff. Although often seen by parents or outsiders as saintly figures, the headteacher had to remind herself that they too could become frustrated, impatient and unsympathetic to someone who was continually unpleasant and personally abusive. As a staff they had to be constantly encouraged to respond positively to Mark and extend to him the quality of support they offered to others.

The consistency of approach and communication across these three social contexts, the family, the peer group and the staff group, set the context for Mark to change and to develop as a social being. It was also the necessary precondition for staff to begin to assess his number skills, his potential for competence in reading and writing, his talking and listening, and then to choose the tasks and targets which would help him move on.

The acid test of 'success' will be in terms of what happens to Mark, and his peers, when school is left behind. It will be tested by their capacity to lead independent lives, to be socially accepted and to make friends, to cope positively with their own sexuality, to have opportunities for further learning, work and leisure.

Parents and staff are acutely aware of the lack of opportunities that lie beyond the school perimeter. The local economy has little room for these young people and the scope for continuing education is poor. Parents and staff alike are keen to see the momentum

of success being sustained after school. They work hard at placements in work and further education but suffer disappointments
when employers or other educational establishments cannot assist. For
the school board this issue is at the top of their priority agenda.

The school may feel it has got it right in respect of the ethos,
learning, teaching and relationships, but they are conscious that
there is still a lot to be done in respect of the world outside. There
is encouraging evidence of progress. A local resident, who does not
have children at the school, describes her own changing attitudes:

> 'When I used to see one of these kids in the street I'd be embar-
> rassed. I didn't know where to look. I didn't know what to say.
> Now I can make eye contact and speak, smile and respond like
> I would to any other child or human being.'

The 'special school' stigma has not only disappeared from the
school name but increasingly from the way people think about it:

> 'Parents are proud of their children and proud of the school.
> They used to be embarrassed about saying where their children
> went to school. Now they are proud to say "My child goes to
> Lochgelly North".'

There are other key people in the community who have the power
to undo, sometimes very quickly, the long, painstaking work of the
staff. A single confrontation with the police, for example, could re-
ignite Mark's earlier abusive behaviour and provoke an escalation
of serious trouble. The school cannot take on its shoulders responsibility for the world outside but it can develop its links with outside
bodies. It can educate attitudes through the local press and through
community events which make the pupils more visible.

A SPECIAL CASE?

It might be argued that this small school with its generous staffing
and its peculiar needs is such a special case that its success could not

easily be replicated elsewhere. It is important to acknowledge the force of that argument, but we must also be alive to the educational values which shine through every facet of Lochgelly North's day-by-day practice. The educational principles by which it lives are principles which ought to apply to every school. Baskwill, in *Parents and Teachers: Partners in Learning*, published in 1989, describes what he sees as the key to effective schools and effective learning:

> 'What we need is a shift in thinking about the nature of the effective home/school communication, a new model of reciprocal responsibility based on a mutual understanding of what learning is; teachers communicating with parents on a regular basis, sharing everything they noticed about their child's growth in learning. Indeed, even more important . . . parents doing the same with teachers, feeling it was their place – and their right – to do so.'

That is a most valuable lesson to be learned by others from the success, against the odds, of this one small Scottish school. We are left, however, with a disturbing question which applies to all schools but is specifically acute in this special case: what is the difference between 'success' for a school and 'success' for the individual who passes through it on the way to a lifetime in the community?

Success for the individual is measured by what the community and the wider society can do to sustain and promote growth, to maintain the quality of relationships and to sustain opportunities for achievement and fulfilment. The danger is that these particularly vulnerable young people who have enjoyed such a high quality of care in childhood and adolescence will, as adults, find their expectations sadly deceived. The 'market' is too self-interested an entity to be trusted with that responsibility. If we are still to believe in something called an educational system we will need to take a closer, more critical look at what we can legitimately expect of schools like Lochgelly North and what can be done in the wider social, political and economic context to support their endeavours.

LOCHGELLY NORTH SCHOOL

An LEA-maintained mixed special school for 2–19-year-olds

The school

Headteacher appointed	1992
Number of pupils	18
Number of teachers (full-time equivalent)	4.5
Pupil/teacher ratio	4:1
Average class size	6
Annual school budget	£0.17 million

Pupils in the school

Registered for free school meals (%)	100
With statements of special educational needs (no.)	18
Ethnic background (%)	
White	95
Afro-Caribbean	0
Asian	5
Other	0
With home/community language other than English (%)	5

6

BURNTWOOD SECONDARY GIRLS' SCHOOL

Wandsworth

Peter Mortimore, Howard Davies and Sarah Portway

Burntwood School was formed in 1986 by the amalgamation of two neighbouring girls' schools. In 1992 it became grant-maintained, for a reason markedly dissimilar from that of most schools that made application for that status: Burntwood wanted to continue to offer a broad and balanced curriculum contrary to the LEA policy of developing specialist or magnet secondary schools. The success of this multi-ethnic school can be judged not only from the fact that it is heavily oversubscribed but also from its excellent academic record.

INTRODUCTION AND OUR APPROACH

We began our task by formulating a strategy. We wished to meet representatives of all the key players: the principal and the senior management team; the governing body; the staff; and the students. From these representatives we wished to hear whether they considered the school to be successful and, if they did, what particular factors contributed to this success. In order to deploy our limited resources to the best effect, we agreed to specialise: Howard Davies would focus on management and organisational issues; Sarah Portway would focus on the way the school responded to parents and the community; and Peter Mortimore would focus on the academic life of the school.

We wanted the opportunity – no matter how limited – to see the school at work in order to sense its ethos and, if possible, to observe the learning and teaching taking place. We also wanted to find a way to tap into the views of ordinary Burntwood students in order to supplement our interviews and observations.

WHAT INFORMATION WAS COLLECTED?

During the course of our investigations we visited the school on seven separate occasions and met with approximately 130 individuals. We had discussions with governors, the principal and her senior management team, staff and students from three year groups (9, 10 and 11) and the sixth form. Observations were made of teaching in classes in Years 7, 9 and 10 and on one of the two days in the year in which the students were given specific academic counselling on their reports.

We called upon the National Foundation for Educational Research (NFER) to help us capture the views of students. In 1993, on behalf of the National Commission on Education, it had drawn up a questionnaire to elicit the attitudes to schooling from a representative national sample of just under 1,000 Year 9 students. We commissioned the NFER to use this questionnaire to collect information from the whole of the Year 9 group in Burntwood. This information would give us an idea of what Burntwood students thought about schooling and it would also enable us to make comparisons with the national sample.

In addition, we analysed much of the paperwork associated with the school, including the prospectus, annual report, various brochures, policy documents, minutes and discussion papers.

THE NATURE OF OUR EVIDENCE

We were conscious that our task of uncovering the ways in which this school achieved its success necessitates dealing predominantly with the perceptions of its students, teachers and governors. We needed, therefore, to take all appropriate steps to ensure the validity and reliability of these perceptions.

With regard to information given to us by the students, we think the overwhelming agreement between the opinions expressed by the relatively small groups which we met and the NFER survey of Year 9 provides sufficient confirmatory evidence to assure us of its validity.

With the groups of governors and staff we had no way of testing how fairly we could generalise from their views and had to rely on the technique – common in the social sciences – of triangulation, whereby we compare the views of different groups on the same issues and only accept their veracity when we have found agreement. If the governors, the principal and the senior management team all indicate the same interpretation of school policy, there can be little doubt of its reality for the school. Similarly, if students and staff both draw attention to a particular aspect of the school organisation which they see as positive, it seemed sensible for us to pay attention to it. Of course, in some areas of our enquiry we would expect there to be genuine differences between the experiences and views of staff and students – for example, over the policy on uniform which staff thought was reasonable but students thought was excessive.

In general, we consider that the objective evidence about outcomes and the more subjective views we gathered about the school fitted well together and gave us a broadly realistic picture of Burntwood School as it is today.

BACKGROUND AND HISTORY OF THE SCHOOL

Burntwood was founded as a new school in 1986 following the amalgamation on the site of two neighbouring girls' schools. The building occupies a site of 13 acres of attractive grounds and was awarded an architectural prize in the 1950s. It consists of campus-style buildings. Two blocks house teaching rooms. There are dining rooms, science and technology areas, a library, a physical education block containing three gymnasia and a swimming pool, and a separate sixth-form suite.

The two schools that were amalgamated to create Burntwood had been very different. One was committed to mixed ability teaching, the other used a banding system; one had uniform, the other did not; one was democratic, the other was run on more authoritarian lines. Yet despite these obvious differences, the amalgamation and formation of the new school is generally acknowledged to have been highly successful.

Two factors are thought to have helped what, in other circumstances, has proved to be a very difficult task. Paradoxically, one was a delay in the appointment of a new headteacher. For one term the new staff, assisted by a talented and experienced advisory head, had the unusual opportunity to plan the school. This involvement and collegial planning seems to have left its mark and is still apparent in the staff's willingness to take on planning issues today. The other factor was that the chosen headteacher had had no previous connections with either school. She did not bring with her old loyalties, and could genuinely seek to create a new institution which would draw on the best aspects of both of the former schools.

The school became grant-maintained in January 1992 following a rejection by the governors of the LEA's plans for specialist secondary schools. The governing body wished to preserve the ability of the school to offer a broad and balanced curriculum. The vote to opt out of the control of the local authority was supported

by 80 per cent of the parents and 60 per cent of the staff. Two grants, of £500,000 and £800,000, for capital developments have enabled the facilities for technology and for science to be brought up to modern standards. The technology development includes a state-of-the-art languages suite in which the latest technology is available to students and teachers.

CATCHMENT AND COMMUNITY

The immediate neighbourhood of the school consists mainly of Victorian residential property. There is a large hospital adjacent to the site. Although most of the school's students live within the borough of Wandsworth, the shape of the borough means that many have an awkward journey to and from the school. The route is not well served with buses and, unusually for inner London, there is not a tube station within the vicinity of the school. There is a bus specially arranged before and after school, but the lack of good, normal transport links has a negative effect on after-school activities and on parents' attendance at meetings.

ADMISSIONS POLICY

The school admits 283 new students each year. Until 1995 all students were admitted without reference to their ability. Because the school receives about 70 per cent more applications than it can take, it offers places according to three criteria based on having a sibling already at the school, any special medical or social grounds and proximity of home.

Parents are invited to visit the school and meet the staff and students. For those who are unable to visit the school during the day, sessions are arranged during an evening and on a Saturday. All students who are offered a place at the school are invited to attend special interviews and are given an induction day and evening in the July prior to their starting at the school. Some students enter the sixth form directly.

From 1995 onwards, the school has been given permission to admit up to ninety places on the basis of ability. Girls whose parents wish to enter them for this competition are required to take quantitative, non-verbal and verbal reasoning tests.

THE STUDENTS

There are currently 1,500 students aged eleven to eighteen at the school. Two hundred are in the sixth form. They come from sixty or so different primary schools. Eighty per cent of them live in the local borough. About 70 per cent have family backgrounds from minority ethnic groups.

THE STAFF

There are currently ninety-five members of the teaching staff although they are not all full-time. The principal, three deputy principals, and four senior teachers make up a senior management team. Fifteen of the teachers are men. A third of the teachers were members of the staff of one of the two amalgamating schools. There are also twenty-eight support staff.

THE GOVERNING BODY

There are twenty-one governors, including the principal. Five are parent governors and two are teacher governors. The remaining fourteen governors represent the business community, the local community, journalism and education. Only one governor remains from either of the two amalgamated schools.

THE PRINCIPAL

Brigid Beattie has been principal since the creation of the new school in 1986. Prior to this she was the deputy headteacher of Holland Park School in West London and for the previous twelve years had worked in secondary schools in Haringay, Oxfordshire and in Inner London, where she had taught history. She is a Fellow of the Royal Society of Arts and a Fellow of the Management Centre at Roehampton Institute as well as a member of the BBC Council for Education Broadcasting. She is a non-executive Director of Wandsworth Community Health Trust.

THE SCHOOL TODAY

The school budget for 1994–95 is £3.8 million. The average class size is twenty-four. Students follow the National Curriculum and a special extended curriculum for students of marked aptitude.

There is setting by ability in most subjects. Special support is provided for those whose first language is not English and for those with special learning needs. Music, drama, dance and art activities are encouraged. There is a student council. The latest attendance figures for the school show that only 7.7 per cent of the total available schooling was missed because of authorised absence and a mere 0.2 per cent through non-authorised absence.

STUDENT INTAKE

According to the report on the school inspection carried out by Her Majesty's Inspectors in 1990 (the year of entry of the current Year 11 students): 'The school takes about one half of its students from economically disadvantaged areas, and the remainder from areas described as neither prosperous nor economically disadvantaged.' One-third of the students are entitled to free school meals. Although no data are available, anecdotal evidence suggests that a much smaller proportion of parents own or have access to a car than is normal in this part of London. Forty per cent of the current student body speak at home a language other than English.

In terms of the educational performance of the student intake, the school regularly commissions an analysis by the Research and Evaluation Unit of the local borough. This shows that reading scores have fluctuated around the national average but in recent years have been significantly below the average for girls. Mathematics scores have been below or just at the borough average. Scores in abstract reasoning have also been around the borough average but the proportion of girls in the most able group has declined. Interestingly, the educational performance of those students coming from outside the borough has, in recent years, been considerably worse than that of local students.

The characteristics of the intake of the school, therefore, whilst not approaching the levels of disadvantage of some inner city schools, are below average in national terms.

STUDENT OUTCOMES

The 1994 examination results show that almost 50 per cent of students obtained five or more of the higher (A*–C grades) in the General Certificate of Secondary Education (GCSE); also the national average for girls. Of all students 92 per cent obtained one or more of the higher grades and almost 89 per cent obtained five or more of the A*–G grades in the GCSE examinations. Given the somewhat disadvantaged nature of its intake, the school appears to be academically successful and to be providing a substantial value-added component to the achievement of its students.

In comparison to the success achieved by the school in the GCSE results, the 'A' level results seem disappointing. The average 'A' level points score achieved by each student was 8.6 (the equivalent of one grade D and two grade E passes or a combination of A/S levels). One factor influencing this result is the struggle the school has had, up until now, to retain its most able students in the face of competition from two successful tertiary colleges in neighbouring boroughs. In addition, forty-one students gained good qualifications in vocational examinations.

The indicators of success are, therefore:

- an oversubscribed entry;
- GCSE results above the national average;
- very low average absence rates;
- higher than average participation in further education (though not necessarily in the school).

ATTITUDES OF STUDENTS

As noted earlier, we invited the NFER to repeat the National Commission's survey of the attitudes of Year 9 students. The full findings from the national survey can be seen in *What do Students Think about School?* (Keys and Fernandes, 1993). The findings from the national survey enable a reasonable comparison to be made of the attitudes of the Burntwood students and those of female students in general. The NFER report on our Burntwood exercise makes the following points.

The main topics covered in the questionnaire were:

- background variables, including: gender; surrogate measures intended to provide an approximate indication of the cultural level of the home; perceived ability and behaviour in school; and post-16 educational intentions and attitudes towards school and learning including views about the value of school and school work, liking for school, interest and boredom with school work, and opinions on the purposes of schooling;
- perceptions of teachers and lessons, including: liking for teachers; teachers' support of pupils' learning; teachers' maintenance of discipline; individual discussions with teachers about school work; and liking for different types of lessons;
- pupils' self-reported behaviour in and out of school, including: behaviour in school; punishments; truancy; participation in lunch hour or after-school activities; reading for pleasure; length of time spent doing homework, and watching television or videos;
- perceptions of parental interest and home support, including: parents' opinions about the value of education; parental interest in pupils' progress at school.

Compared with the national sample of girls:

- 'the Burntwood girls were more likely to believe in the value of school and education and to believe that their school should teach them what would be useful for their future careers. They were also more likely to agree that school work was worth doing and that homework was important in helping them to do well and more likely to say they intended to continue their education after Year 11. However, they were slightly less likely to express positive attitudes towards their school and less likely to intend to stay on in the sixth form of their own school;

- the Burntwood girls were more likely to say that their teachers praised them when they produced good work. They were more likely to say that they talked to their teachers about their work, but less likely to say that they talked to their teachers about their future careers. The Burntwood girls were less likely to say that they liked all or most of their teachers;
- the Burntwood girls were more likely to say that they behaved well in school, but also more likely to say that they had received punishments (such as lines, detentions or being kept in). The Burntwood girls were more likely to say that discipline in their school was too strict and that there were too many rules. Their greatest objections were to rules concerned with school uniform;
- the Burntwood girls were less likely to say that they had played truant this year and slightly less likely to say they had been bullied;
- the Burntwood girls were more likely to say that they worked hard at school but had slightly lower perceptions of their own ability and of their teachers' perceptions of their ability;
- the Burntwood girls spent more time each day on homework and slightly less time reading for pleasure; they also spent more time watching TV and videos (but this could have been because the Burntwood survey took place in the winter, whereas the national survey took place in the summer);
- the Burntwood parents were seen by the daughters as slightly more supportive of the school, but there were no differences in the perceptions of the two samples in terms of parental interest in their future.'

These results provided us with some fascinating information about the school. They illustrate the positive way in which learning, good behaviour and academic achievement are viewed by the parents, students and teachers. It also shows us that the strictness associated with the teachers (and probably needed in order to achieve these good outcomes) is not always appreciated by the students.

Similarly, the finding of a commitment to further education and a willingness to transfer to a college at sixteen also illustrates the difficulties of retaining students in a single-sex school situated within relatively easy reach of large coeducational colleges with good reputations.

THE NATIONAL COMMISSION'S FACTORS OF SUCCESS

The school rated highly in relation to the ten features of success described in *Learning to Succeed*. There was manifestly strong positive leadership exerted by the headteacher and senior staff. We were also impressed with the good atmosphere that we experienced in the school. The physical environment had been enhanced and the grounds of the school were well kept; interestingly, the students were critical of the appearance of the buildings and felt they could be tidier. From our discussions with the teaching staff, we identified a clear and consistent focus on learning. High expectations were held on behalf of students who were, themselves, expected to take responsibility for their learning and to participate fully in the life of the school.

It was difficult at the early stages of our enquiry to know whether there were well-developed procedures for assessing the progress of students, whether there were rewards and incentives to encourage success, and whether parents were encouraged to involve themselves in their daughters' education. It was clear, however, that the staff provided several extra-curricular activities to suit students' interests and to expand their opportunities.

THE SCHOOL'S PUBLICATIONS

The prospectus gave details of the history of the school, its facilities, its curriculum, organisation of time, the extra-curricular opportunities and administration and included a section for parents. The text was clear and there were excellent photographs of life in the school. The prospectus also contained a supplement which listed the names and qualifications of staff, and provided a detailed breakdown of courses and the information required for the Parents' Charter, including a full analysis of examination results.

The official annual report from governors to parents was similarly well produced. It provided a description of life during the last school year. Dealing in particular with sensitive topics such as religious education, sex education and (anti-)bullying measures, the school strove to explain its policies clearly and succinctly. The report also provided a considerable amount of information on the work of the governing body and its sub-committees and included a breakdown of the financial costs of the school. The school development plan priorities for the next year were also listed and included the key policy of striving to reduce under-achievement. A full income and expenditure account was given in the report, as were the attendance figures.

Finally, details were given of outings to the theatre, exhibitions, museums and other special events of the school's sporting activities, musical achievements (including two choirs and an orchestra) and of additional clubs in mathematics, science, computing, languages and technology. School journeys and field trips in England as well as to Venice, Paris and Madrid were also listed.

THE SEARCH FOR AN EXPLANATION

The preceding sections provide the background with which we began our series of visits (apart from the NFER pupil attitude survey which is reported later on in our programme). We accepted that Burntwood was an effective school in that it was achieving reasonably good academic results with an intake of students that was somewhat disadvantaged. Our job, therefore, was to collect as rich information as we could in order to tease out the reasons for its success against the odds.

We have chosen to group the reasons that we identified mainly under the headings of values and mechanisms. We do so because we wish to draw attention to the way the school staff endeavour to link the school mission with very practical ways of achieving that mission. We are conscious, however, that other, equally satisfactory ways of organising the material could have been found.

VALUES

Clarity of aims and ethos of the school

We think the clarity of the aims of the school (built around the mission statement of the school, 'the best education today for the women of tomorrow') is crucial to the success of the school. We have been struck by the commitment of staff, students and governors to the principles and values embodied by the school community: the use of the school name as an adjective (and, at times, as an abstract noun) is a good example of the way this commitment reveals itself ('. . . a Burntwood identity' and '. . . that is not very Burntwood').

The way students appear to accept and identify with the school's aims and values seems to us likely to encourage their acceptance of responsibility and to create general good will. Compared to students elsewhere, they are more likely to see the value of education in general even though they complain about the school's strictness.

We have also considered the particular ethos of the school. In our view the Burntwood ethos is now a self-reinforcing system in which high expectations and enthusiasm generally lead to positive and constructive attitudes to learning and to better-than-average behaviour. These positive attitudes appear, to us, to be exhibited by both staff and most of the students (interestingly, not all students are positive, as the survey demonstrated) and to result in generally constructive and warm relationships. These are recognised and valued by the governors.

Focus on learning and achievement

The focus on learning throughout all aspects of the life of the school appears to be fundamental. It is apparent in the literature about the school. This focus was apparent in the sample of lessons observed. It was stressed in discussions with all our respondents. It appears to have been the dominant driving force of the school since its creation.

As evidence of the commitment to learning of the school governors and staff and of a lack of complacency, we noted that two of the three major priorities listed in the current school development plan are focused on the curriculum and on the organisation of learning.

We also considered it significant that the pastoral support system is nested in an academic structure. We also found that the parental involvement in the school is primarily focused on the educational development of their children.

We think these factors help to translate the rhetoric about learning into reality. The fact that teachers and managers demonstrate this shared understanding of the priority of learning over all other activities powerfully influences the ethos of the school. In comparison with other institutions which we know, there appears to be remarkably little evidence of territorial battles being waged between different segments of the school community.

The time and attention given to the reporting on progress also impressed us. The systems appear well thought out and effectively executed. The students obviously value the feedback they receive.

It became clear to us that not only is learning valued but also that the ethos of the school celebrates achievement. Governors, teachers and students all stressed the positive attitude to achievement that has been established and which is constantly reinforced. Learning is valued for its own sake but is also seen as the key to achievement. Students want to succeed in public examinations and thus equip themselves to do well in a career. The large amount of homework undertaken – with over 20 per cent of Year 9 students reporting over three hours each night, in comparison with a national figure of less than 2 per cent – illustrates the point.

High expectations

Expectations affect everyone involved with the school and are reflexive in their nature: they work in both directions. The governing body, for example, has expectations of the principal but she, in turn, has expectations of it. The governors have taken their role in the school very seriously. Led by their chair, they have participated in both collective and individual training programmes which have given them the opportunity to develop their contribution to Burntwood.

Similarly, both staff and students have expectations about the way the other party will behave towards them. The Burntwood Agreement, signed by each new student, parent and the principal of the school, lays out the rights and responsibilities of each of these parties and is, in effect, a formal expression of these expectations.

We have been struck forcibly by how frequently we heard high expectations being expressed of other people in this school. An extension of the policy on expectations has just been formulated on the principle that successful education requires students to co-manage the process. (We were surprised, therefore, that the NFER survey showed, on average, that Burntwood students had lower perceptions of their ability – and of their teachers' perceptions of this – than was the case nationally.)

We were impressed that both students and staff have had the opportunity to make explicit their expectations about the other party. We have come across schools where the teachers had produced expectations about their students but not where the process was reciprocal. We understand that, initially, some members of staff felt uneasy about the wisdom of providing an opportunity for students to comment on staff behaviour. We also understand this uncertainty and commend the staff for taking this risk. The highly positive reactions to the exercise that we elicited from students augurs well for future interactions between staff and students. The involvement of students in the formulation of the policy on expectations is an indication of the strength of the school's collective confidence.

We have also been struck by how 'hard-nosed' the expectations policy is. It even provides guidance on what happens if either students or staff fail to meet their expectations. It seems to us that exercises of this sort provide an excellent basis for the creation and maintenance of a positive ethos. We are conscious, however, that it takes time and energy to carry it through and that, to a certain extent, the ethos will have to be re-created from time to time as new students and new teachers join the school.

Focus on quality

We observed only a minute proportion of the school's teaching and discussed the matter with only a fraction of those involved, but the impression that we have gained, and which was supported by the views of students, is that the general quality of teaching in the school is high. We see the quality of teaching as being a supremely important aspect of the life of the school. Because it is high, the students feel confident in the ability of the staff to support their learning. In turn, because the students expect good teaching, the staff are more likely to continue to deliver it and, therefore, to gain more satisfaction in their daily work. The system thus becomes self-reinforcing.

We also detected a sense of healthy competition between members of departments and among 'clusters' (a group of departments is known in the school as a cluster) over the promotion of good teaching. This acts as an incentive to individual teachers who do not want to let the side – or their students – down.

Striving for quality does not stop with teaching. The school takes obvious pride in the way it presents itself and the quality of its collective behaviour. The carefully maintained grounds and the politeness and efficiency of the student receptionists illustrate a sense of professionalism and a quiet confidence in the way the school conducts its activities. Again, we were struck that the students – in comparison to their peers in other schools – did not judge the building to be particularly clean and tidy. This may, of course, reflect a more critical stance or higher expectations than found elsewhere.

Collegiality

We were impressed by the existence of a particular form of collegiality amongst the staff. This collegiality appears to operate at both the department and cluster level as well as across the school as a whole. Given the dispersed nature of the buildings, and the tendency of staff to take breaks in their cluster room, the collective, whole-school feeling is perhaps surprising and even paradoxical. Our impression is that the basis of this form of collegiality is a strong commitment to the underpinning values of the school.

We are conscious that some staff feel the pressure to be task-centred is so great that it does not allow time for social activity. This can be counter-productive in that problems that might be sorted out informally in staffroom conversation have to be resolved through the use of memos or formal meetings. At the same time we know there is a view that one of the benefits of life at Burntwood is the absence of a strong staff-room culture with its attendant rivalries and cliques.

It seems to us that the single-sex composition of the school and the predominance of women in senior positions on the staff provides a strongly unifying focus (encapsulated in its mission statement) for this girls' school. Given the mood in society, generally, that women need to assert their entitlement to an equal opportunity for achievement, this focus appears to generate considerable energy which the school is able to channel towards achievement.

Comradeship is also discernible amongst the students. Tolerance, patience, the valuing of diversity and a pride in the corporate success of the school were obvious amongst the representatives of the student body that we met. We are conscious that we have had the opportunity to discuss these issues with only a very small number of students. Without exception, those students were positive and articulate; we recognise that others may be different. The survey of the whole of Year 9, however, made clear that, whilst there is a range of opinion on most issues, the views of those we talked to generally reflected the views of the majority of students.

MECHANISMS

Leadership

It seems clear that the stable and secure leadership exhibited by the principal is a key factor in the success of the school – the absolutely key factor, according to some respondents. The determination of a respected leader to push the achievements of the school to the maximum appears to us also to be a major factor in the success of the institution. We have not had the opportunity to study in detail the style of leadership adopted, but we have heard from our respondents that commitment, attention to detail and high expectations are three of the characteristics much in evidence. We believe that the ability to judge the quality of job applicants is also important, and there is evidence that the principal possesses this skill to a high degree and uses it most effectively. A vital characteristic of leadership, in our judgement, is the way the principal is able to delegate to, and support, the various post-holders with leadership roles within the school. We think this has led to a willingness to take ownership of developing school policies and is clear evidence of staff appreciation of this support.

Deciding who does what, in terms of the leadership of a large organisation, is obviously crucial. We think the skill of knowing when the decision needs to be taken by the whole staff, the middle managers, the senior management team or by the principal herself is extremely valuable. The evidence given to us suggests that, on the whole, decisions have been taken correctly. There is also evidence that the principal's habit of thanking and congratulating staff for particular achievements is highly reinforcing. We were interested that this began as a joke with the principal using stationery with the picture of a tiger but that it has become part of the school tradition. Now tiger-sticker headteacher awards are highly sought after.

Management

The school is clearly managed very efficiently. A senior manager with a financial background was recruited at deputy principal level and has invested his time and energy in creating good systems and sound financial policies. The organisation appears well structured and professional: communications are generally clear; responsibilities are well defined; and services are managed competently. There is a strong corporate identity that appears to have been reinforced, if not created, by a number of related elements, including the logo, the uniform and the newsletter. The general view seems to be that this strong corporate identity helps the school to function well. It seems to us that the emphasis within the school on what are sometimes called short-term reinforcers of appropriate behaviour also promotes successful functioning. A considerable amount of corporate effort appears to be invested in rewarding students and staff for outstanding achievement or particular efforts. We think this is a sensible strategy and consider that the benefits for the school repay considerably the efforts of the principal and senior staff.

We were also interested that the school appears – collectively – to be able to cope well with change. The transition to grant-maintained status appears to have been smooth. The recent change of entry policy to include a selected group of pupils might have caused considerable turbulence but appears not to have done so. Similarly, we have been struck by the way administrative systems are regularly changed and improved.

Communications

In many institutions one of the most common complaints is about the lack of good communications. This has not been the case at Burntwood. Communications appear to be good, and it is obvious that considerable time and energy have been invested in creating and developing appropriate channels. Examples of such channels are the cluster meetings and the feeding of views up to the senior management team and, reciprocally, from the senior staff down to the clusters. Special consultation exercises (such as the diagnostic windows sheets which the principal uses to take a 'rain check' on staff views of different aspects of the school) are also used fairly frequently.

Monitoring

We are only too conscious that the systems we have seen require careful monitoring in order to retain their effectiveness. Whether it is the amount and quality of homework being undertaken by the students, the level of GCSE results or the quality of the individual feedback given in the biennial reporting sessions, there appears to be evidence of good monitoring systems at work. The frequency of monitoring does not appear to be resented; it seems that both staff and students see its value and appreciate its purpose within the overall goals of the school.

Participatory decision-making

As we have noted earlier, we were impressed by the amount of participatory decision-making that takes place. The advantages of this can readily be seen in the high proportion of the staff accepting ownership for policy decisions. Because the debates surrounding those decisions have been well conducted and there have been opportunities for exploring the advantages and disadvantages of particular courses of action, the decisions appear to have been made on rational grounds even in areas of policy which, in other schools, have been seen as highly emotional. The involvement of students in decision-making – where this is appropriate – also appears eminently sensible, as do the attempts to seek, and listen to, the views of parents.

Parental and community involvement

The relationship of the school with parents is deemed important and is still being developed. The strategy to engage parents in year groups and in the educational processes of the school is clearly sensible. We suspect that, if the achievement of all or a great majority of the student body is to be raised significantly, current strategies for parent involvement will have to be enhanced.

The relationship with the community, however, appears still to be at a relatively *ad hoc* level. There are examples of links with local businesses (for example, through the British Telecom scheme and GNVQ programmes) but these do not yet seem to be part of a fully planned outreach programme.

In our judgement, the school has pursued an intelligent policy in seeking to establish its emphasis on learning as its major priority. It may be that it is now at a stage to develop its outreach potential in a rather more coordinated way.

OTHER CONTRIBUTORY FACTORS

Grant-maintained status

The circumstances in which the school became grant-maintained are unusual. A Wandsworth Borough strategy for the creation of specialist schools, modelled on North American Magnet Schools, was rejected by the governing body, and, incidentally, by all other governing bodies of secondary schools, the parents' consultative committee and the headteacher.

The governors of Burntwood then acted in order to protect the autonomy of a girls' school to offer a broad and balanced curriculum. The result was that a school which – had it been located in another part of the country – might well have rejected grant-maintained status, embraced it in order to protect its character. This history, together with the extra funds made available because of the change of status, has proved uniquely favourable to the development of the school. Significant changes in the philosophy of the school have occurred without a great deal of disruption or ideological tensions. The school has remained in harmony with itself. The extra capital funds have been used to upgrade its facilities and now include a computer network and very impressive science facilities.

The first year of the new status is said to have been an exhilarating one. The services of the LEA were not missed greatly. Only educational psychologists, welfare personnel and one adviser (who is carrying out an evaluation of the appraisal system) have been carried over from the old to the new system. Under grant-maintained status small but significant changes have been introduced at a speed previously deemed to be impossible. There is a feeling that the school is now free to develop, unhampered by political agenda.

The decision to apply to the Secretary of State for permission to accept 30 per cent of the entry on the basis of academic selection was taken on pragmatic grounds by the governing body as the only way to protect the balanced intake of the school.

Buildings and site

The advantages of a relatively large site with its extensive landscaping and its campus-style environment are considerable. Games facilities on-site also increases the attractiveness of the school. The buildings, which in the 1950s were considered outstanding, are considerably better than those of many other urban schools. Recent capital grants to improve and extend the facilities have enhanced the opportunities open to students of the school.

WHERE NEXT?

Maintenance and enhancement of current standards

As we have made clear, we believe that this school is successful and that it has succeeded against the odds in an exceptional way. We have sought to explain our understanding of why the school is in this position. Given the investment we have made in seeking to understand the institution, it would seem foolish not to go one step further and identify three further challenges.

In our view the first challenge will be the maintenance and enhancement of current standards. Given the pressures on urban schools with disadvantaged intakes, sustained effort is required even to stand still. The work of an effective school succeeding against the odds is never over as, each year, new students and new staff will join and have to be convinced that success is possible for them. These newcomers will not share ownership of the way the school functions even though they may well have been attracted by it. They will need to be socialised into the norms of Burntwood. The way we have described the school's ethos as a self-reinforcing system illustrates the importance of continuity. Continual efforts and further innovations involving new staff and students are essential.

The sixth form

The current size of the sixth form of about 200 students has enabled it to function, in our judgement; it is not really large enough to flourish. In order to offer a sufficiently broad choice of 'A' levels, GNVQs and various other vocational qualifications, a larger sixth form base would be beneficial.

We have been impressed by the way in which the school has changed its strategy on the sixth form. Whereas at one time the policy was to isolate sixth formers and imitate the ethos of a self-standing mini sixth form college, the current view of staff is that this was counter-productive. Such a sixth form could not compete with other, much larger colleges in neighbouring boroughs and able students constantly drifted away.

The new policy seeks to strengthen – rather than to diminish – the links between the sixth form and the rest of the school. It aims to impose prefectorial duties and to associate each sixth former with a class of younger girls. Rather than focusing on the separateness of the sixth form, the school now seeks to integrate it with the rest of the school and to provide opportunities for leadership for older students.

Families from minority faith groups find these arrangements attractive and safe for their daughters. Where there is a strong preference for all girls' education, the arrangement is also likely to be attractive to other families. We think, therefore, that with this strategy the school may well be able to expand its sixth form and to provide a firmer academic setting for both the study of 'A' levels and GNVQs.

For this strategy to succeed, however, it will be necessary to raise the current levels of achievement. More top A and B grades will be needed if the school is to establish itself as a serious rival to the local colleges and to independent schools. Currently, as we have noted, the achievement at eighteen is not as impressive as at sixteen, and this is clearly a weakness. In our view the senior management team would be wise to review 'A' level teaching techniques and ensure that appropriate staff are recruited in order to bring about an improvement.

Outreach

We learned of a number of interesting activities involving local business companies but were struck by the lack of an overall policy for outreach work. We recognise that the first priority for a school must be its focus on learning and achievement within the curriculum. Now that this appears secure – at least up to the age of sixteen – we think this should be the moment to improve and consolidate relationships. Links with local companies could be enhanced and pupils' work experience integrated into this arrangement. Staff work experience in different fields might also be included if this was deemed appropriate.

Parents

It might be time to rethink the school's policy towards parents. It will obviously be necessary to reconsider any new policy in the knowledge of the difficulties that many families have in getting to school functions because of work or family commitments and poor evening public transport. Innovative approaches may need to be undertaken. It might, for instance, be worth making a series of Burntwood videos to accompany options choices or applications to the sixth form. The promising results of year group, as opposed to the whole school, parents' meetings will need to be evaluated and, if appropriate, further developed.

CONCLUSION

Like almost every other school in the country, Burntwood is not perfect, and we have set out three areas in which we think improvements are both necessary and possible. Nevertheless, in conclusion, we wish to reiterate the fact that, in our judgement, success has undoubtedly been achieved. One of the key ingredients of success has been the ability of the leadership of the school to motivate the

staff to plan for further improvements. It is this continual seeking for improvement that we see as the main source of energy in the school.

In carrying out an investigation of this sort, and in writing a positive report on the school, we are aware that we may be encouraging complacency. We trust that the staff will resist this temptation and – with the knowledge that we have been impressed – continue to strive for excellence and to refuse to accept that anything less is good enough for their students. Urban schools are demanding places in which to work. Successful ones demand more of both staff and students than is sometimes thought reasonable. For the students, however, such schools can have a very powerful positive influence on their life chances. At a time of such radical changes in the patterns of work and in society in general, the benefits of attending an effective school are likely to be of even greater value for urban pupils coming from disadvantaged backgrounds. This is why schools which succeed against the odds are important and why governing bodies, headteachers and their staff deserve to be congratulated on their success.

BURNTWOOD SCHOOL

A grant-maintained comprehensive girls' school for 11–18-year-olds

The school

Headteacher appointed	1986
Number of pupils	1,469
Number of teachers (full-time equivalent)	90
Pupil/teacher ratio	16.3:1
Average class size	24.5
Annual school budget	£4.04 million

Pupils in the school

Registered for free school meals (%)	30
With statements of special educational needs (no.)	9
Ethnic background (%)	
White	34
Afro-Caribbean	17
Asian	29
Other	20
With home/community language other than English (%)	56

School outcomes

% of 15-year-olds in 1994
achieving GCSE passes

5+ A*–C grades	48
5+ A*–G grades	91
1+ A*–C grades	86
1+ A*–G grades	96

% of Year 11 (1993–94) students
who are now

In full-time education and training	98
In employment with training	0.5
In employment without training	1.5
Other	0

% of 16-year-olds entered for 'A'/'AS'
level (or equivalent) in 1994   21.8

Average points score for
'A'/'AS' results (1994)   8.6

7

HAYWOOD HIGH SCHOOL
Stoke-on-Trent

Michael Barber, David Carr
and Margaret Carter

There was a time, in the early days of comprehensive reorganisation, when the amalgamation of two schools was a challenging experience, given new buildings and additional funding. In the 1980s, when Haywood High came into existence without those advantages, amalgamation was more traumatic; and, in an area of considerable social deprivation and low parental interest, the challenge was of another kind. The way in which this school has responded to the low esteem in which it was held and the low expectations of its pupils is the key feature of this case study. One of the most significant features is the high percentage of pupils who now remain in education after the completion of compulsory schooling.

Haywood High School, situated as it is in High Lane, has views over much of Burslem and the rest of the Potteries. The school playing field looks on to the stadium, if that is the appropriate term, of Port Vale football club, an organisation that knows all there is to know about the vagaries of league tables.

The school serves two large housing estates, both of which are predominantly council-owned and are representative of the more deprived parts of the Potteries. Behind the school a gloomy shopping street runs down the hill towards Burslem. The shops are of the small, local variety and each of them has its own one-armed bandits aimed, according to Yvonne Jeffries, the headteacher, to persuade pupils to part with their limited funds on their way home. Some years ago the fish-and-chip shop there did a roaring trade during the school lunch hour, and bought a row of game machines to exploit the pupils while they were in the queue. Yvonne Jeffries, who was appointed in 1989, decided, as part of her improvement strategy, to prevent pupils leaving the school at lunch-time. The chip shop owner was outraged. He said the school was putting him out of business. The school was unmoved and the chip shop is still there. The incident is a sharp reminder that being responsive to the local community, as the jargon has it, is not always plain sailing.

The school buildings themselves are a mixture. The site, because of its wide views across the area, feels more expansive than it is in reality. The current school is the result of a traumatic amalgamation on to the present site in the late 1980s. Most of the buildings are post-war but there is a beautiful new block, built in the last three years, paid for from Staffordshire LEA's (local education authority) capital programme. Building on sites in the Potteries is not always easy since there are often abandoned and long-forgotten mineshafts to avoid. This explains one or two unusual environmental features at Haywood. The last phase of the building work is still in progress and will affect the administrative offices and entrance hall. The recent building programme has made an important contribution to raising morale at the school and thus to improvement.

In 1994–95 the school had more than 830 pupils. Of these 200 take free school meals, and approximately 100 are from minority ethnic communities – in the case of Haywood, overwhelmingly Asian. One important sign of returning community confidence is that each year the intake has risen. Thus the school has 122 pupils in

Y11, 167 in Y10, 170 in Y9, 176 in Y8 and 197 in Y6. There are 45.1 (fte) qualified teachers and the school had a budget for the 1994–95 financial year of £1.5 million, though like many schools is facing cuts this year, and has little in the way of reserves. The average class size is thirty pupils. In fact, as pupil numbers have grown the pupil–teacher ratio has worsened from 14.7 in 1991 to 19.4 in 1994.

The GCSE examination results in 1994 were a disappointment to the school. About 20 per cent of pupils aged fifteen at the start of the school year 1993–94 achieved five or more grades A*–C; 80 per cent achieved five or more grades A*–G; and 100 per cent of those entered for City and Guilds were successful. This represented a setback from two years previously (1991–92) when over 25 per cent of pupils had achieved five grades A*–C at GCSE. Interestingly, in terms of four grades A*–C, as opposed to five, the school has continued to improve.

The headteacher and her colleagues expect to see a significant step forward in the 1995 results, and indeed their confidence in the improvement strategy depends upon it. When we asked the headteacher whether the 1995 results would be better than 1994, she replied firmly, 'They have to be.'

The school's own analysis of the 1994 results suggests that at least part of the explanation of the dip lies in the trauma of amalgamation five years previously. The school reached a low ebb during the amalgamation, with poor staff morale, high levels of truancy, poor pupil behaviour and a complete loss of any sense of identity. Its reputation in the community fell catastrophically, and indeed a powerful part of the improvement strategy since then has been aimed at rebuilding community confidence. In 1989 there were only just over 100 pupils in the intake instead of a standard number of 180. The consequence was that the 1989 year group had entered the school with very poor levels of literacy and minimal parental support at the start of their secondary schooling, since more supportive parents or parents of able children had taken their custom elsewhere. The 1994 results are therefore, the school would argue, atypical. They have good reason to believe that results in each of the next three years will be considerably better. That is not to say there is any sense of complacency at the school. The staff at Haywood do not think they are yet working in a successful school; but they are convinced it is an improving school. The hall-marks of the school's response to last year's examination results were analysis, thought and practical steps for moving forward.

The extent to which pupils from the school remain in education after they leave Haywood High School has also increased dramatically over the last four years. The improvement in the staying-on rate at Haywood outstrips that in the rest of Stoke-on-Trent, in Staffordshire as a whole and indeed across England and Wales. The staying-on rate has improved from 21.9 per cent in 1989 to 51.4 per cent in 1994. It peaked in 1992 at 55.6 per cent but the school expect the figures for 1995 and 1996 to exceed this level. In an area of historic low expectations this is a remarkable achievement. Of course, as in the rest of the country, the shift is not the sole responsibility of the school: a combination of the recession and changes in the benefit regulations made a contribution too.

The school faces its future with a good balance of newly

qualified and experienced teachers. During and just after the amalgamation there was significant turnover, but in recent years the staff has been stable. Interestingly, however, there is still a significant number of staff who taught at the school before and during the amalgamation. They are now amongst the most powerful advocates of the school and mention repeatedly the transformation in the morale of the staff and the expectations and demeanour of the pupils that has taken place in the last five years.

THE LIFE AND WORK OF THE SCHOOL

In our visits to the school and in examining its documentation, we looked explicitly for evidence of the ten characteristics of successful schools set out in the report of the National Commission on Education, *Learning to Succeed* (see Appendix A). This section reports on the school against those criteria.

Strong, positive leadership by the headteacher and senior staff

We had no doubt at all that this characteristic was in evidence. All the staff we spoke to recognised the important role the headteacher had played in the progress the school had made. They shared her vision of an improving school with high standards and expectations, a positive reputation in the community and a staff who enjoyed being at work. They also believed that the headteacher had made a vital contribution in radically improving relations between pupils and staff.

They mentioned repeatedly three particular characteristics of the headteacher's management style. First, she knew each of the staff well as a person, remembered to thank people for their special contributions and attended to those critical personal details which matter so much. We were told, for example, that whenever a member of staff moved to another school they would, on their first day in the new post, receive a personal note wishing them good luck.

Second, the headteacher was praised for her ability to delegate. She did so not only through the formal hierarchy but also through responding to the initiatives of individuals and through asking teams of volunteers to take responsibility for drawing up school policy on important themes. We spoke, for example, to two teachers who had volunteered to draw up the school's anti-bullying policy though it was not formally part of their responsibility. They had taken the initiative to attend relevant courses, had led consultation with pupils and staff, and drafted a policy which had recently been approved by the whole staff. We encountered a number of similar examples.

Third, all the staff recognised that the headteacher was prepared to take responsibility for tough decisions, when they were necessary. These included decisions relating to staff performance and under-performance.

The headteacher appeared to be well supported by the deputy heads and other senior colleagues. The deputy heads clearly took responsibility for the detailed administration and worrying about vital but routine issues such as attendance, the timetable and overseeing the ongoing building contract. Their attention to the detail of these issues provides the headteacher with the opportunity to be an effective educational leader.

A good atmosphere generated by shared aims and values and an attractive physical environment

Both pupils and teachers believed that the school had a positive and cheerful atmosphere. Certainly, in the classes we observed, in the corridors and in the formal meetings we attended, we gained the impression of a warm and happy community.

In addition, there was a shared emphasis on high expectations. The pupils spoke of the consistent pressure from the headteacher and the staff to achieve. It has to be said that the same pressure was not present in the home environment of some of the pupils. The staff were convinced that during the five years in which they have made such significant progress the social problems of drugs, crime, unemployment and family breakdown confronting the school have intensified. For a significant minority of pupils this contrast clearly presented them with an almost irreconcilable conflict. The headteacher and many staff therefore often found themselves in counselling mode and believed that in the vast majority of cases the pupils trusted them sufficiently to share their personal dilemmas. Similarly, the evidence we gathered suggested that the pupils respected the teachers' contributions, both academic and pastoral.

The physical environment had clearly received a great deal of attention during the past five years. The new buildings provided a superb learning environment and some excellent new facilities such as a drama studio. Much of the rest of the buildings had been improved too. There were, for example, carpets in places and numerous displays of pupils' artwork. Not all of the facilities were excellent by any means and inevitably finance is strictly limited. Nevertheless, the surroundings have clearly been improved throughout the school and transformed by the investment the LEA has made in new buildings and the refurbishment of part of the old buildings.

In most of the classrooms we visited there were displays of posters, pictures or pupils' work, although there probably was room for further improvement in this respect.

High and consistent expectations of all pupils

The high expectations of pupils that appeared to be a feature of the school have already been commented upon. It is obviously difficult to judge consistency on the basis of a few visits within a short space of time. Nevertheless, the issue emerged repeatedly in discussions with staff and pupils. In the lessons we observed it was evident that teachers made attempts to motivate pupils across the ability range and that they expected a great deal from each of their students. The pupils themselves testified to the pressure they believed themselves to be under. The evidence of high expectations came through in the marking of work, the school's approach to assessment and in the ways in which teachers used questions in classrooms.

There were also some cameos we came across which provided evidence of the point. A group of pupils had taken an interest in a local man, Jack Baskeyfield, who had been killed in action during the Second World War and posthumously awarded a VC (Victoria Cross). They had interviewed his widow who still lived locally and discussed his war record with his regiment. They had then not only prepared a written report about his life but also, in cooperation with a leading Potteries company, designed and produced a memorial plate which the company and the school were about to market. This is a remarkable example of the full exploitation of an idea and of the best form of cross-curricular activity, bringing together history, design and business.

Well-developed procedures for assessing how pupils are progressing

Limitations of time meant that we discovered less about this aspect of the school than we would have liked. Nevertheless, we know a significant amount about it from previous contacts with the school. A vital feature of life in the lower school is the day book. This is a Filofax-style document which each pupil always has to hand. In it they note what work is to be done, while teachers and parents use it to comment on a pupil's progress. A similar idea exists in many schools; the key to its success is whether it is rigorously used by all parties and particularly whether form tutors and subject teachers ensure that it is kept up to date and remains a living document. The evidence we saw suggests that this is the case at Haywood High School.

In Years 10 and 11 pupils work towards records of achievement which record not just their academic performance, but performance across the whole range of school activity. Parents receive detailed and regular reports. The school examines the prospective grades of Year 11 students and targets those who appear to be performing below the school's assessment of their potential in the months leading up to GCSE. This is an example of the school's careful record-keeping and the use it makes of its assessment data.

Responsibility for learning shared by the pupils themselves

Here the evidence we have was probably not adequate to reach a rounded judgement. Certainly, in the lessons we saw pupils were active participants in the learning process and appeared, in the main, to be well motivated. The evidence from a survey of pupil attitudes in the school conducted at Keele University suggested that pupils at Haywood are significantly better motivated and more positive about school than those in many comparable schools.

The day-book system also acts to encourage pupils to take responsibility for their own learning. This is reinforced powerfully by the availability of additional voluntary classes after school. This encourages young people to choose to learn more and thus to take responsibility for extending their progress. The staff considers this to have been an important element in changing peer-group pressure.

Participation by pupils in the life of the school

Haywood High School constantly impressed us with regard to this aspect of successful schooling. Perhaps the best example of it in action was the prefect system. In Year 11 there were between forty and fifty prefects, roughly one-third of the year group. They had been appointed through a full-scale appointments procedure towards the end of Year 10 when the posts of prefect had been advertised. All those who believed they were able to fulfil the requirements of the person specification and the job description were encouraged to apply. Each application was considered and then candidates were interviewed formally by a member of staff. There was no strict limit on the number who could be appointed and therefore all those who met the criteria were appointed. The few who were not appointed were told that this was due to doubts about their commitment or behaviour (or both), but that if there was evidence of change over the next two to three months, then their applications would be reconsidered. This process was open and encouraging, and, of course, involved important learning experiences in relation to preparing for life after school.

It was, however, by no means the only evidence we saw of pupil involvement in the life of the school. Pupils had been involved in drawing up the behaviour policy and the anti-bullying policy, for example. The prefects themselves took responsibility for contributing to many features of school life such as the supervision and stocking of the library under the supervision of the full-time librarian. Not all the prefects participated fully, pupils told us, but many did. What was impressive, however, was the clear sense that the pupils felt that this was their school.

Rewards and incentives encouraging pupils to succeed

The school had placed great emphasis in its behaviour policy and in its overall approach to achievement on providing positive re-inforcement and incentives to succeed. Young people's achievements are recognised through an awards evening, through assemblies, through a range of certificates, through letters home and through the many day-to-day interactions between pupils and teachers. Rewards are available not just for absolute performance but for improvement and across all aspects of school life, including attendance and behaviour, not solely academic success.

It was difficult to reach firm conclusions, but we gained the impression that the rewards system, which needs in any school to be permanently under review, was not always entirely consistently applied.

Parental involvement in children's education and in supporting the aims of the school

The staff of the school emphasised the efforts they had made to encourage parental involvement. The day book was perhaps the most concrete evidence of their efforts, although it was clear too that attendance at parents' evenings had improved significantly, with the overwhelming majority now attending.

Overall, there is no doubt that there is extensive parental support for the school. Yvonne Jeffries says that one of the key indicators of their changed attitudes is that she no longer has to deal with a stream of angry and sometimes aggressive parents as she did in the late 1980s. Conversely, whereas then a complimentary thank-you letter from a parent was rare, she now receives a steady stream of them. She and other staff also pointed out that the parents on the governing body and involved in the 'friends of the school' were always constructive. Nevertheless, the most powerful message from our days in the school was that involving parents was a demanding uphill struggle in which success was at best limited. The school clearly does not believe it has solved this problem, a view shared by many urban schools.

There were two problems teachers remarked on repeatedly. One was the historically low expectations in the community. They saw part of their mission as being to transform attitudes outside as well as inside the school walls but they were far from convinced they had succeeded. In this aspect of their work they have been greatly assisted by their participation in the Two Towns Project referred to in detail later which brings together three high schools, the FE (Further Education) colleges, the two local universities, the TEC

(Training and Enterprise Centre) and the LEA in a school improvement project. The signs are that attitudes to education in the Potteries are changing, but only slowly, even with these combined forces working on the issue.

The second problem was what Yvonne Jeffries referred to as the decline of parenting. All too many parents, the school suggested, had not provided the secure, supportive upbringing that young people need in areas where drug-related crime has steadily increased over the last few years.

It seems that, however successful a school is, it will not be able on its own to overcome these wider and deeper social currents. It can, however, play its part in changing the culture while in the meantime doing its best for the young people during their time at school.

The school will hope to benefit in the next few years from Stoke-on-Trent's success in gaining funding from the government's Single Regeneration Budget for the Cobridge area, which includes part of Haywood's catchment.

Extra-curricular activities which broaden pupils' interests

The school provides an extensive range of extra-curricular activities at the end of the school day. These include homework clubs and additional classes as well as traditional extra-curricular activities. Great emphasis is placed on these after-school activities and many pupils choose to participate in them. The school sees them as an important part of the process of changing.

There are also numerous individual projects. For example, the school has been involved in an art project with the Royal Academy and with local Potteries firms on various design and production projects. The Jack Baskeyfield project has already been mentioned. They also designed and produced a series of plates for the 1991 Milk Race which passed through Stoke-on-Trent.

Collaborative activities with companies had also taken place, for

example, with Royal Doulton, TSB and H&R Johnson. These companies, and many others, also provide work-experience places and contribute to the range of work-related activity the school provides.

Other factors

It would be possible to list a number of other aspects of success in Haywood. Here it is our intention to refer to just one. School improvement is hard work and makes huge demands on the staff in terms of energy, skill and commitment. We were impressed by the positive attitude of staff, including teaching support staff, and by their dedication. It is surely a central part of successful school management to create the conditions to enable the staff to make this kind of commitment. One example of the extent of Haywood's success in this respect is the range of after-school provision which is provided by teachers out of sheer commitment to the school.

SCHOOL POLICY

In the previous section various aspects of school policy have already been examined. This section supplements them by examining:

- the school's decision-making process;
- its approach to teaching, learning and the curriculum;
- the school's policies on attendance, behaviour and bullying;
- the school's participation in the Two Towns Project.

The decision-making process

As we have seen, Haywood's management approach involves extensive delegation and encourages staff to take the initiative in promoting development. It is important to bear this context in mind because the formal structure of policy-making is only part of the story. In many ways the informal 'can do' culture is more important to the success of the school.

A management team, consisting of the headteacher, the two deputies and the senior teachers, meets regularly. There are also monthly meetings of heads of departments and of the middle managers with pastoral responsibility. Approximately twice a term there are full staff meetings.

Yvonne Jeffries also emphasised the importance of the daily briefing. This lasts five to ten minutes and is an opportunity to exchange information. She also uses it consciously to build the sense of team work and to focus on the positive. She takes the opportunity to congratulate colleagues publicly for recent achievements. It is also an opportunity to share a joke. She says that in her early days as a headteacher she spent a great deal of time every evening planning that brief ten minutes, seeing it as a vital opportunity to shift the culture.

We were able to talk to representatives of the governors. They clearly have absolute faith in the headteacher and are committed to supporting her philosophy and her policies. They see their role more in terms of linking school and community than as a formal decision-making forum. In decision-making, the governors are relatively passive. The deputy heads are involved in the governing body's committees and have played an active part in building the cooperative relationship that exists between governors and staff.

The approach to teaching, learning and the curriculum

Haywood High School's formal curriculum varies little from that available in many comprehensive schools. All pupils study the full range of ten National Curriculum subjects and religious education in the first three years. During Year 9 young people and their parents make choices about what to study in Year 10 and Year 11. All follow appropriate Key Stage 4 courses in English, mathematics and science. Most continue to do a modern foreign language. Beyond that, pupils have a wide choice, which includes some vocational options. Where GCSE is considered inappropriate there are other externally accredited options available. For example, in 1994 thirty-three pupils were awarded a City and Guilds Foundation Certificate.

The school's approach to teaching and learning is built on the notion of high expectations. As the school aims state, it wishes 'to stimulate the highest possible standards of academic and personal achievement'. As becomes apparent in visits to the school, high expectations are a matter of detail as much as of general aspiration. It involves positive responses to pupils' questions about career options: it is not simply a case of answering their questions but of challenging lack of aspiration where it is apparent. It also involves teachers being constantly aware of the importance of their countless interactions with pupils during the course of the school day. These are crucial issues, evidence of which would take much more time to gather than we had. Nevertheless, the evidence we do have is broadly positive.

The approach to teaching and learning, according to the school's aims, emphasises the development of basic communication and literacy skills, and involves 'active learning methods, the appropriate use of homework and the encouragement of the use of library and computer facilities'. We saw some evidence of this in practice. The school has, for example, a full-time librarian who apart from meeting the needs of a full house at lunch-time, also provides support and assistance during lessons.

In the lessons we observed there tended to be a combination of formal, direct teaching of the whole class and active individual and group work. Pupil behaviour, once order had been established, was on the whole good.

The school's policies on attendance, behaviour and bullying

The school's policy on attendance is the responsibility of one of the deputy heads. It emphasises the importance of punctuality and attendance. The deputy head monitors carefully the attendance levels in each class and liaises appropriately with form tutors. Individual pupils with poor attendance records are carefully followed up and the deputy head has a weekly meeting with the LEA's education welfare officer. This relationship is an exceptionally good and effective one. The school's approach involves the careful monitoring and follow-up which must be the central plank of a policy on attendance. It has not chosen the approach of publishing throughout the school class-by-class attendance figures, though this strategy is considered effective by many schools. On the other hand, it has laid emphasis on public acknowledgement and praise of high levels of attendance by individuals.

The behaviour policy was arrived at through widespread consultation among staff. It might be described as mainstream if not traditional. It stresses that pupils are expected to 'recognise the authority of the teacher' and to 'behave in a courteous and orderly manner and show respect for others, their property and the environment'. Again there is a strong emphasis on praise and on accentuating the positive. Through the prefect system there is also an element of pupil involvement.

The key to successful behaviour policy is consistent application. This is difficult to evaluate in fleeting visits. Again the evidence we did see of pupil behaviour in classrooms and corridors was largely positive. Certainly staff testify to a huge improvement in pupil attitudes to school over the last few years. Poor behaviour and attendance threatened to overwhelm the school around the time of the amalgamation. While it would be an exaggeration to suggest it was no longer a concern, certainly it is now a manageable problem and the general tenor of the school is one of calm purposefulness.

The recent development of the school's policy on bullying has already been referred to. Bullying is not currently considered to be a major problem although its existence in the school is openly acknowledged. The process of developing the policy has opened up the issue in the school, and ensured that it is not hidden from view as it is in so many schools. The policy aims to involve pupils as well as staff in challenging bullying and to monitor it through confidential questionnaires as well as recording the follow-up to them. It is too early to say how effective the new policy will be but its development is certainly consistent with what is currently considered to be best practice.

The school's participation in the Two Towns Project

The Two Towns Project is a school improvement project in the Potteries towns of Burslem and Tunstall. Haywood, along with two other secondary schools, has been involved in the four-year project, which ended in 1995.

The project was initiated by Philip Hunter, the Chief Education Officer of Staffordshire, and the then Professor of Education at Keele, Tim Brighouse, and was funded by the Staffordshire TEC and the Paul Hamlyn Foundation. The additional funding paid for a project coordinator based at Keele and for each of the schools to have a small but significant sum for innovation and development at school level.

Targets for the three schools were set through a process of discussion and proved to be under-estimates of what was possible. In terms of GCSE results, staying-on rates and truancy rates, progress in the three schools has been significantly greater than either Staffordshire or national averages.

Yvonne Jeffries acknowledges the importance of the Two Towns Project in helping Haywood to improve. Her view is reinforced by the senior teacher with responsibility for coordinating the Two Towns Project at school level. The collaboration with other schools, the sharing of ideas, the pressure of meeting publicly agreed deadlines and the inspiration of working with nationally known figures are all significant aspects of the project's contribution to the school. In some ways they are more important than the obvious material benefits.

The headteacher of one of the other schools expressed a view which Yvonne Jeffries shares: that the project did not so much persuade them to do what they would not have done anyway but it did enable them to do them more quickly and effectively. As she put it, 'we achieved in three years what might otherwise have taken ten'.

ACCOUNTABILITY IN THE SCHOOL

The issue of accountability in education is a complex one. A powerful element of the reforms of recent years has been an attempt to make schools more accountable to parents and the public. There have been four pillars of this drive for accountability: the National Curriculum, national assessment, the performance tables and OFSTED inspection. It might be added that predominating over each of these four is the idea of market accountability: the pressure on schools, following the 1988 Education Reform Act, to recruit pupils if they want to maintain a viable budget.

The underlying shift in this policy thrust is the notion that it is the individual school that is accountable for raising standards and not the LEA or any other organisation. Since this shift in the point of accountability has been accompanied by the delegation of budgets (which has been particularly extensive in Staffordshire) and many personnel powers, it has caused a transformation in the role of headteachers.

An interesting aspect of our visits to Haywood is that this series of changes, perhaps the most important revolution in education this century, was barely referred to in our discussions with the headteacher and teachers. It seems that the reforms have simply been taken in their stride as staff focus on the higher goals of school improvement. In this process the changes have been largely positive as far as Haywood is concerned. The management of the budget, for example, has fitted well with the school's clear sense of direction and its emphasis on delegating power throughout the staff.

It is possible to look at the school's response to accountability in relation to the four pillars. The National Curriculum caused similar trials and tribulations in Haywood as elsewhere and the school's response to national assessment at KS3 was similar too. Meanwhile the school has yet to undergo OFSTED inspection though it was inspected by HMI in 1991–92, a report which assisted the headteacher's efforts to bring about change.

The performance tables, however, have had a significant impact. We have already seen the threat they posed after the school's relatively disappointing results in 1994. On the other hand, the publication of results probably does help to galvanise the staff in its determination to improve. Perhaps this is so because the school has a target-setting culture which originates with its involvement in the Two Towns Project. The project targets, unlike the national performance tables, emphasise improvement against previous best rather than any given absolute levels. The extent of improvement is monitored at both school and departmental level.

Market accountability has also been a powerful influence. The community's loss of confidence in the school was identified by Yvonne Jeffries as a high priority in the improvement process. It must have seemed possible at the time that the school's reputation in the community would become irreparably damaged. This has happened to another Stoke school involved in the same reorganisation. In fact Haywood's reputation has been painstakingly rebuilt with the result that, judged in market terms, it has been remarkably successful, as its intake figures reveal.

The headteacher and staff, however, would see accountability going far beyond the market or the four pillars. They recognise the importance of governors and they see the school as having an important, indeed leading role, in the community. It would not be an exaggeration to suggest that the staff see themselves as having a mission to transform expectations in the community. This has been very much part of the Two Towns philosophy which underpins their approach to school improvement.

Beyond these forms of accountability there is an overt sense in Haywood High School of an assumption, often among teachers, that they are accountable to the students they teach. This is a matter of detail as well as generosity. The specific request for careers or academic or personal advice from a particular pupil matters and deserves attention. It is interesting, for example, that the school ensures that a nurse is available regularly for young people to consult about health or personal problems.

Finally there is a strong sense of professional accountability. All members of staff are aware of their responsibility to colleagues. And while all staff would no doubt accept that they were accountable to the headteacher, the day-to-day experience appears to be the opposite. The headteacher has a strong sense that she is answerable to the staff for representing the school to the world outside and for maintaining the course the staff have collectively chosen.

SCHOOL IMPROVEMENT

Though research is able to tell us what characterises effective schools, it is important to remember that effectiveness is not a static state. Even a school which against all the criteria had achieved success could not rest on its laurels. The education service changes. The demands of society change, staff move on, the intake alters. Put another way, the process of becoming effective – of improving – never ends.

Haywood High School is certainly an improving school, and has travelled a long way from the gloomy place it found itself to be in the late 1980s. This improvement can be seen in its results, its staying-on rates, attitudes within the school and community attitudes to the school. The school hopes that the investment of thought, commitment, energy and insight that it has made will also bear fruit in terms of those stubborn, hard statistics of examination achievement. It is hard to be certain, but the evidence indicates, in our view, that the process of improvement will indeed continue in the next few years.

There is a growing body of literature about 'what works' in school improvement, much of it referred to in the opening chapter of this book and in some of the case studies. It is our intention in this concluding section of this chapter to identify those factors that appear to us to be at the core of Haywood High School's improvement.

One that is evident is the value to the school of participation in an improvement network with other schools and organisations. From the Two Towns Project the school has derived ideas, encouragement, affirmation, positive publicity and some helpful additional funding. The project has been a catalyst in establishing the process of success breeding success.

Another, evident throughout the chapter, is the quality of leadership of the headteacher. The clear, firm, collaborative style that characterises Yvonne Jeffries' approach appears to have worked. It is worth noting in passing that the hard, lead-from-the-top, I'm-the-boss approach would have been unlikely to have been effective in the late 1980s when so many staff and pupils had been bruised by the process of reorganisation.

A further evident quality in the school is what might be termed a consistent striving. The staff we met were, as far as we could determine, seeking improvement at the level of detail as well as generality. In other words, it affected their approach to teaching, day-to-day interactions with pupils, and their planning. There was no sense of either complacency or hopelessness. To some extent this was a result of the headteacher's conscious effort to empower others, both staff and pupils. The culture of the school encouraged people to make change happen rather than to wait for others to do so.

Finally, the school's culture was built upon excellent interpersonal relationships. Many schools state that they aim to achieve mutual respect, a sense of quiet purpose and positive relations between teachers and pupils. Haywood, even in its difficult social setting, has achieved this in reality. Educators have sometimes been criticised for putting 'caring' before 'achievement'. The Haywood experience suggests that not only is it possible to have both but also that the two can be formed in a virtuous circle.

HAYWOOD HIGH SCHOOL

An LEA-maintained mixed school for 11–16-year-olds

The school

Headteacher appointed	1989
Number of pupils	832
Number of teachers (full-time equivalent)	45.1
Pupil/teacher ratio	27.7:1
Average class size	30
Annual school budget	£1.51 million

Pupils in the school

Registered for free school meals (%)	24
With statements of special educational needs (no.)	13
Ethnic background (%)	
White	88
Afro-Caribbean	0
Asian	12
Other	0

With home/community
language other than English (%)   12.5

School outcomes

% of 15-year-olds in 1994
achieving GCSE passes

5+ A*–C grades   20
5+ A*–G grades   81
1+ A*–C grades   40
1+ A*–G grades   92.6

% of Year 11 (1993–94) students
who are now

In full-time education and training   52
In employment with training   17.5
In employment without training   11.7
Other   18.8

8

HAZELWOOD INTEGRATED COLLEGE

Northern Ireland

Anthony Gallagher, Robert Osborne, Robert Cormack, Irvine McKay and Stephen Peover

In the part of the United Kingdom most riven by religious differences, and troubled by a quarter of a century of terrorism from both Protestant and Catholic extremist groups, the move towards integrated schooling is most welcome. As the introduction points out, the percentage of young people being educated across the sectarian divide is small, but growing. Hazelwood was one of the first such schools. Its achievements in a relatively short time are noteworthy. Almost all entrants would not have qualified for a grammar school place, yet academic standards are high. Even more important, in the light of the province's history of conflict, is the growth of religious tolerance that has developed from the mixed community.

INTRODUCTION – THE NORTHERN IRELAND CONTEXT

The Northern Ireland education system differs from that of the rest of the United Kingdom in important respects. The Department of

Education for Northern Ireland (DENI) has overall responsibility for education. Executive authority for educational administration is shared between the DENI, five Education and Library Boards (ELBs) and the Council for Catholic Maintained Schools (CCMS). The DENI is currently responsible for the overall education budget and for the capital grant allocations to all schools. In addition, the DENI is responsible for the recurrent budgets, under separate formulas, of voluntary grammar schools and grant-maintained integrated (GMI) schools. The ELBs, which receive a block grant from the DENI, fund all other schools with each ELB having a separate formula. The ELBs provide professional support to all schools. The CCMS is responsible for the employment of teachers in Catholic maintained schools and advises the DENI on other matters relating to these schools.

Under arrangements similar to those in England and Wales, schools, through boards of governors, are now responsible for delegated budgets. The structure of boards varies by type of school, but church representation is high.

Under the Education Reform (Northern Ireland) Order (1989) a Northern Ireland common curriculum has been introduced with the specification of attainment targets at key stages and the associated assessment tests. The Northern Ireland curriculum has a number of statutory cross-curricular themes, including Education for Mutual Understanding and Cultural Heritage. The new curriculum is being phased in a year behind the equivalent measure in England and Wales.

The education system in Northern Ireland is characterised by the retention of selection at age eleven. Most pupils in their final year of primary education sit two tests, the results of which influence their selection for places in grammar schools. These tests are separate from the assessment arrangements for Key Stage 2. Although open enrolment has been introduced, as in England, only grammar schools are permitted to use academic performance as a criterion of entry.

An additional feature of the education system in Northern Ireland is the *de facto* segregation of pupils by religion. Although the integrated sector has expanded in recent years, still only about 2 per cent of pupils attend these schools. The integrated schools, which explicitly seek to educate Protestant and Catholic young people together, originated through parental action in the early 1980s: at the time of writing there were four post-primary integrated schools and about twenty primary integrated schools, with more expected to open in September 1995. In the early days, the integrated schools relied heavily on British charities, but since the 1989 Education Reform Order they have received government support. The Order also imposes a duty on the DENI to encourage integration. The integrated schools are supported by the Northern Ireland Council for Integrated Education (NICIE).

HAZELWOOD INTEGRATED COLLEGE

Hazelwood College is an integrated, non-selective, mixed secondary school for pupils aged eleven to eighteen. The school was founded in 1985 by a group of Protestant and Catholic parents from north Belfast assisted in the early years by the charity BELTIE (Belfast Educational Trust for Integrated Education) and was the second such school to open in Northern Ireland, the first being Lagan College. It opened in temporary premises and in 1986 moved to its current location. In 1988 government, under regulations that then existed, recognised the school's educational viability and granted it maintained status. This meant that all recurrent costs would be met, as would 85 per cent of authorised expenditure on capital projects. Under the terms of the 1989 Education Reform (Northern Ireland) Order the school applied, with the support of parents, for Grant Maintained Integrated status (GMI), and this was attained in 1989. GMI status entitles the school to 100 per cent funding for recognised recurrent and capital expenditure. With this status the school deals with the Department of

Education for Northern Ireland (DENI) for all funding matters rather than with the local authority.

As an integrated school, Hazelwood has a number of founding principles. These are:

- the school should give equal status to the two major cultures in Northern Ireland;
- the balance between Protestant and Catholic children should ideally be 50:50 and every effort is made to keep within a 60:40 band;
- teachers should be similarly balanced between the two major traditions;
- the school should educate and cherish all children of Protestant, Catholic, other faiths and none on a footing of equality;
- the school should be Christian rather than secular in character;
- religious instruction should be provided according to the wishes of parents. To ensure that the children are properly instructed, practical arrangements should be made with the clergy of all faiths;
- parents have the primary responsibility for the education and welfare of their children and this should involve them in the planning and content of the education of their children.

LOCATION

Hazelwood occupies a 9-acre site in north Belfast in the premises of a former secondary school for girls. The ward in which the school is located has a male unemployment rate of 18 per cent and a female rate of 12 per cent which, although high, are lower than in some wards in the west of the city where rates for males are around 50 per cent. The area from which the school draws most of its pupils, however, includes the most deprived parts of north Belfast where unemployment rates exceed 30 per cent, and includes areas which saw a very high proportion of the deaths and violent incidents during the twenty-five years of the civil disturbances.

The school premises consist of a main building, which had deteriorated badly after the closure of the original girls' school. This building, although substantially upgraded, has a poor exterior. The school relies extensively on 'temporary' mobile classrooms. In early 1995, however, the DENI indicated that Hazelwood's £9.9 million proposal to improve the school buildings substantially was to proceed. The school anticipates that this work will commence towards the end of 1995. There can be little doubt that the current state of the premises at Hazelwood do not provide the type of physical environment that is normally believed to assist in the creation of a successful school.

HAZELWOOD IN ITS EDUCATIONAL CONTEXT

Although Hazelwood is a non-selective school, it exists in a system which is essentially selective. The results of the transfer tests can be used to provide a picture of the entry levels of Hazelwood's pupils, as can be seen below in Table 8.1. Comparatively few of the entrants to Hazelwood have achieved grades which would normally gain them entrance to grammar schools (grades 1 and 2). A substantial majority of entrants did not sit the transfer procedure. This group is composed of two elements: those who were not entered for a mixture of educational and social reasons, and those, believed to be the larger group, who do not need to sit the test since their first preference is for Hazelwood as an integrated and non-selective school. Many of this latter group will have attended Hazelwood Integrated Primary School, which is situated quite close to the Hazelwood College site. In general, most pupils who do not opt to take the transfer tests would not have been expected to receive one of the higher grades had they taken them.

However, it seems likely that the 'not entered' pupils who transferred from Hazelwood Integrated Primary School to Hazelwood College would cover a wider range of ability and a proportion

Table 8.1 Grades in the transfer procedure for entrants to Hazelwood College and Belfast ELB non-grammar schools, 1991–93

			GRADE			
	1	2	3	4	*Other*	*Total*
1991	2	3	20	38	53	116
1992	1	2	15	45	43	106
1993	2	4	11	57	52	126
BELB average*						
1993	1	3	14	56	43	117

Note: *Based on 22 non-grammar schools

might have obtained one of the higher grades on the transfer tests, if they had taken them.

The profile of Hazelwood's entrants is very similar to the average position for secondary schools in the Belfast ELB. Another indicator in examining the profile of Hazelwood's entrants is the proportion of pupils entitled to free school meals. This measure is used as an indicator of social deprivation by the DENI and the ELBs, and is used to give some additional resources to schools under formula funding. The figures for Hazelwood reveal that 184 pupils (31.5 per cent) are entitled to free school meals. Although this is high, it is considerably lower than the average figure for non-grammar schools in the Belfast ELB. For controlled (*de facto*, Protestant) secondary schools the average is 42.4 per cent, while for maintained (Catholic) secondary schools it is 56 per cent. Hazelwood, therefore, does not have the excessively high proportion of pupils from socially deprived backgrounds common to most secondary schools in Belfast but nevertheless has almost one in three pupils falling into this category. Hazelwood, thus, has a much wider cross-section of pupils than most secondary schools or grammar schools in Belfast.

Hazelwood has a policy that all pupils are timetabled for nine subjects at GCSE level and encourages as many of the pupils as possible to sit the examinations for all these subjects. Hazelwood's first cohort of 'A' level students was introduced in 1992. Sixteen students had completed their 'A' levels by the end of the 1993–94 school year, with nine obtaining two or more passes at grades A–E. Pupils who wish to take 'A' levels in the college are required to have obtained at least five GCSE passes at grade B. In the same year the college offered GNVQ Intermediate and Advanced level courses for the first time. Students hoping to enter GNVQ Intermediate level are required to have obtained four or five GCSE passes at grade E, while those wishing to take GNVQ Advanced are required to have obtained four or five GCSE passes at grade C.

Table 8.2 GCSE examination performance, 1992–94

	Entered for 5+ subjects	Entered for 1–4 subjects	% achieving 5+ grades A–C	A–G	% achieving 1–4 grades A–C	A–G	% no grades A–G
1992/93							
Hazelwood	98	2	48	93	35	5	2
BELB Secondary	72	19	20	67	37	20	13
NI Secondary	78	16	25	73	41	18	9
1993/94							
Hazelwood	89	5	34	85	35	6	9
BELB Secondary	78	18	21	69	36	21	10
NI Secondary	80	15	27	74	39	19	7

Because the first year of new examination systems provides only a limited picture of a school's performance, we here concentrate on Hazelwood's performance at GCSE level. The data for the last two years are presented above in Table 8.2. The data suggest a good performance from Hazelwood when compared with the BELB and the Northern Ireland non-grammar averages for those two years.

Hazelwood competes for pupils with a range of grammar and secondary schools in its local area. There are both Protestant and Catholic grammar schools in relatively close proximity. One of these is a coeducational Protestant grammar school, and there are separate boys' and girls' Catholic grammar schools. Of the Catholic secondary schools in the area, the girls' Catholic secondary has a good reputation, whereas that of the boys' secondary school is perceived to be weaker. This may explain the preponderance of boys amongst the Catholic pupils in the school. The school has experienced difficulties in gaining access to Catholic primary schools in the past in order to give presentations to parents and pupils. This is beginning to break down but is still a problem.

HAZELWOOD'S STATED AIMS

The school's broad educational aims are published in the prospectus and include:

- the achievement of understanding through the encouragement of mutual respect;
- ensuring that all pupils reach the highest level of personal, intellectual and academic development of which they are capable;
- ensuring that every pupil leaves the college with the knowledge, skills and strategies necessary for living in a changing world;
- emphasising that pupils' personal development is as important as their intellectual development in the preparation for adult life;
- enhancing the pupils' self-esteem and therefore their ability to cope with and accept other people;
- developing an understanding of the world as a threatened environment;
- developing an open system of school organisation emphasising the partnership and interdependence of parents, pupils and staff.

The creation of an 'atmosphere based on trust, openness, honesty, justice and co-operation' is emphasised, and it is stressed that all are participants in the educational process. Thus:

'Pupils, teachers, parents and governors are encouraged to maintain this ethos. Homework is regarded as a fundamental process with each pupil having a homework timetable with the expectation that parents will supervise homework and ensure that they are completed.'

INSPECTION REPORTS

The school was inspected in May 1993 with special reference to science and technology. The report suggests:

'There is a friendly and supportive atmosphere in most classes. Pupils are well motivated and enjoy their work.

Standards achieved by the majority of pupils are satisfactory in home economics and science and are high for practical work in home economics.

Teachers are suitably qualified and deployed. The quality of teaching ranges from satisfactory to good.

The quality of teaching and learning in technology and design and the GCE A level courses in science is affected adversely by major deficiencies in the provision of specialist equipment and materials.

An encouraging start has been made to improve coordination and curricular coherence within this area of study.'

In response, the school detailed specific actions taken to meet the matters criticised in the report and took issue with some comments. The issue of inadequate facilities was enthusiastically endorsed as strengthening the school's approach to the DENI for additional funding: this resulted in a grant of £50,000 for design and technology and, more recently, £94,000 for information technology. The inspection report was taken very seriously by the school and prompted a considered series of responses. It was perceived as an opportunity for dialogue concerning the activities of the school in one area of the curriculum. In addition,

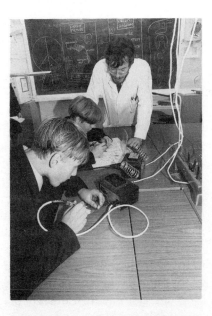

the opportunity was used within the school to carry out internal inspections in each area of study.

METHODOLOGY AND EVIDENCE

In order to collect data for the National Commission on Education investigation, a series of meetings and visits were undertaken by the research team. In October 1994, an initial meeting was held with Tom Rowley, the principal, to outline the purpose of the proposed enquiry and invite the college's participation. Agreement to participate was confirmed at a meeting with the principal during November. During this visit an additional meeting was held with Noreen Campbell, the vice-principal, to discuss specific plans for further visits to collect research data. When these arrangements were made the researchers spent some time discussing the background and development of the college with her, and she outlined some of the distinctive features of practice in the school which she felt contributed to its success.

As an immediate consequence of this visit we were invited to attend the presentation evening run by the college for parents and pupils in November. The presentation evening provides an opportunity for the principal and board of governors to report on school activities to parents, and school prizes and examination certificates are distributed to pupils. On this occasion particular pride was evident in the fact that 'A' level certificates were being awarded for the first time to college pupils.

The research team spent a full day at the end of November in the college. We talked with pupils of all ages, toured the college, met with the senior management team and had individual discussions with other key members of staff, including the special needs co-ordinator and the bursar. In December we were invited to a preview, to which teachers and pupils from other Belfast schools had been invited, of a one-hour television programme on Hazelwood College which was followed by a discussion. In February 1995 the research team attended a lecture to PGCE (Post-graduate Certificate of Education) students at the School of Education, Queen's University, Belfast, in which the college principal presented the fundamental beliefs.

Later in February we met with the former chair of the board of governors, who had been involved with the school from its earliest days and was able to offer an alternative perspective on its development to that provided by teachers. The final element of the fieldwork for the project came when we attended the annual Assembly for Peace held by the college in March. This marked a particularly appropriate point at which to complete data collection for the case study. The Department of Education in Northern Ireland had just announced a substantial capital grant which would permit the college to build sorely needed new premises. During the welcoming address the vice-principal pointed out that the 1995 Assembly marked the tenth anniversary of the college, the eighth Assembly for Peace the College had organised and, most significant of all, the first to take place while Northern Ireland was at peace.

THE ETHOS OF HAZELWOOD COLLEGE

In discussions on education in Northern Ireland the notion of 'school ethos' frequently arises even though it is often ill-defined or loosely conceptualised. By contrast, the ethos of Hazelwood College is unusually clear and unambiguous to the extent that its underlying principles are contained in a manual which is provided for new teachers entering the school. In this part of the report we outline the rhetorical dimensions to this approach while in later sections we examine the extent to which the rhetoric is matched by the reality of practice in the school.

It is worth noting that the basic elements of the Hazelwood approach were put together by the current principal and two vice-principals of the school, even though one of the vice-principals has not worked in the school from its opening. These principles found an echo among parents and the original governors, as we shall see below. We found this significant, as it suggested that at the heart of Hazelwood lies a collegial identity and commitment.

The starting point for the Hazelwood approach is that schools can and should contribute to social change. To that extent senior staff within the school argue that they are attempting to make it a microcosm of what wider society should be like. The approach highlights the claim that the school curriculum contains two main domains, the formal and the hidden curriculum, and that affective learning takes place within the hidden curriculum while cognitive learning takes place within the formal curriculum.

Given the level of violence suffered by Northern Ireland over the last two decades and more, and the understandable belief by many that schools can and should contribute in some way to the promotion of community reconciliation, it is not surprising that a number of different approaches have been adopted at different times. In essence, three broad strategies can be described: first, approaches aimed at changing the curriculum of existing, *de facto* religiously segregated schools; second, attempts to encourage greater contact between pupils in segregated schools through joint programmes of work; and finally, the development of religiously integrated schools. The approach adopted by Hazelwood College sits firmly within the third approach and is based, at least in part, on a critique of some of the alternative approaches to reconciliation, especially those which suggest that the problem of prejudice is largely cognitive. The Hazelwood approach argues that the real issue lies in people's perceived level of threat: the higher the perceived level of threat, the narrower, and hence more prejudiced, the general perceptions. It is argued that the level of threat is directly linked to self-esteem, and it is this focus on the self-esteem of pupils that provides the central plank of the college's approach.

The Hazelwood approach is that all organisations have a therapeutic and a moral environment. By introducing into the classroom practice the principles of unconditional positive regard, empathy and genuineness, high self-esteem is promoted. For moral development, at both individual and institutional levels, it is not enough to 'obey the rules' because this is simply the proper thing to do. Understanding *why* both raises self-esteem and enhances the acceptance of others. Hazelwood sets out to make explicit the nature of its moral environment through the practice of its members, staff and pupils alike, in both the formal and hidden curriculum.

The written documentation available within the school points to a number of specific practical consequences. School reports, it is suggested, should focus on achievement and provide each pupil with a positive account of what they can do across a range of domains. The need to work towards the enhancement of pupils' self-esteem is seen to have implications for the assessment and counselling systems operated by the school, and for the nature of staff–pupil relationships. Maintaining close involvement of parents in the school is seen to contribute to enhanced self-esteem, as is the provision of mixed-ability teaching.

Given the explicit nature of the Hazelwood approach, the documentation also highlights the importance of staff development. In this section of the report we have outlined the characteristics which Hazelwood College explicitly defines as its guiding principles. These might be best summarised by two particular features that make Hazelwood College distinctive in the context of Northern Ireland: first, it is a planned religiously integrated school which sets a high regard for moral values while not privileging any specific moral system; and second, it is a comprehensive school operating in a largely selective educational environment and with a strong commitment to mixed-ability teaching. The two main sources of evidence at this stage lie in a manual produced by the college and a lecture given by the principal. To that extent this outline has focused on the rhetoric of the Hazelwood approach. In the next part of the report we turn our attention to the practice within the school which was observed and assessed through fieldwork research.

STAFF–PUPIL RELATIONSHIPS

One of the first things to strike a visitor to Hazelwood College is that, while the school operates a strict uniform policy, pupils and teachers address each other by first names. At first sight this must seem to many as a curious affectation, harking back to the heyday of progressivism. Our observations in the school suggest that the practice tells us more about the confidence that exists in the relationship between pupils and staff. This confidence, which spoke to us of a strong sense of community, was manifest in a number of ways. We were struck by the number of pupils who said they liked the school because of the way they 'got on with' their teachers. Some of the older pupils said that their teachers respected them, and described their relationship as 'friendly and close'. Perhaps more pragmatically, one of the younger pupils said that he liked being at the school 'because the teachers are less strict than those in other schools'. On one level, then, we saw evidence of an open and friendly relationship between staff and pupils.

A further striking example of the positive relationship between staff and pupils was seen through the openness displayed by the staff and their readiness to give voice to the pupils. During the day we spent in the school we visited a number of classes to discuss issues with the pupils. Although the teachers were aware that we were in the school, they were normally unaware that a visit had been planned to their class until we arrived. Despite this, not one objected to our presence and in all cases they offered to leave us alone with the pupils during the discussion. This openness is a particular feature of the school in a more general sense: not only do they receive a large number of requests for visits to the school but the general approach on the part of the senior staff appears to be to agree to such requests unless there are very good grounds not to agree. The television crew had fairly unrestricted access to the pupils and to school life for an extended period, despite the undoubted irritations they were causing to some towards the end.

That the school would allow the possibility of some of its pupils inadvertently to say something controversial or distressing on national television speaks volumes for the confidence placed in the pupils by the school. Indeed, on two occasions comments made by pupils and broadcast on Channel 4 did cause some distress within the school, but this did not cause the senior staff or governors to 'pull the plug' on the programme or even, as far as we could tell, consider this possibility. By contrast, and as further evidence of an open and confident community within the school, both occasions were taken as opportunities for discussion and exploration of difficult topics rather than as situations demanding censorship.

STAFF–STAFF RELATIONSHIPS

We have described above the open and friendly relationship that we found between staff and pupils. Our observations suggest that a similar situation exists within the teaching staff in their relationship with one another. Although our direct evidence is limited, we did gain the strong impression that an important contribution to the success achieved by Hazelwood College can be attributed to the quality and commitment of the teaching staff.

A somewhat informal atmosphere is evident among the staff, but this should not be taken to imply a casual approach to their work. In fact, on the basis of our observations such a conclusion could not be further from the truth. The monitoring systems operated by the school, which we consider in more detail below, devolve many administrative duties to individual teachers. No teacher complained about this paperwork; moreover, they consistently highlighted the value of the procedures in helping them to do their job.

A number of teachers suggested that a particular characteristic of the school was that it constantly looked at innovations and new ideas. In part this may be explained by the history of the school in that innovation might have been seen in the early days as necessary to survival, and more recently as a necessary concomitant to rapid growth. For the present purposes the most significant aspect of this approach is that it appears to place an additional set of tasks on teachers, requiring them to spend many hours in meetings and discussions after normal teaching hours. Once again, the teachers we talked to tended to value this involvement rather than see it as a burden.

If the situation among the staff is as we describe it above, we felt the need to ask how this has been achieved. Our clear sense was that two main factors seemed to contribute to the positive picture we found. First, we gained a clear sense that the staff feel involved in the decision-making processes of the school and are kept informed about what is going on. The second main factor was our impression that the staff had a common sense of purpose. In part this can be attributed to the ethos promoted by the school, the values and principles of which did occur and recur in conversations with teachers. Different teachers placed different emphasis on aspects of this ethos. For some it was the commitment to a comprehensive, mixed-ability approach to teaching that was most evident, while for others it was the integrated nature of the school that was given greatest emphasis; but what they had in common was a sense of what they were trying to achieve, how they would go about achieving these ends and, that as individuals, their contribution to this process was both valued and worthwhile.

THE ATTITUDE TOWARDS ACHIEVEMENT

During our fieldwork in the school we gained a very strong impression that an important part of the explanation of the success of Hazelwood College lay in the attitude held towards achievement. In a range of different ways it was clear that expectations placed on pupils are high, that the school consciously and deliberately celebrates achievements by pupils, and that achievement is defined by the school in a variety of ways.

One way in which these features were clearly underlined was at the presentation evening. The principal's speech to parents pointed to a number of successful achievements by the school and its pupils, including increasing pupil numbers, successes in public examinations, groups from the school competing in drama, verse-speaking, debating and public-speaking competitions, in addition to awards under the Duke of Edinburgh scheme. Perhaps even more significant was the wide range of prizes distributed to pupils later in the evening. Six awards went to young pupils who wrote and prepared their own books, as judged by the newly arrived teachers in the school. During the event particular attention seemed to be given to the college community awards, which went to pupils 'whose actions and example have brought great credit to the school'. There were twenty-two awards for pupils with 100 per cent attendance records during the year, and personal progress awards for 'the most committed pupil in each class'. Thereafter a series of prizes were awarded to pupils who had achieved success in academic, vocational, sporting and competitive activities, with evident pride being displayed in the presentation of the first 'A' level and GNVQ certificates to college pupils.

If the approach adopted by the college during the presentation evening reflected a diverse interpretation of achievement, it is important here to underline the clear importance that is attached by the school to academic achievement. This was clear from our conversations with teachers who expect their pupils to work hard and strive for excellence, but perhaps even more important, believe they are capable of so doing. This can be seen in more immediate procedures within the school: in line with its explicit comprehensive approach and mixed-ability teaching the expectation on the part of the school is that all pupils will study and enter for a range of public examinations. We have examined earlier the comparatively high academic achievements of Hazelwood pupils in public examinations: as a demonstration of the school's expectations of its pupils it is perhaps as significant that a higher than average proportion of Hazelwood pupils enter five or more GCSE subjects, in comparison with other non-grammar schools.

Relevant to the discussion on achievement is some consideration of the school's commitment to mixed-ability teaching. On one level this is seen within the school as reflecting an important part of its ethos, and there are a number of practical advantages perceived to derive from the approach. At the level of ethos, mixed-ability teaching is seen as important in counteracting any potential labelling effects where the identification and grouping of, in particular, low-ability pupils can, it is argued, become a self-fulfilling prophecy. This principle applies also to teachers, all of whom carry an equal teaching load and all of whom are expected to teach at all levels within the school: this is particularly important now that the school has developed an 'A' level programme to which all teachers will be expected to contribute.

At a more practical level, mixed-ability classes make it easier to move pupils between classes, a strategy that is sometimes used to cope with disciplinary problems, as we discuss below. In addition, it means that teachers can see tangible success in each class of pupils they take and they avoid unconsciously labelling particular class groups as 'bad classes'.

MONITORING WITHIN THE SCHOOL

It will be clear from the report so far that we were very impressed by the attitudes and practices we saw during the fieldwork for this report. We were equally, if not more, impressed by the monitoring procedures we saw in operation. The monitoring procedures addressed two areas, pupils' work in school and discipline, and appeared to be characterised by two main features: first, they operated on a system of early identification of problems and thus early intervention; and second, the procedures seemed to prefer rewards for approved behaviour as opposed to punishments for inappropriate behaviour. We will discuss the systems as operated for schoolwork and discipline separately.

The monitoring procedure for pupils' schoolwork is based around the class tutor system. Each designated group of pupils is assigned a class tutor on entry to the school. A key aspect of Hazelwood's system is that this group will continue with the same class tutor for the five years of their compulsory education. As we discovered when talking to some of the class groups, this ideal is not always achieved as the duties of some teachers inevitably alter over time.

On a day-to-day basis the key role of class tutors is to meet their classes at the beginning of each day. Each pupil has a homework diary and, for pupils up to Form 5, there is a designated slot in each day for silent reading for which pupils can select their own preferred book. During the class assembly and registration session the class tutor takes the roll for the class, checks the homework diary to ensure that the pupils have completed all that they were assigned, and checks that each pupil has a suitable book for the silent reading period. The key advantage of this system is that a designated teacher has a daily overview of the schoolwork of a group of pupils and, unlike a subject teacher, is in a position to identify if individual pupils are beginning to slip behind in their work. In addition, the class tutor reviews the class record book, which is used to build up a picture of the behaviour in each class, with a written comment being made by each teacher taking the class. This system permits the class tutor to maintain a regular review of the class of pupils as a group.

Alongside this system of daily monitoring, and consequent on it, the class tutor has an important pastoral and support role for the class. The ability of a teacher to fulfil this role is enhanced by the fact that their tutoring responsibility does not change each year, but covers an extended period for a distinct group of pupils. This makes it more likely that a relationship of trust will develop between pupil and teacher. In addition, the class tutor is the first

point of contact between the school and parents: if the daily monitoring identifies a problem and the class tutor feels that the pupil's parents can throw some useful light on the problem, can contribute to a solution or simply ought to be brought into discussions, then contact is made with the parents. Once again, a relationship of trust can develop between teacher and parents because the period of responsibility for pupils held by class tutors extends over a period of years.

Clearly, we could only see aspects of this system in operation during our fieldwork. However, it was evident that class tutors do maintain fairly regular contact with parents. In our discussions with one of the class groups we asked the pupils for some aspect of the school they did not like so much: to the amused endorsement of his peers, one pupil complained that his class tutor 'was never done calling my mum and dad on the phone', although said with an air of insouciance rather than frustration or anger.

Firmer evidence of parental involvement is provided by the report system. Each month a progress report is sent to the parents of each pupil. The report contains two main sections. The first section, on the pupil's achievements that month, is completed by the pupil. In addition to identifying up to four positive achievements, pupils complete a section on their personal evaluation (excellent, good or poor) of their homework, uniform and punctuality. The second section is completed by the class tutor and indicates if the pupil has been meritorious in their behaviour, attendance, time-keeping, homework and academic work. The final part of the report allows the pupil, class tutor and parents to make any additional comment they wish.

In addition to the monthly reports, school reports go to parents at key points during the year; and at the end of each year an interview is held between the class tutor, pupil and parents, at which personal goals and targets for each pupil are discussed and agreed.

Similar features can be seen to characterise the college's approach to discipline. The system appears to be based on the following principles: early identification of problems is encouraged in order to permit early, and hence more benign, intervention; pupils are encouraged to alter their behaviour, although sanctions of various kinds can be and are used; and early intervention permits a series of graduated steps in order to achieve the desired ends. In practice it appears that the class tutor is able to identify and deal with many of the problems that arise. When the problem becomes more serious a pupil can be put 'on report'. A pupil on report must get a report card signed by each teacher in each class over a period of up to a week: the daily briefing meeting for teachers is an opportunity to let all teachers know which pupils, if any, are on report. While a pupil is on report other sanctions can apply: a pupil who plays for a school sports team, for example, may be banned from training for the week. A record of satisfactory behaviour over this period permits a pupil to come off report and any additional sanctions are removed. If the problem still persists then additional measures can be employed.

Clearly, in order to arrive at a firmer assessment of the discipline system in the school a more extended period of fieldwork would be necessary. That said, we were impressed by the range of measures available in the school and by the fact that this range seemed to be enabled by the system of early identification and intervention. We have described the basic system as we found it: in addition, the school is prepared to move pupils between classes as a way of encouraging better behaviour by changing their immediate environment; classroom assistants are also used to help pupils complete homework when persistent lapses have occurred. In the words of one of the vice-principals, the school 'tries to identify and target pupils who are having problems as quickly as possible, and, by keeping a close eye on them for a time, tries to sort the problem out as quickly as possible'.

THE ATTITUDE TO RITUAL

All schools have rituals and Hazelwood College is no exception. Our fieldwork observations, however, suggest that the role accorded to ritual in Hazelwood is both more explicit and direct than may be the case in most other schools. Our fieldwork was topped and tailed by two ritualistic events, the presentation evening and the Assembly for Peace. This proved to be fortuitous, to the extent that both events highlighted the twin themes that run through so much of the Hazelwood experience: the priority attached to high expectation and achievement through a comprehensive educational strategy; and the priority attached to reconciliation through religious integration. The Assembly for Peace, in particular, was a highly emotional event centred on a confluence of three historical commemorations: the 150th anniversary of the famine which devastated Ireland, a commemoration of the Shoah based on the fiftieth anniversary of the liberation of Auschwitz, and a commemoration of those who died in the twenty-five years of the conflict in Northern Ireland. Dealing with any one of these would be difficult enough, but the Hazelwood event addressed their combined significance with extraordinary professionalism and in a remarkably thought-provoking manner.

During our period of fieldwork Hazelwood College was visited by a number of dignitaries. Lady Mayhew, wife of the Secretary of State for Northern Ireland, the President of the Methodist Church in Ireland, an Assistant Chief Constable of the Royal Ulster Constabulary and others attended the Assembly for Peace. The Lord Mayor of Belfast also visited the school. Perhaps most significant during this period, however, was the visit to the school of Mary Robinson, President of the Irish Republic. This was the first visit of any kind by any President of Ireland to any school in Northern Ireland. We were told that this visit provoked discussion among the pupils in the school, not least because some of them come from a tradition which would perceive President Robinson as the Head of State of a foreign country with irredentist claims on Northern Ireland. From the present point of view the key points are that the visit happened and that the discussion was encouraged.

The key point in this section of the report lies in the broader significance of ritual to the school: like many schools in Northern Ireland Hazelwood receives many requests for visits; as an integrated school in the province Hazelwood possibly receives an above-average number of requests. The senior staff of Hazelwood normally agreed to these requests, a fact which, in itself, probably acts to increase the number of requests in the first place! The rationale of this is quite explicit: visits by important people to the school are encouraged because it is seen to contribute to the pupils' self-esteem. The intention is that the pupils become aware that the visits are important not only because the visitor is important, but also because the visited are important. Once again we see how decisions about the day-to-day activities in the school, and here specifically in relation to ritual, are consistent with an agreed set of principles that underpin the school ethos.

THE BOARD OF GOVERNORS

The board of governors played a central role in the development of Hazelwood College both as an integrated and as a comprehensive school. The board of governors were substantially motivated by a sense of being pioneers. The governors, with senior staff and a group of parents, shared a vision of creating a school which embodied the dual philosophy which was, and is, so distinctive in the Northern Ireland context. The board of governors, therefore, has played a central role in the overall shaping of the school, a role which many boards of governors play in the developing integrated sector in Northern Ireland. The commitment in terms of time and emotional energy required in such circumstances was extensive. While adopting a very much 'hands-on' approach to their work in the school, the senior staff of the college appreciate the fact that the governors gave them the freedom to translate consensually agreed principles into practical measures. With the school now established, and with the £9.9 million capital programme about to start, there is a sense in which the governors can sit back a little, but there is also a clear sense that they remain highly supportive of the senior staff and committed to the general direction and ethos of the school. Currently the board meets on a monthly basis with high regular attendance, and the individual governors are regular participants in a variety of internal school meetings and events.

EXTERNAL RELATIONSHIPS

In the early days the board of governors of Hazelwood, as with all integrated schools, relied extensively on British charities, such as the Nuffield Foundation, which provided much of the initial start-up finance for these schools. The charities, apart from establishing basic financial accountability, operated a 'hands-off' approach, allowing the school to strike its own priorities and ethos. The relationship with the umbrella organisations for integrated schools has continued cordially. For example, the school sought assistance from NICIE to launch its 'A' level and other sixth form work, having failed to convince the DENI of its initial viability, and received a grant of approximately £20,000. Sixth form work is now financed by DENI.

A strong point made by senior staff was that the school has always felt a great deal of independence and freedom in decision-making. In the early days before achieving maintained status the freedom was so great that it was described as 'almost scary'. With GMI status, the school continues to have a great deal of independence, dealing with the DENI for all financial matters and with the Belfast ELB for professional educational support.

There is a more general point relevant to this part of the discussion. The integrated schools in Northern Ireland developed in difficult circumstances. Tensions in Northern Ireland were high throughout the 1980s because of the period following the Republican hunger strikes in the first half of the decade, and Unionist opposition to the Anglo-Irish Agreement in the latter half. Hazelwood itself was located in the area of Northern Ireland that has seen the highest extent of random sectarian assassinations throughout the quarter-century of the conflict.

At a more benign level, the integrated schools were opening during a period of declining rolls, which made some people in the educational system question the need for a 'third sector'. Others perceived the integrated schools as making an implicit judgement on their role in reconciliation. Whether or not these perceptions were accurate or not is irrelevant to the present discussion except in so far as they highlight the potentially inauspicious environment within which Hazelwood developed. Despite the undoubted success of Lagan College, the first post-primary integrated school, it was unclear in 1985 whether Hazelwood would follow the same path. For this reason the staff in Hazelwood at the time perceived that some educational bodies did not provide an entirely support-ive hand to the college until such time as it had demonstrated its viability. This may help to explain also why the school developed a pattern of relying on its own resources, as referred to above. At the presentation evening the chair of the board of governors under-lined this by declaring that Hazelwood 'could no longer be dis-missed as an eccentric experiment'. The school is an undoubted success, and with that success has come the confidence, on all sides, for Hazelwood to participate fully in the support systems provided by the local ELB and other educational bodies.

An important decision of the board of governors was to recruit a professionally qualified bursar to augment the work of an individ-ual governor who had acted as treasurer. As the retiring chair of the governors put it: 'while our treasurer had done sterling work in the early days as we began to develop and grow, it was vital that the board of governors and senior staff had a clear picture of our day-to-day financial circumstances'. The bursar plays a central role in the financial management of the school.

The current resources of Hazelwood College are derived from the DENI under the terms of the formula for GMI schools. There is little evidence that Hazelwood as an integrated school is being advantaged.

An important resource implication for Hazelwood arises from its commitment to keeping class sizes small. Small classes, it is argued, facilitate mixed-ability teaching and the monitoring systems designed to check on pupils' progress. With few staff changes, the staffing budget grows as teachers move up the salary spine towards their maximum. This, and the further development of sixth form teaching with its disproportionate staff, will test the ability of the college to maintain small classes, and the school may have to rethink its overall approach.

THE NATIONAL COMMISSION CRITERIA FOR SUCCESS

We have highlighted the most significant aspects of Hazelwood we found during our fieldwork. The National Commission criteria were identified as conducive to school success. The criteria have been implicit in our considerations, but in this section of the report we comment briefly on their explicit relevance for Hazelwood. Our conclusion is that all ten features, which concentrate on the spirit and atmosphere of schools, pupil expectations, assessment procedures, parental involvement and strong positive leadership, can be found operating strongly within Hazelwood College.

The National Commission pointed also to a range of other features which it felt was likely to promote successful schools, which we did not find so evident in Hazelwood. One problematic area was in staff development: newly appointed teachers to Hazelwood are given an induction programme to introduce them to the distinctive policies and practices of the school. Beyond this, however, senior staff accepted that the college's staff development procedures were weak, in part because of the pressing need to allocate resources to other priorities. Some of these problems have arisen because of the rapid growth of the school and the consequently high proportion of new staff being inducted into the school on a regular basis.

Until relatively recently the management system for the school operated on a fairly informal basis, in part also as a consequence of the continuation of practices that had their origin in the early days of the school when pupil and staff numbers were small. Within the last couple of years the management structure has been formalised. The principal, two vice-principals and three teachers appointed by the board form the senior management team. Eleven teachers, with varying posts of responsibility, form the middle management, while a further eight teachers hold posts of junior responsibility and form the tier below middle management.

One final point concerns the Hazelwood premises. Of the many features which strike any visitor to the school, perhaps one of the most evident is the dilapidated nature of the premises: indeed, on the day we spent in the school one of the vice-principals had to leave us to deal with a threatened failure in a heating boiler. The premises currently occupied by the school are woefully inadequate but, as we indicated above, the removal of a moratorium on capital development in schools has provided Hazelwood with the opportunity and resources to build new facilities. For the present, Hazelwood stands as a clear example that, while a lack of resources is not to be recommended, it does not, in itself, doom a school to failure. If Hazelwood tells us anything, it is that human resources provide the bed-rock for a successful school.

HAZELWOOD COLLEGE

A grant-maintained integrated mixed school for 11–18-year-olds

The school

Headteacher appointed	1985
Number of pupils	600
Number of teachers (full-time equivalent)	40
Pupil/teacher ratio	27.2:1
Average class size	25
Annual school budget	£1.5 million

Pupils in the school

Registered for free school meals (%)	27
With statements of special educational needs (no.)	0
Ethnic background (%)	
White	99.1
Afro-Caribbean	0.6
Asian	0
Other	0.3
With home/community language other than English (%)	0

School outcomes

% of 15-year-olds in 1994
achieving GCSE passes

5+ A*–C grades	29
5+ A*–G grades	79
1+ A*–C grades	71
1+ A*–G grades	95

% of Year 11 (1993–94) students
who are now

In full-time education and training	62
In employment with training	6
In employment without training	5
Other	27

% of 16-year-olds entered for 'A'/'AS'
level (or equivalent) in 1994 — 40

Average points score for 'A'/'AS' — 7 (first year of 'A' level examination by the school)

9

ST MICHAEL'S ROMAN CATHOLIC COMPREHENSIVE SCHOOL
Billingham, Cleveland

Gerald Grace, Diane Bell and Bill Browne

Billingham lies to the north of the River Tees in the north-eastern county of Cleveland. The county is relatively small in area, but was once prosperous as a base for heavy industry. There is now widespread unemployment in the county as a whole, and Billingham is largely dependent on the continuing level of employment in the petro-chemical industry, its economic mainstay. The school was likely to close ten years ago as a consequence of falling rolls and poor leadership. It is now regularly over-subscribed and a 1994 OFSTED report praises the school leadership and its pupils' concern for their school and community. The research team describe it as having Catholic values which help to promote the common good.

CATHOLIC VALUES AND THE COMMON GOOD

The school was selected on the basis of confidential performance data available to the National Commission which demonstrated that St Michael's School, following objective analysis of intake and outcome data, was 'a remarkably effective school'.

This judgement was confirmed by a subsequent OFSTED inspection (Inspection Report, 907/4630) of the school which took place between October and November 1994, and which reported as follows:

> 'GCSE results have shown a steady improvement and have been consistently above local and national averages in recent years. In 1993 they were exceptionally good.'

Table 9.1 Comparative summary of GCSE results, 1990–94 (percentages)

Pupils	Entered for 5+ GCSEs	Achieving 5+ A(*)–C	Achieving 5+ A(*)–G	Entered for 1+ GCSEs	Achieving 1+ A(*)–C	Achieving 1+ A(*)–G	No A(*)–G GCSEs
St Michael's 1994							
Totals	98.0	49.7	96.6	100.0	79.2	98.0	2.0
Boys	98.7	44.7	97.4	100.0	75.0	98.7	1.3
Girls	97.3	54.8	95.9	100.0	83.6	97.3	2.7
Cleveland 1994		34.3					
England 1994		43.3					
St Michael's 1993							
Totals	97.7	61.4	97.0	98.5	81.8	97.7	2.3
Boys	94.9	50.8	93.2	96.6	72.9	94.9	5.1
Girls	100.0	69.9	100.0	100.0	100.0	100.0	0.0
Cleveland 1993		31.3					
England 1993		41.1					
St Michael's 1992							
Totals	92.0	46.3	87.8	99.0	73.2	96.7	3.0
Boys	86.0	38.0	82.0	98.0	64.0	94.0	6.0
Girls	96.0	52.0	92.0	100.0	79.0	99.0	1.0
Cleveland 1992		29.8					
England 1992		38.1					
St Michael's 1991							
Totals	94.7	46.8	86.2	100.0	70.2	98.9	1.1
Boys	96.0	44.0	86.0	100.0	66.0	100.0	0.0
Girls	93.2	50.0	86.2	100.0	75.0	97.7	2.3
Cleveland 1991		27.5					
St Michael's 1990							
Totals	91.0	33.0	87.0	100.0	68.0	95.0	5.0
Boys	88.0	32.0	82.0	100.0	62.0	94.0	6.0
Girls	95.0	34.0	95.0	100.0	78.0	98.0	2.0
Cleveland 1990		26.0					

'Very good attendance and behaviour contribute to the very sound education provided by the school.'

'Positive leadership over several years has ensured that the school is held in high esteem by the local community.'

'The school provides very good value for money.'

'The aspirations of the school's mission statement derived from Christian values are visible in the daily life of the school.'

'Pupils demonstrate respect and responsibility for others within the school and its wider community.'

The effectiveness of St Michael's School was, in other words, a comprehensive effectiveness in the judgement of the OFSTED inspectors. While its most visible achievements were demonstrated in exceptionally good GCSE results (Table 9.1), it was clear that the school was also successful in the areas of personal and social education, the generation of community responsibility and an awareness of Christian values.

St Michael's is an 11–16 school, and a significant proportion of its pupils go forward for sixth form and further education. The selection of the school for the project is particularly justified by its recent history. Having been on the verge of closure in 1984–85, with a falling school roll and leadership problems, St Michael's School is now a school highly regarded by Catholics and non-Catholics alike, with a rising school roll and a currently over-subscribed intake status. The school in the last ten years has been 'turned around' from incipient failure, and possible closure, to visible success. In the three reports which follow an attempt is made to assess and evaluate the factors involved in this transformation. The approach has been to adopt a triangulation of research perspectives. The first member of the research team has compiled a report based on perspectives from the school, the second on perspectives from the community and the third on perspectives from local industry. It is important to note that some contradictions and differences in emphasis arise when using fieldwork triangulated perspectives. However, to preserve the integrity of the data it is necessary to show that different constituencies of respondents and evaluators do rate the components of school effectiveness in particular ways. Nevertheless, what is apparent in reading these reports is the large amount of agreement which they demonstrate about the effectiveness of St Michael's School, while showing interesting differences of emphasis.

THE SCHOOL IN ITS LOCAL CONTEXT

St Michael's School serves the local Roman Catholic population in the districts of Billingham, Norton and Port Clarence in the County of Cleveland. Although the immediate area of the school is a pleasant 1960s 'green field' site in the 'new town' of Billingham, the area in general is highly industrialised with ICI and other chemical industries much in evidence. The school is situated to the north of the River Tees and it serves areas of social and economic deprivation as well as areas of moderate prosperity.

Male unemployment rates in 1994–95 for the areas served by the school were Billingham (15 per cent), Norton (16 per cent) and Port Clarence (20 per cent) (Cleveland CC Statistics). In Year 7, 11 per cent of pupils are reading at levels two or more years below their chronological age and the school estimates that 11 per cent of pupils across the age range have special educational needs (SEN). SEN refers to any pupil, across the entire pupil population of the school – that is, all year groups – who is assessed as being likely to benefit from additional curricular support, by falling into one or more of the following categories:

- learning-related problems;
- behavioural problems;
- social problems;
- medical problems.

The number of pupils qualifying for free school meals at St Michael's was 19 per cent in 1994, which is above the national average of 15 per cent but below the Cleveland average of 28 per cent (Cleveland CC Statistics).

Although on a number of national indicators St Michael's School can be seen to serve a relatively deprived population it must be noted that other Catholic and County schools in the area served more deprived populations. Nevertheless, when intake and outcome measures are examined, St Michael's School demonstrates a high profile of success across a comprehensive range of educational achievements.

The majority of the school's pupils come from the five Roman Catholic feeder primary schools in the area. For the 1995 intake, 119 Catholic pupils from these schools will be admitted, without interview. For 1995 the school also received 106 applications for 52 places which are available for families in the community who express a preference for the school and who are sympathetic to Roman Catholic values. These entries are decided on the basis of interview. The school is, therefore, over-subscribed and there is strong competition to gain admittance.

It is sometimes claimed that denominational schools use such interviews to practise a covert form of selection. This suggestion had no validity for admissions to St Michael's School, as the head-teacher made clear:

'It is a cynical view, and one, it might be suggested, expressed by those who are envious of the success of Catholic schools, that where there is a surfeit of applications for a particular Catholic school, selection is made on the basis of ability and social origin. It is a failure on the part of those who express this view that they have a complete ignorance of the values and community factors which play such an essential part in Catholic establishments. At this school there are three major elements in the process whereby pupils whose parents express a preference for admission to Year 7 are awarded a place.

The first major element is the preference form. This is a document in which the parent or guardian expresses his or her reasons for wishing to send their child to the school. Prior to its completion, the parent or guardian is presented with a school prospectus which highlights the mission statement, the Catholic Christian basis of the school's existence, and the clearly-defined criteria for entry. The preference form is of great significance since, through it, the crucial factor in the exercise can be assessed, that is, to what extent the parents are in sympathy with the aims and objectives of the school. However, it does rely heavily on articulacy in the written word, therefore the insistence at St Michael's on meeting face-to-face with every applicant.

Secondly, there is the interview, which is a meeting with the parent and child. Representatives of the school can discuss and ascertain the reasons why a preference has been expressed, and assess how valid the Christian expressions of support are. It should be emphasised that: no contact is made with the child's primary school to discuss ability or attitude; no reports or work from the child are seen or requested; and no questions beyond "what is your favourite/least favourite subject?" are asked.

The final stage in selection is a meeting of the staff admissions panel, after the interview process has been completed. This is the stage where decisions for allocations are made, and where all the information from the preference forms and interviews is brought together. A decision is made after very long and detailed consideration of those we can best estimate fulfil the true spirit of the admissions criteria and who would be best suited to the school.

An estimate would be that, of the fifty-two pupils who have been accepted for St Michael's in September 1995, approximately thirty-two of these live in council rented accommodation.

The Cleveland County Admissions Officer, who sat as the county representative on the appeals committee for the school, was quoted as follows:

"My experience as someone who has attended appeals hearings at St Michael's is that places are not awarded on the basis of ability or social status. In a number of cases, candidates recently who were not awarded places at St Michael's made appeals at another local school which enjoys some reputation, and that school and its appeals committee were impressed by the very high academic ability and skills of two of the candidates who had been refused a place at St Michael's. I have no doubt in my mind that St Michael's applies the criteria, as laid down by the governors, consistently and fairly."'

The total pupil roll in 1994 was 849 (411 boys and 438 girls). There were 45 full-time equivalent teachers and the pupil–teacher ratio, including the headteacher, is 17.9:1. The average teaching group size was 23.2 (OFSTED Report 1994).

THREE PERSPECTIVES ON THE SUCCESS OF ST MICHAEL'S

Each member of the research team investigated the ways in which the success of the school was described by one of three constituencies: school members; community members; local employers and former pupils. Data were collected by semi-structured interviews and in some cases by telephone conversations. In addition to describing the features of school success which respondents perceived, they were also asked to provide their explanations for this success. In the reports which follow, the research team present these data along with their own evaluation judgements.

PERSPECTIVES FROM THE SCHOOL – REPORT ONE

The evidence base for this report consists of reading the available documentation provided by the school, the OFSTED Inspection Report (1994) and statistics provided by the Research and Intelligence Unit of Cleveland County Council and by Teesside Training and Enterprise Council. Research interviews were held with the following members of the school:

- the headteacher (10 years' experience at the school);
- the deputy headteacher (pastoral, 28 years);
- head of history (24 years);
- head of drama (5 years);
- joint head of technology (21 years);
- head of English (1 year);
- a supply teacher (2 years part-time);
- the school secretary (20 years);

- eight pupils from Years 10 and 11 – that is, in the fourteen-year to sixteen-year age range chosen to represent a cross-section of ability and of attitudes to the school.

Five observational visits were made to the school over a seven-week period.

SUMMARY OF FACTORS RELATED TO THE SCHOOL

The effectiveness of any institution is always the outcome of the legacy of its history and of its contemporary mode of operations. In the case of St Michael's School, Billingham, the legacy of its history can be seen to have contributed to its contemporary effectiveness in two ways.

The school, from its original foundation in May 1965, was characterised by a reputation for strong discipline but, at the same time, by an ethos of caring for its pupils, especially those from socially deprived backgrounds. This culture of caring in an atmosphere of firm discipline was to an important extent the creation of the school's first headteacher. It is a feature of the school which, although changed in style and form in recent times, remains distinctive of its contemporary culture and local reputation.

After a successful foundation and a rise in the school roll to 954 pupils in 1976, changes in the demography of the local Catholic population resulted in progressively falling school rolls. By the mid-1980s the number of pupils had dropped to around 500, and this situation, taken together with a lack of leadership from within the school or from within the Diocese, brought the school under the threat of closure by 1984–85.

This fundamental threat to the school's existence produced a response in the local Catholic community, with the establishment of an action group, St Michael's Against Closure (SMAC). Strong community support for the school was generated by an alliance of school staff, parents and community members. The present headteacher (then a parent of two pupils at the school) was prominent in the campaign to save the school. The effectiveness of the SMAC campaign not only saved the school from closure but also established a powerful network of community support for the school which operates to the present day.

This crisis situation demonstrated a visible level of support for the school which had a very good effect upon staff and pupil morale and also upon the school's image and reputation in the locality. Experienced members of staff at the school have commented upon this period in the school's history as a period of 'shared ordeal'. Out of this shared ordeal came a strong bonding of school and community which has lasted.

The historical legacy of St Michael's School, therefore, with its established reputation for firm discipline and caring for pupils and its strong community and parent support networks underpins and continues to shape its contemporary effectiveness.

ST MICHAEL'S SCHOOL: CONTEMPORARY EFFECTIVENESS

The listing of the correlates of effectiveness can become a sterile exercise unless some attempt is made to come to an informed judgement of the relative significance of particular factors in particular social and educational settings. However, this is a difficult enterprise because of the inevitable interaction of effectiveness correlates. While recognising the complex interaction of effectiveness factors at St Michael's School the following may be regarded as the building blocks of its success, expressed in a tentative rank ordering.

Community support network (factor 1)

This refers to the network of interlocking support for the school provided by parent, community and parish networks in the area.

The network, originally established to defend the school from closure, now operates to underpin and to facilitate the school's evident success. Billingham as a community is a stable and cohesive social area and many of the current parents were themselves educated at St Michael's School. There are strong bonds of loyalty to the school.

The effect of this in practice is that parents support the school, not only by sending their children there but also, in the great majority of cases, by their active involvement in supporting its spiritual, moral and social objectives and its educational and sporting programmes. There is thus a powerful alliance of teachers and parents working for common objectives in the education of the pupils of St Michael's.

The community support network which has its locus in the Catholic population is the source also of significant financial support for the school, through an active Parent-Teacher Association (PTA), which has had a good effect upon the physical environment of the school and upon its resources and facilities. Through judicious use of public relations and media information about the school's successes, it has extended its appeal beyond the Catholic community to the wider community of the area. This results in a contemporary situation in which the school is over-subscribed, with about one-third of its pupils coming from non-Catholic homes.

Strong parental and community support may thus be said to be the foundation stone of St Michael's School effectiveness. However, such support has not been forthcoming simply out of loyalty to the school. Community support is informed and strengthened by a shared perception of the positive features of its contemporary culture and profile of operations.

St Michael's as a caring and ordered community (factor 2)

An ethos of caring, derived from Catholic and Christian values, is apparent in the school, and this is commented upon by both staff and pupils as central to the success and effectiveness of the school. It is particularly noticeable that those staff who are able to make comparative judgements about school ethos in the area, newly appointed staff and part-time supply staff, give special prominence to the sense of an ordered, calm and caring community which characterises St Michael's. This is seen to be the fundamental institutional underpinning of the school's success.

This sense of an ordered and caring community in the school is constituted and reinforced in various ways. The basis is to be found in the religious, moral and social values which are expressed in the school's mission statement:

> The purpose of St Michael's RC School is to serve the whole community from which our children are drawn by offering them an extensive range of educational, pastoral and liturgical experiences within a caring Christian context. We aim to develop a sense of true community spirit which will form the foundation for each individual's future in the wider community and to do so in an overtly Christian environment, where charity, forgiveness, use of talents, mutual respect and the dignity of the individual provide the impetus for all endeavour.

The school's mission statement is not a formal piece of rhetoric devised by the 'senior management' but an agreed statement of religious, moral, educational and social aims produced after widespread consultation. It is, as one staff member noted, 'a living statement' which permeates the life and the work of the school. It produces a definable ethos which is commented upon by visitors, staff, parents and pupils.

Caring, mutual respect and the dignity of the individual are made manifest in the pastoral care system and the effective use of the house/year blocks as a social base; in the system of pupil grouping in which mixed-ability classes are a significant part; in the steady insistence upon standards of personal appearance, including the wearing of school uniform, and of courtesy and politeness and in friendly teacher–pupil relations both in the classroom and in extra-curricular activities. The pupils perceive that they are respected because their teachers demonstrate careful preparation of lessons; detailed follow-up of work completed, or not completed; and a general climate of high expectations for achievement and performance. Staff involvement in extra-curricular activities, especially sport, has a very positive effect upon school ethos and relationships and is clearly appreciated by the pupils:

'The teachers put on sports activities after school and they join in as well.'

(Pupil, age fifteen)

The disciplinary system of the school works in a quiet and understated way but it is particularly effective. In the language of its pupils, the disciplinary system is 'dead strict – but fair'. The pupils know that infringement of the rules for behaviour and appearance will be systematically followed up and that this follow-up activity will involve their parents or care-givers. Parents and pupils know that failure to cooperate with the school in disciplinary matters can result in sanctions of various kinds. They also know that these sanctions will be applied as necessary.

> 'The school has high standards and strict rules. I would send my children to St Michael's because it is a Catholic school that teaches morals, kindness, consideration and confidence to the pupils.'
>
> (Pupil, age fourteen)

In operating its disciplinary system, St Michael's School has three advantages which not all schools possess. It has an established core of long-service teachers who are well known to the parents and the pupils. It has purpose-built house/year blocks which provide smaller disciplinary and social units, described by one staff member as 'schools within the school'.

Perhaps its greatest advantage is that the great majority of its pupils want to be at St Michael's rather than at other secondary schools in the area:

> 'It has good exam results and the pupils and teachers have quite good relationships. . . . I feel that it is better than any of the other secondary schools around this area.'
>
> (Pupil, age fifteen)

The great contribution which the disciplined and ordered community atmosphere of the school makes to its effectiveness, especially its academic effectiveness, is that, in the words of one staff member, 'it allows teachers to concentrate upon their teaching rather than simply "containing" pupils'.

Staff quality and staff commitment (factor 3)

If factors one and two jointly provide the conditions for the effectiveness of St Michael's School, factor three, staff quality and commitment, is the active constituent for realising that effectiveness in practice. Quality staff in this context implies teachers who demonstrate high levels of professional conscientiousness and commitment to the interests of the pupils. These interests may be academic, social/personal, sporting, artistic/creative, and so on. The teachers of St Michael's School take equal opportunities for all pupils seriously and this is manifested in a climate of high expectations for all.

A core of long-established teachers (twelve with over twenty years' service at the school and fifteen with ten to twenty years' service) provides a cohesive base for staffing, and these long-service teachers have generated a culture of loyalty and commitment to the school and its pupils. More recently appointed teachers comment upon the fact that such loyalty and commitment are quickly learned by new staff members. Internal staff rapport and morale are good.

The existence of quality teaching staff is in part the fortunate historical legacy of St Michael's but in more recent times it is also the outcome of a consciously applied staffing policy. The headteacher has operated a strategic policy for retaining and promoting quality staff and for careful selection of new appointments. Members of staff, on appointment, are made aware of the required commitment and the high standard of expectations. In the view of the present headteacher the current effectiveness of St Michael's School is the achievement of a committed and cohesive staff.

The concept of quality and committed staff extends, however, beyond the teachers to include all other support workers within the school. These support staff, in particular the school secretaries, are seen to be vital to the school's success. This manifests once again the powerful idea of the school as a total working community which characterises its ethos and operations.

Headteacher leadership and management style (factor 4)

All observers and commentators attribute much of the school's recent success to the qualities, commitment and leadership style of the headteacher. The headteacher is commended for his open, approachable and consultative style of leadership. The headteacher perceives his own role to be fundamentally about enabling others to do what they are good at doing. By universal consent, he has been very successful in his policy of enabling and empowering others to work more effectively for the good of the pupils.

The leadership of empowerment which characterises St Michael's School involves identifying, with others, what needs to be done and then providing the motivation and the resources to carry out the project. The prime role of the headteacher as school leader has been to provide a sense of purpose and focus for the school's activities. This has involved a steady focus upon what is in the best interests of the pupils and of the community.

Experienced staff at St Michael's School have been able to compare previous leadership regimes which were restrictive, dogmatic, uncreative and hierarchical with the present leadership style, which has reversed all of these features. A particular strength of the current leadership style is that it has rejected traditional hierarchy and also more recent notions of senior line management to celebrate shared involvement in leadership and management.

It is significant that the term 'senior management team' is not used in the school. The headteacher believes that contemporary ideas of 'senior management' can be divisive of staff unity and collegiality. In place of a senior management team, the school has a 'school manageable group' (the headteacher's creation) which consists of senior post-holders but which is open to any other staff who wish to contribute to policy formulation. The group has no executive powers but it functions as a regular forum for consultation and for staff involvement.

The effect of the headteacher's open style of leadership and management, referred to frequently by the staff as an 'open door' policy, is that staff feel that they are listened to and that their views are respected. It is recognised that the headteacher is politically shrewd and skilled in human relations and that many decisions are therefore shaped in accordance with his diagnosis of the school's needs. This quality of informed and committed leadership is both respected by and expected by the staff. At the same time, all staff members have a sense that their views count and that policies are open to negotiation and modification.

Headteacher–teacher relationships are good. Among the contributory elements of these good professional relationships are an absence of hierarchy, friendly and informal social relations, and a strong sense among the teachers that if a good case is made for extra resources to support particular projects, these resources are likely to be found. It must be said that the headteacher's ability to make extra resources available is an asset and an advantage not possessed by all headteachers in the area.

The headteacher's leadership is firmly premised upon strong support for teaching and learning quality in the school. He is known to monitor the performance of various departments, and heads of department are clear about their responsibilities for quality control within their various subject areas.

Staff value the fact that the headteacher has a regular teaching commitment and that the headteacher and the deputies regularly provide cover in the case of staff illness. This preserves the sense that all are members of the teaching team in the school and avoids a 'management' (non-teaching) and 'workers' (teaching) culture from developing in the school.

The headteacher also adopts a policy of 'being about the school', and there is a regular morning briefing to all staff by the head-teacher and the deputies before the start of the day's timetable. Headteacher–senior staff–staff interaction is therefore a frequent occurrence.

The leadership of the headteacher is widely acknowledged to

have had a considerable influence upon the school's current effectiveness and reputation in the community. His considerable personal and professional commitment to the school and its pupils has provided a model for all staff. His leadership style has done much to bring out the strengths of all the staff and the pupils.

The headteacher expressed his views on leadership and management in education in these terms:

> 'I see my role as headteacher as being one who steers and directs the school towards a particular vision which I have. That vision is to make, with the help of others, St Michael's the best school in the country, one in which the Gospel values are well entrenched and practised, and where there is a maximisation of talents. After that, everything which I do in order to achieve this vision, whether it be managerial leadership or educational leadership, is to progress towards this ideal. It would seem to me to be a little bit naive and simplistic to try to categorise headteachers into being entirely managerial or educational: the two are inextricably entangled. Having established the vision, then I must work with others, through consultation and debate, to put in place the management structures, and to implement policies. I do not see myself as being a headteacher who directs in a managerial fashion. Besides setting up the structures to implement the policies, then the educational policies themselves must be carefully considered and debated, and I would consider that I play a central role in establishing the initiatives, giving advice, and promoting good educational practice. An essential aspect of my leadership style is to establish which members of staff are capable of initiatives, and then to give the encouragement and advice to see initiatives through to a conclusion. In purely practical terms, a headteacher gains a great deal of respect and credibility from staff by being involved in the actual educational process through teaching to a level where he or she can be seen to be accountable, and in sharing the workload of supervision

for absent colleagues. To those outside of the school community, this latter exercise might seem a little unimportant, but it assumes a significance far beyond that which it may seem at first sight. The failure of senior management to participate fully, on a regular basis, to the cover for absent colleagues is probably the greatest cause of ill-feeling between staff and management in schools today. In conclusion, there are various dimensions of headship: the vision; the managerial; the educational policy-making and involvement; the action; and what forms the basis of any successful leader, the interpersonal skills which are developed through experience and common sense.'

Teaching and learning environment (factor 5)

The sense that the headteacher and staff of St Michael's School believe in the capacity of all of their pupils to learn and to make progress is symbolised most clearly in the school's use of mixed-ability classes for a large part of its educational programme. The strong educational philosophy of the school is the maintenance of opportunities for all. The advantages of mixed-ability teaching and learning in the view of the headteacher and other teachers is that it builds self-respect among pupils and avoids the creation of alienated, low-stream, low-expectation groups among the pupils.

A strong academic work atmosphere exists which is maintained by regular homework and follow-up of homework. Pupils' work is liberally displayed throughout the school, and regular communication of school and pupil successes is made to the parents by a 'Home Links' newsletter, ten years in existence, and by regular media coverage of the school's achievements.

The pupils interviewed all had a very clear sense of their school's public image and particularly of its academic and sporting successes. They had a sense too that they would, in their various ways, find some success in the school:

'The school is very fair and understanding. Whenever I have had problems, I've discussed them with teachers and they have been solved.'

(Pupil, age fifteen)

'The school is excellent because it sets high standards for pupils to follow whatever their ability is. Pupils with less ability get the same attention as normal pupils so everyone is equal. Respect for all is taught at St Michael's.'

(Pupil, age sixteen)

The quality of teaching and learning at St Michael's School is enhanced and amplified by access to appropriate educational resources and equipment. The prime conditions for success are set by professionally skilled and committed teachers meeting average teaching-size groups of twenty-three pupils. The educational results are, however, enhanced by the school's possession of appropriate equipment in information technology, science and technology and art, music and drama:

'The teachers are kind and understanding and we have good facilities to work with.'

(Pupil, age fourteen)

'St Michael's is a good school . . . it has a broad range of subjects on offer and they are taught very well by a great range of teachers. St Michael's is also a very tidy and clean school in appearance.'

(Pupil, age sixteen)

Buildings, work environment and resources (factor 6)

The well-designed and well-maintained buildings of the school seem to bring out the best in the pupils. There are hardly any graffiti and very little vandalism. The physical structure of the school is respected. This respect arises partly from the sense of ownership which pupils feel for 'their' school, especially 'their' year block, but it also seems likely that their awareness of their own parents' contributions to the maintenance through the fund-raising of the PTA is a factor:

> 'Our school is like a family community. We have good sports facilities and interesting things to do. We also have a lot of computers. We get good exam results.'
>
> (Pupil, age fourteen)

The pupils interviewed had a sense that in every year in which they had been in the school there had been a visible improvement in the school's facilities.

The school has been fortunate in its possession of a budget surplus in the local management of schools (LMS) allocations. The deputy headteacher and others have also been resourceful in generating extra income from the adjacent leisure centre and from external agencies. These resources have been used to make the school an attractive and pleasant work environment for everyone.

PERSPECTIVES FROM THE COMMUNITY – REPORT TWO

The evidence base for this report consists of reading relevant documentation and publications produced by the school together with the OFSTED Inspection Report (1994). Research interviews were held with the following:

- the headteacher;
- a parent governor;
- the ex-chair of the PTA;
- a careers officer;
- an education social worker;
- a post-16 college principal;
- a feeder primary school headteacher.

SUMMARY OF FACTORS RELATED TO THE EFFECTIVENESS OF THE SCHOOL

The factors presented here are given in a tentative rank ordering which reflects the emphasis assigned by members of the wider community when evaluating the success of the school.

Strong, positive leadership by the headteacher and senior staff (factor 1)

The headteacher of St Michael's School is perceived, in the wider community, as a charismatic and entrepreneurial manager who secures effective performance from staff and pupils alike. All interview discussions highlighted the importance of the headteacher's leadership role but stressed also the sense of involvement arising from his open-door policy with staff, pupils, parents and external agencies. Management competencies would, therefore, appear to be a critical success factor in achieving a high level of school effectiveness.

Teaching staff who have worked within the school for over twenty years still display a high level of commitment and enthusiasm. A significant percentage of the senior staff and of the teachers lived within the locality and were integral members of the local community in terms of sporting and social activity. This was thought to be very different from other schools in the area where very few staff members lived in the locality.

Parental involvement in children's education and in supporting the aims of the school (factor 2)

A particular factor is the Home/School Contract for Partnership, which has to be signed by parents or care-givers in Year 7 and which pledges parental/care-giver support for the ethos of the school and for its requirements in terms of school rules, uniform, appearance and work.

A strong and active PTA is apparent, with a good representation of teachers as well as parents. Parents are empowered to participate actively in school life through sporting activities, pupil work-experience placements and by providing additional learning support for slow learners.

Regular communication with parents was evident in the provision of termly assessments of pupil performance as well as full yearly reports, all of which invite the comments of parents or care-givers. The production and circulation of the 'Home Links' newsletter, together with the St Michael's School *Year Book* to all homes, was particularly appreciated and commended.

The St Michael's Leisure and Community Centre creates a defined community focus for pupils, parents and local organisations. A member of staff has been appointed to develop specifically the community aspects of this facility.

Extra-curricular activities (factor 3)

The involvement of St Michael's pupils in strategies to achieve effective primary school liaison was commended. Year 10 pupils from St Michael's are involved in coaching the football team at one of the feeder primary schools and Year 11 pupils are involved in promoting reading and writing skills within primary education.

Post-16 liaison is also enhanced through involvement in the student mentoring programme at the local sixth form college. Close working links between St Michael's School and Bede Sixth Form College ensures effective transition at sixteen for many Year 11 pupils.

Strong school/community links also arise from Catholic parish activities, pupil involvement in the St Vincent de Paul organisation and the involvement of the school orchestra in support of local community events.

It was noted that a named member of staff was responsible for community publicity, community involvement and liaison with

external agencies such as the local Training and Enterprise Council (TEC). This was thought to be crucial to the success of school/community activity.

A good school atmosphere generated by shared aims and values (factor 4)

St Michael's School is perceived, in the local community, as transmitting a distinctive Christian and intellectual ethos. Although a Catholic school by denomination, the approach to community involvement is undoubtedly ecumenical. The ecumenical spirit of the school can be seen to be not only a progressive feature of its ethos but also part of its own institutional success from the period of threatened closure in the mid-1980s. Esteem for the school is such that non-Catholic parents are keen to reside within the school locality to enhance the chances of entry for their children.

An attractive and stimulating physical environment (factor 5)

The school has made a determined attempt to create a well-equipped, well-furnished and welcoming environment. This has been achieved with the support of the PTA and local and national agencies. All community commentators mentioned the favourable impression created by the clean and attractive working environment of the school.

CONCLUSION OF REPORT TWO

Although much of the success of St Michael's School can be intrinsically linked to its active Catholic/Christian ethos and values, significant acknowledgement must also be given to the management competences of the headteacher. These competences include his entrepreneurial approach in gathering Christian commitment, regardless of denomination, into the school; his harnessing of staff commitment and enthusiasm; his structured approach to promoting the achievement of all pupils' potential and his undoubted ability to earn respect for the school in the local community. In the words of a local education social worker:

> 'St Michael's touches all parts of the community from a strong Christian perspective and it brings out the best in everyone.'

PERSPECTIVES FROM LOCAL EMPLOYERS AND FORMER PUPILS – REPORT THREE

The evidence base for this report consists of reading relevant documentation. Research interviews were held with the following:

- the headteacher;
- the deputy headteacher (pastoral);
- eight former pupils of the school;
- six local employers.

It should be noted that responses from local employers were generally obtained by telephone conversations.

SUMMARY OF FACTORS RELATED TO THE EFFECTIVENESS OF ST MICHAEL'S SCHOOL

The factors presented here are given in a tentative rank order which reflects the emphasis assigned by local employers and by former pupils when evaluating the success of the school.

Firm and fair disciplinary system (factor 1)

This was regarded as the foundation stone of the school's success by employers and by former pupils. Pupils are encouraged to report instances of bullying in the school and action is taken following these reports. The influence of the deputy headteacher (pastoral) and the influence of the pastoral house block system was regarded as fundamental to the good disciplinary ethos in the school. Local employers commented that St Michael's School ex-pupils stood out by their demeanour, their disciplined manner but also by their confidence and articulateness.

Highly positive management team (factor 2)

The school's success owes much to the exceptional commitment and enthusiasm of the headteacher and the senior staff. This commitment has a positive effect upon other staff and upon the pupils. Careful selection of staff also ensures a high level of involvement.

Ethos of care in the school (factor 3)

The best is achieved from both staff and pupils because both groups experience positive and caring relationships in the school. The Catholic/Christian commitment of the school is evident in the quality of the relationships in the school.

High level of expectation and generation of pupil confidence (factor 4)

The school is perceived to operate on a 'high expectation' policy. Strategic use is made of praise and of public recognition of the full range of pupil achievements.

The use of drama to encourage pupils to express themselves and to become more confident in public relations was commended. It was thought that this approach had beneficial effects in the interview situation for later employment.

St Michael's: an over-subscribed school (factor 5)

It was known that the school was currently over-subscribed and this was taken to be evidence of its visible market success. It was observed that if St Michael's School were a business, in the world of commerce, it would now be expanding its operations with a building programme and the admission of increased numbers of pupils.

ST MICHAEL'S SCHOOL: AN OVERVIEW OF EFFECTIVENESS

In a major research study of the effectiveness of Catholic schooling in the United States, (Bryk *et al.*, [1993] *Catholic Schools and the Common Good*, Harvard University Press) have concluded that many Catholic schools benefit from:

- the presence of an 'inspirational ideology' derived from a Catholic/Christian view of the purposes and values of education;
- a dedicated and committed school personnel (school leaders, teachers, assistant staff, and so on) who contribute more than a contractual obligation to the schools;
- a community ethos characterised by shared values and shared activities within the school and outside it which bonds students and teachers;

- high educational and academic expectations set in a framework of firm but caring discipline; and
- a community education network in support of the schools arising from a partnership of governors, priests, teachers, parents, Catholic employers and parish members.

All of these factors can be seen to have worked to help make St Michael's School an effective institution in personal, social and moral formation, in the generation of community responsibility and in the achievement of academic, creative and sporting goals. The school has achieved success 'against the odds' of threatened school closure and against a rapidly worsening economic and social situation in the Teesside area.

ST MICHAEL'S ROMAN CATHOLIC SCHOOL

A voluntary-aided mixed school for 11–16-year-olds

The school

Headteacher appointed	1985
Number of pupils	849
Number of teachers (full-time equivalent)	45.8
Pupil/teacher ratio	18.53:1
Average class size	22.3
Annual school budget	£1.48 million

Pupils in the school

Registered for free school meals (%)	20

With statements of special educational needs (no.)	1
Ethnic background (%)	
White	99.7
Afro-Caribbean	0
Asian	0.3
Other	0
With home/community language other than English (%)	0.3

School outcomes

% of 15-year-olds in 1994 achieving GCSE passes	
5+ A*–C grades	49.7
5+ A*–G grades	96.6
1+ A*–C grades	79.2
1+ A*–G grades	98
% of Year 11 (1993–94) students who are now	
In full-time education and training	77.3
In employment with training	15.6
In employment without training	1.5
Other	5.3

10

SUTTON CENTRE
Mansfield, Nottinghamshire

Jean Ruddock, Kate Clarricoates
and Reg Norman

Sutton-in-Ashfield lies in the heart of the county of Nottinghamshire in the North Midlands. The design of Sutton Centre was revolutionary when it opened over two decades ago; and its place in the heart of the community is still rivalled by a mere handful of similar educational, social and recreational institutions. Although there have been, as may well be expected, major changes in its management style in over twenty years, the principles of concern for the well-being of its pupils and its openness to the community have endured.

A SCHOOL IN THE MARKET PLACE

On arriving at Sutton Centre you don't see the usual institutional trappings of a school. There is no gate to pass through; no iron railings mark it off from its surroundings; no high walls contain the students, or keep local people out. There is no concrete playground, no tarmac drive. It is difficult to know whether you are on the school premises or not. And when you are inside, the windows look directly on to the marketplace, the town library, a newly refurbished shopping centre, a health centre and a pub. Three paths wind through the buildings, taking members of the community across the site or into its buildings, for the school is also the local community and leisure centre. The 760 students share the facilities with the 2,000 or so adults who come each week to learn, to practise their hobbies, to take part in sports and health activities, or to visit the theatre, which doubles as the school's assembly hall. It is a very accessible site, with around forty doors: 'It's got access from all round – and that's been our philosophy – open all the time, from early morning to late at night,' said the chair of governors, who went on to recall a time when a member of the local community wandered into the headteacher's room from the pub on the corner: 'Now this is a fellow that's had too much to drink and he's sat down in a chair there, "Eh up, me duck", he says to the headteacher, "I've just been defending your school in the pub. Some people don't think that it's like what a school should be like. I think you've got a great school and I'm proud of it" – and then he went!' A key theme in our story is the view of the school held by members of the community.

A tour of Sutton Centre takes us from a large, carpeted foyer, welcoming and in no way intimidating, along corridors with large wall spaces covered, floor to ceiling, with evidence of students' activities and successes: residential trips abroad, a basketball tour of the Greek island Cephalonia, a day trip to Boulogne, drama and dance performances, walking expeditions and voluntary work in the community. The displays of students' work are no less colourful and energetic. The original open-plan spaces have, over time, and at the wish of both students and staff, been given more structure and a bit more privacy. Teachers have small rooms and niches clustering round their departmental resources centres. There is a small in-service suite where groups of teachers can hold meetings, and a communal area used by teachers and other workers at the centre, and for meetings between teachers and students; there is no traditional 'enclosed' staffroom as such: 'This building', said the chair of governors, 'was built for kids and for teachers to teach kids. We wouldn't have a room cut off from the rest of the school where the staff sit.' Teachers queue up alongside students in the dining area and eat with them at the same tables.

In that part of the site which houses the joint-use leisure facilities we saw about thirty members of the community on an indoor bowling green, about fifteen men were in the technology area, constructing small pieces of furniture and toys, or shaping walking sticks; twenty or so people, mainly, if not all, women, painting and drawing – and the health and fitness suite was full. There was activity on the ice rink, which is free to students during the lunch break, and a basketball match was going on in the sports hall. From a window we saw a mini-bus bringing disabled people on to the site. There is no playground and the sports fields are a mile or so away. During short breaks young people can walk around inside and get coffee from the snack bar or vending machines. At lunch-time they can go out into the town unless they are in Years 7 and 8, for the headteacher has an agreement with parents that younger students will not move off site during the school day. Staff are very aware of their 'duty of care' for all students and want to be sure that the younger ones have learned the school's social code of responsibility for oneself and concern for others before they are allowed to wander out into the town during the day.

A recent LEA inspection (1993) reports that:

> 'the campus reflects the philosophical and architectural vision of its founders to provide a true community school with a range of facilities and a caring and egalitarian ethos, to meet the needs of a community which had inadequate provision of social facilities'.

THE EARLY HISTORY

As a consequence of the industrialisation of the western area of the county, a number of small villages found their boundaries

Sutton Centre seen from the Idlewells shopping centre

becoming blurred, and an urban area now developed, housing 50,000 people, around two centres of employment – coal-mining and hosiery. With the expansion of employment and housing, new facilities were needed for the community, including a school, and in 1971 the county LEA and the Urban District Council started to look at the possibility of providing a full community centre in the town.

The school's first intake of students transferred from other secondary schools in 1973. At that time, the area had one comprehensive school, formed in 1969 from a merger of a very small grammar school for girls and a secondary modern school. In 1977, as the final phase in the LEA's plans for secondary reorganisation, Sutton Centre absorbed students from two other small secondary schools and about twenty of their teachers. At the point of absorption Sutton Centre had about 1,400 students. A range of factors, including demographic, have resulted in falling rolls, and in

September 1994, at the start of the new year, the school had 760 students aged 11–18. It was not full but the centre is thinking constructively how to increase its recruitment which suffered a dip recently. The present headteacher, who had been a local inspector, seems to be making steady progress in reversing this trend and his obvious pride in the school and gentle authority will be very reassuring to parents.

The early history of the school was chequered and the reverberations have taken a long while to fade, despite some very favourable comments in an early HMI Report (1978) which were echoed in the 1993 LEA inspection report. Nearly everyone consulted during our study talked about the 'vision' of those who founded the school. But at the time the predominantly traditional working-class community wanted a new grammar school on a green-fields site. What it got instead, in the words of the deputy headteacher who joined the school in the early 1980s, was the equivalent in terms of schools of a 'Spielberg Spaceship'! The community responded positively to the leisure facilities which the new complex offered, for these were familiar, but less positively to a school that was modern, trail-blazing, but not the school of its hopes. The first headteacher, by all accounts a charismatic and persuasive man who shared the vision of the creators of the new complex, enthused the new staff, most of whom came from outside the immediate township. A significant element of the school's philosophy was its trust in the rhetoric that the new CSE examinations at sixteen would be regarded and accepted as the equivalent of the GCE 'O' levels; in the minds of employers and aspiring parents 'O' level retained its supremacy – and the new school did not offer 'O' levels. In the early years Sutton Centre lost some students to schools that did.

That alone was enough to cause concern. But a particular incident fanned the concern: a lesson on swearing and the origin and analysis of swear-words, which a parent heard about and questioned. Unease about the school being 'different' found a focus in this incident which got full media coverage, and the LEA felt obliged to request a visit by HMI. The report was positive in many respects and should have quelled the turbulence but, as one of the deputies said, the observations of professionals are often less influential within a community than the images offered in the local press and through local stories.

Another factor contributing to the school's struggle to convince its community of its worth is the morning-to-night exposure to public scrutiny. Working here is indeed like being in a goldfish bowl. The headteacher commented:

> 'This is a very public site. People going to the shops go past the classroom windows. They are literally two feet away from the children doing their lessons. There is no playground. The letting-off steam area is in fact the building itself. We don't exclude the children from the building on any occasions whatsoever; it is their building. They're remarkably good. It warms my heart. Whenever you walk round the school most times you will see something which makes you think, "I'm not totally sure about that", but most of what you see is really positive.'

The headteacher's judgement is confirmed by the early HMI report (1978), which points out how responsibly young people behaved in relation to buildings which are there for them and for their community:

> 'HMI would like to record the fact that it would be hard to find a school which had been open as long as the Centre in which the premises still retained such freshness of appearance. There is not only an absence of any serious signs of vandalism, there is less evidence of wear and tear than might have been expected, although the premises are heavily used throughout the day and the evening. The unobtrusive way in which all users have contributed to a well kept building deserves high praise.'

Our own visit, seventeen years later, confirmed that impression. The buildings are weather-beaten and show the wear and tear of twenty-four years of constant use, but buildings are well cared for, there are some exciting new areas (the IT suites, for instance), the spaces are bright and clean, and students move round the building comfortably and easily.

VALUES, AIMS AND FOCUS

When the school first opened, the values that defined both its social and academic aims were created by the staff and there was, in a sense, no need for them to be written down formally in a single document. HMI, inspecting the school in 1978, made explicit the aims after talking with staff and reading various documents:

- to teach a common, balanced curriculum, which will provide an appropriate education and an equality of esteem for all students;
- to teach so as to meet the individual needs of the students, within mixed-ability social groups but using flexible teaching strategies;
- to integrate educationally with the community by providing opportunities for adults and adolescents to work and learn together and to enable the community to join with the school in making the best use of the centre's accommodation and facilities;
- to organise a system for the pastoral care of each individual student which enables the development of self-discipline by emphasising the personal responsibility of the individual to the community and consideration for others as the basic principle of conduct.

The HMI report also notes that the school has not tried to be 'aggressively innovatory' but has tried to put into practice ideas which have been 'widely discussed and supported in educational circles'. And it goes on:

> 'The school's greatest success lies undoubtedly in the way it has achieved in its comparatively short existence, a high standard of personal relationships, of cooperation and commitment

to learning from its students, and of community responsibility. These could not have been attained without the exceptional hard work and devotion of the staff. The visitor is impressed with a feeling of buoyant vitality.'

The (1993) LEA inspection report also notes that students' 'relationships with each other and with teachers are very good' and that

'the school is meeting its behavioural aims successfully through an emphasis on counselling and rewarding effort and behaviour. The dual system and the influential role of the tutor also contribute to an orderly school. Students know the school well and understand the values it promotes. They are courteous to visitors and respond well to additional responsibility.'

This report did not list the school's aims and values, but it is clear from the comments, and from our own observations and discussion two years later, that the staff has sustained its commitment to the values that gave, and still give, the school its distinctive character.

WHAT DO THE AIMS LOOK LIKE NOW?

In reverse order, the fourth aim is to do with pastoral care, and the system seems to operate consistently at different levels, suggesting that there is a strongly held principle that is unifying practice. On entry, each group of students is assigned two tutors (usually one male and one female) who stay with them throughout their time at the school. The dual tutoring system is demanding of staff time but is considered worth the investment. Where some schools may have cut back on the PSE/tutor time session because National Curriculum subjects were fighting for space, Sutton Centre kept it going. The dual system ensures that all students have regular opportunities to talk with a tutor: 'If you have any questions, problems or difficulties – or good ideas – you should see your tutor or co-tutor and talk about them,' advises the booklet for new students. The tutor system is complemented by the learning support system. All students judged by their tutors to be in need of help, and about 40 per cent of Year 7 students have a reading age two years below their chronological age, have sessions with the learning support team. Students may be supported in class or withdrawn, but if any student feels humiliated by being seen to be receiving extra support, then she or he can opt for support during the evening classes (the 'eleventh session') when teaching groups and teaching patterns are extremely varied and support can be offered inconspicuously.

Primary–secondary transition is taken very seriously. Staff teach occasional half days in the six primary schools that mainly feed Sutton Centre, and while still in Year 6 students are invited to the centre for sessions on IT and drama – and 'an orange juice and a large biscuit' (these recruitment events are not of course without an element of self-interest!). Tutors try to learn the names of the new students before they start in September and the first three days of the new school year are spent largely with the tutors and tutor group. Within the first month there is a three-day residential trip, made as a tutor group; all the cooking is done by the group and students learn to work together, to support one another and to value one another – team work and loyalty set a pattern for the future. The site is quite close, and parents know that they can visit if their child is troubled at being away from home, and students know that they can return quickly if they really want to. In themselves, the strategies are not unusual, but it is the consistency of the overall framework of relationships that helps students, many of whom lack secure frameworks in their lives out of school, that is impressive.

The third aim is to do with effective use of the site and the provision of opportunities for adolescents and adults to learn and work together. Any consideration of the impact of the centre on the local community and vice versa must start by recognising that the centre is in an area of high unemployment and with few significant employers. It is an enormous challenge for the school to help students see that education and training can prepare them for a worthwhile and occupied adult life. The centre is a constant reminder to students of the adult world: and about 2,000 older members of the community, some bringing young children to the centre's crèche, come to the centre each week, many for further education and many for leisure activities. There are common policies for all – to do with dress, noise, courtesy and protection of the equipment and fabric. 'There's always something to do at this school,' said the students we interviewed, with enthusiasm.

The most distinctive feature is the 'eleventh session' – the term being a throw-back to when the school had ten morning and afternoon teaching and learning blocks (it now has twenty-five sessions): the 'eleventh session' is the generic term for the evening and Saturday morning classes attended voluntarily by many of the students as well as by older members of the community. Students can do homework, getting extra help with something they are puzzled by, get on with a hobby or join a sports activity: 'You can choose what you take part in, and your parents and family can come too,' says the brochure for new students. A deputy comments:

> 'After fourteen years I still find it remarkable that children will come back voluntarily (500–600 attendances each week) and not so much for the exotic elements; but for more maths, more English, more languages, more science. They come back for the curriculum.'

The library also provides a service during these sessions. The well-structured programme of extra-curricular activities demonstrates that education does not stop at sixteen or eighteen – a concept that is not always easy to communicate to students while they are still at school.

The successful management of any organisation requires that there is effective management both of people and of the financial resources to support their activities. At Sutton Centre there is a very clear understanding of the financial situation and there was clear evidence of good management both in terms of forward planning and control of current expenditure in relation to budget. The school clearly benefits from its strong presence in the community centre; and it has a high level of involvement in adult education activities which are funded by both the LEA and the Further Education Funding Council (FEFC). The skilful integration of school and further educational activities results in some benefits to the school: availability of additional equipment; the presence of a maintenance team that can keep fabric and facilities in good order. The joint use of the site makes good economic as well as educational sense. The success of the integration is clearly helped by the staff's willingness to lead some evening or weekend sessions, with remission from weekday teaching, and by the general spirit of enthusiasm and good will that prevails in the school.

The second aim focused on mixed-ability work and the need to respond to students as individuals. The opening remarks of the pamphlet 'Welcome to Year 7' convey the message that 'everyone counts' in good, straightforward words: 'I know that each of you will bring your own particular skills and talents to Sutton Centre and that your individual personality will help our school to grow and develop during your time with us.' This is not rhetoric; this is the reality of the place. The commitment of the school to non-uniform clothing is part of the overall frame. The logic of the dress code is clear once you are in Sutton Centre: the centre is a shared facility and open to all, and the code of conduct (to show courtesy and respect for others) holds for all users of the centre, both young and old. There is no dress requirement for any particular group except as is necessary and logical for particular tasks or activities. We saw no extremes of dress among the young people; individual style can be managed without departing from the code which stresses that dress should be practical and comfortable, that neither clothes nor badges should give offence to others, and that all should take pride in their personal appearance.

Following the same logic, it would be unacceptable for the school to sort students and label them by ability. Equity has always been, and continues to be, a cardinal principle that runs through and unifies every aspect of work in school. All the centre's spaces are accessible to the disabled. Although relatively little energy has as yet been given to issues of ethnicity, teachers have worked exceptionally hard to try to counter the gendered pattern of expectations in the community, still apparent among the mainly retired people attending the woodwork and art classes, and in the career aspirations of the youngest students we talked with. The English department, praised by the local inspectors for the quality of its work, has been at pains to offer role models of sensitive males and to legitimise reflection and feeling as a way of countering the gendered image of the subject; literature is, as a result, more popular among male students than it is in many schools. All departments are supported in organising single sex groupings where teachers think that such grouping will help to balance out opportunity and help those who are being held back to grow in skill and confidence. Indeed, the headteacher and deputies are confident that the school has, over time, started to unlock some of the stereotypical ways of thinking in the community.

Teachers in this school, as are many others working on equity issues, are well aware of the dilemmas facing men and women in the community. There is a nationwide aggressive advertising culture that urges people to 'buy, buy, buy' – and yet the reality here is that many lives are lived out on welfare benefits in a community that learns not to be adventurous and to make do on little. Men are losing their traditional role as breadwinner; what have been seen as the 'real men's jobs' are decreasing, but it is not easy for men and women to enter into negotiation about changing their patterns of domestic responsibility – and women, in such circumstances, are readily lured into the casual labour, low-wage economy. It is important that the school sustains its efforts at helping young people to rethink roles and responsibilities, to learn to be themselves, and not to model themselves on conventional images of what men and women are and should do. One older student told us that, while he had expected to go into the forces when he left school, he had now decided, as a result of his work in drama, that he wanted to be an actor; to make such a career choice takes courage, and it is a mark of the school's influence that the young people are, by the time they are nearing the end of their time in school, so open and so confident in exploring alternatives.

The first of the school's aims highlights 'equality of esteem for all students' but it is also about offering a balanced curriculum. The school has tried to maintain, as an important educational experience and as a foundation for autonomy and responsibility, a strong principle of choice in the curriculum. This was not easy during the first phase of National Curriculum reform when space for options shrank; but as a result of the Dearing review there is more scope both for students to exercise choice and for the school to maintain its offerings in the creative and performing arts. Indeed, while we were at the school a site in the shopping area was open for displays and performances of the centre's creative work and members of the public were, by all accounts, flocking in!

Sutton Centre is already very pleased with its pilot work on GNVQ (General National Vocational Qualifications) courses in Years 12 and 13. Teachers like the flexibility that allows students, increasingly, to construct exciting and relevant individual pro-grammes of study – choosing, say, from an 'A' level programme, a course offered under franchise by a further education college in the county, and a course run for adults and students in the 'eleventh session' programme. The aim is to bring the GNVQ work down into Years 10 and 11 and to plan a fully integrated programme of equally valued academic and vocational courses (the senior management team was already using the National Commission's thinking on the General Education Diploma as a blueprint here). The principles of balance and choice are also reflected in another distinguishing feature of Sutton Centre: the two activities weeks that happen in late November and early July. Students can choose from a wide set of possibilities and have an experience of sustained, focused work. They can decide to work intensively on a subject in which they know they have weaknesses and where they need to tighten the scaffolding for their learning; or they can concentrate on canoeing, cycling, table tennis and other sports, go camping or youth hostelling, do some forensic science, start new hobbies and crafts, have additional work experience, learn to write ghost stories or make bonsai gardens, do sketching or pottery or creative cookery, make a film or even go abroad.

In many respects, then, the story of Sutton Centre is a story of success, as the early HMI and the recent LEA reports suggest, apart from occasional patches of weakness in particular departments and areas of provision. But times have changed and 'success' has now a singular interpretation. The challenge for the school has been to lift the level of formal achievements at sixteen and eighteen without abandoning the frameworks of individual respect and support that the teachers know are the foundation for progress among their students.

THE FOCUS ON ACADEMIC ACHIEVEMENT

In the early 1990s national concern about the country's economic future led to a cry for higher standards in schools and a public system of scrutiny. The focus was narrow, and was on those aspects of achievement that are measurable and comparable across institutions. For schools like Sutton Centre that had tried to work with students on a broad and consciously enriching front, this meant that the quality of their work with students went unrecognised. However, staff accepted the challenge, and prepared themselves for a thorough-going attempt to raise academic expectations and levels of achievement.

The current senior management team acknowledge that in the past Sutton Centre, along with many other schools serving similar communities, concentrated rather more on what might be called the 'caring' goals. This is not to say that it ignored academic goals: indeed Sutton Centre had, and still has, many distinctive features that testify to its concern to support students in academic work, such as its 'eleventh session' activities and its pioneering work on student profiling. Moreover, there is some evidence to suggest that the school has always tried to be flexible in its support for exceptionally gifted students. HMI noted in their 1978 report that one such student had taken maths 'A' level in the fourth year (now Year 10) and that two others were expected to do the same. This is still happening, as the chair of governors recalled:

'One of the things that I'm always proud of is when one of our students gets their A levels before they should. . . . We put them in as soon as they're ready; they don't wait. There was a girl in the paper last week – her brother went through before her, got his A level at fourteen and became a barrister. She recently finished her final year at medical school and became a doctor – and these are kids that have come from our community.'

But in what sense is this a school that is 'improving', and how do we as outsiders make fair judgements about progress given the proven link between disadvantage and underachievement? Using the national yardstick of percentage of students gaining five A*–C passes at GCSE, the year-by-year figures from 1988 show a steady rise, but with a blip in 1992 (Table 10.1):

Table 10.1 Sutton Centre students gaining five A–C passes at GCSE

| 1988 | 11.3% | 1989 | 16.5% | 1990 | 18.2% |
| 1991 | 23.9% | 1992 | 20.5% | 1993 | 25.5% |

Taking a three-year rolling average for the same period, the scores would be:

1988–90	1989–91	1990–92	1991–93
15.3%	19.5%	20.8%	23.4%

In 1994, the percentage dropped to 21.7 but this is explained by a change from a dual award GCSE modular science course – which, through a combination of clear, short-term targets and rapid feedback, had proved highly motivating – to one that involved a different way of working. In 1995, as the school started to adjust to the new frameworks the score rose again to 22.1 per cent. Of course the use of raw scores as a basis for comparison is, quite properly, heavily contested; we have to take a more context-sensitive approach. Nottinghamshire has levels of social and economic disadvantage that are above the national average, and Sutton Centre has levels of disadvantage in the families of its actual student intake that are well above the average for the county. Overall, the school is about 28 per cent more disadvantaged on the dimension of semi-skilled/unskilled worker families and it is also about 28 per cent more disadvantaged with regard to free school meals.

What we would expect, realistically, is that a school which had put academic achievement on its agenda will begin to show gradual progress over a number of years. The use of a rolling average will help to even out any 'blips' caused by events largely beyond the school's control (blips could, for instance, be the result of a change in a school's student intake, or reflect the time-lag while teachers and students adapt to the demands of an examination-orientated course after becoming used to a coursework approach). Nottinghamshire is one of the few LEAs in the country that can confidently undertake a reliable contextualising analysis, using a multi-level modelling system. Its figures, which are presented to and discussed with each school individually, show that Sutton Centre has been improving its performance slowly but fairly steadily. The Nottinghamshire average has also risen – but Sutton Centre's scores have risen at a slightly faster rate from a lower starting point. At the end of the 1980s (three-year average covering

1988/89/90) the proportion of pupils in the school scoring five or more A*–C passes at GCSE was 15 per cent compared with an LEA average of 25 per cent. For 1992/93/94 these figures were 23 per cent and 33 per cent respectively. Similarly, the percentage obtaining five or more A*–G grades in the school at the end of the 1980s was 61 per cent compared with a county average of 75 per cent. By the mid-1990s these figures had risen to 74 per cent and 84 per cent respectively. And in 1994, the school's science results at 'A' level were slightly above the average for the county: students in the county as a whole averaged 4.2 'A' level points compared with 4.4 points for the school.

The 1993 LEA inspection report on the school includes the following passages:

> 'In comparison with those from schools in similar catchment areas, Sutton Centre's overall examination results were good. . . . Among the school's recent successes are its results in English, drama and science, while results in 3-dimensional art are well above the national average and reflect some outstanding work.'

The poor levels of organisation and aspiration found in two departments were quickly analysed and robustly tackled by the senior management team, and the post-inspection plan is firmly scheduled and manageable and seems to have the active commitment of the staff. The report went on:

> 'The quality of learning was satisfactory or better in eighty per cent of the lessons observed and was good or very good in over half of these. Concerned to maintain improving academic standards, the school is engaging in increasingly thorough and sophisticated analysis of public examination entries and results. The school predicts and evaluates outcomes, identifies concerns, sets targets and produces strategies for improvement.'

Understanding patterns of achievement contextually means, in this case, looking at Sutton Centre's past. Expectations in the community have not been high, for the traditional employment openings in the area did not require high levels of academic performance. Most students stayed in the area and many found employment at fifteen, later sixteen, in local industry where the openings were strongly gendered: boys went into coal-mining, girls into hosiery and allied factory work. 'In fact,' said the chair of governors, 'we're the only one of the nine districts in the county without a further education college – and basically that was because it was never felt to be a need.' Then of course came the collapse of the local economy: 'all of a sudden the pits have gone, the factories have gone'. Now the teachers have the ironic experience of seeing the community beginning to appreciate that what the school can offer is what young people in the 1990s need: courses that are flexible and that allow young people to construct a tailor-made programme, taking what is appropriate from 'A' level, from GNVQ, from RSA and so on. Indeed, the school is considering, alongside its other priorities, asking all its teaching staff (with training support from the careers service) to have a group of about fifteen students each with whom they would work over the years, monitoring their career aspirations and ensuring that they are well informed about requirements and possibilities.

It takes time to change patterns of expectations, and work with students needs to be gently started and firmly supported from early on in their school careers. Many families still do not travel far away from the town and its immediate environs, and the school's concern to provide opportunities for day and residential trips is an attempt to make travel a familiar experience and so to widen horizons for employment. But it is not easy to change conventional ways of thinking about the roles of men and women. As one teacher said, even lower middle class parents continue to have limited aspirations, especially for girls. 'They say, "I think she ought to be a care assistant", and we say, "We think she ought to do

'A' levels and go to university", and they say, "Oh, I don't want to give her ideas beyond herself."' So the school is doing much work with parents, saying to them that their children 'are capable, they can do it' and persuading them that it is a respectable and important thing to aim high and keep options for employment open. The staff are also working on internal attitudes: 'We've done quite a bit of work on raising expectations among teachers, saying that students should be entered for the exams . . . and that's improved quite a lot.'

The school is also putting effort into a small number of well-judged initiatives that are designed to raise expectations and levels of achievement, but that are also consistent with its overall concern to support all students and to avoid creating situations where some students are made to feel that they are failures. Some of these initiatives target Years 10 and 11, but others reflect the school's concern to build steadily towards confidence in self and in school work. For instance, although students are encouraged to keep work diaries throughout their school career, the diaries for Years 10 and 11 have been designed to resemble a filofax. In English, the 100 per cent coursework in Years 10 and 11 has had to give way to only 40 per cent – to the school's extreme annoyance – but, characteristically, it is immediately taking steps to ensure that the damage is contained. The English department has just introduced a 'taster' exam experience at the end of Year 10 designed to acclimatise and sensitise students to the demands without being dysfunctionally threatening. This is seen as a helpful move and will be formalised across subjects as the school's 'end of Year 10 examination'. It is followed in Year 11 by a slightly more formal 'mock' exam. Testing and timed assessments are also being used more extensively to ensure that students are not unnecessarily disadvantaged by the sudden loss of coursework. The commitment is high: 'we have got a responsibility to produce well-qualified students, you know, as well as to develop all aspects that we feel are important for their future' (manager, KS4). A system of interim reports was introduced a couple of years ago – and these are, as far as possible, 'praise' reports – helping students to believe that they can achieve, and helping parents to share that belief; students at risk have opportunities within the tutor system to talk through their problems and to have advice. The parent/student evening about staying on beyond the compulsory leaving age has been given a high profile and is well supported. The school's involvement in the compact scheme, together with the GEST-funded attendance project, has also helped with attendance levels, and students seem as keen as teachers to keep their own attendance records and to ensure that they do not fall below the 90 per cent target.

All departments now have target-setting meetings with the headteacher and the targets have to be realistic: 'we want to improve and we are improving, but if you set something you're going to fail at, the same as for the children, it's a pointless exercise' (manager, KS4). The national target of over 70 per cent of students gaining five GCSE A*–C passes (or equivalent) by 1997 is too remote as yet to be accepted as a realistic target; the school must build up to that, and its action plan is based on a careful analysis of context as well as of psychology!

The task is made more difficult by the time and effort given to young people, some sixteen in the last six months, who have joined Sutton Centre because they were not settling in other schools or because they had been excluded. A government grant made available to a number of schools as part of a national initiative on improving rates of attendance enabled Sutton Centre to give intensive support to these students and to others who were at risk. The school feels that its efforts have paid off except with the handful of students who are on the school roll but who have run away from home. When the grant stops, the school, which is facing the possible loss of five teachers as a result of the shortfall in its budget, may not be able to maintain this intensive support for students who have problems in attending. It is not easy in education to have pump-priming grants unless schools are in a position to be able to raise money for the continuation of successful work from parents or from business sponsorships – and both seem remote possibilities in the case of Sutton Centre. Thus, although bringing long-term non-attenders back into school is a national priority, the source of additional support may dry up and the good efforts of the staff at Sutton Centre may have to be abandoned.

Another bitter irony for the school is the government's drastic cut-back on coursework. If higher levels of engagement and achievement are identified as a national target, why take away, especially from those schools that are already struggling with the effects of social disadvantage, strategies which are successful in helping young people to commit themselves to learning? There is little logic in this. Sometimes, teachers must feel that they are (in Webster's words in *The Duchess of Malfi*) 'merely the stars' tennis balls, struck and bandied which way please them'. Students have responded well to modularised coursework, with stepped targets and a clear grasp of the boundaries of a task. A teacher noted how students will 'spend hours on a piece of coursework, drafting and redrafting it, and coming along to eleventh session to get extra help for it'. And a deputy headteacher spoke feelingly about the modular science GCSE course that the school had introduced: 'The most unlikely students were queuing up for their results'– they were engaged, had a sense of progress and were achieving. The examination results were very good indeed, but the course was withdrawn and teachers now have to construct a new way of working and new strategies for getting the best out of their students. We admire the capacity of the staff at Sutton Centre to reorientate themselves so quickly in the face of set-backs and inequities in the system, to hold on to their commitment and to remain optimistic.

The educational reforms have, however, generally been helpful to the school, as the headteacher and the deputies point out: whereas, formerly, the school was thought by some sections of the community to be doing its own curious thing, it can now say that it is doing the same as other schools in the area – and more! 'Now we can say that we are in the mainstream and doing well in the mainstream,' said the headteacher.

FOCUS, OWNERSHIP AND TIME

It has been argued that the judgement as to whether a change is an improvement depends on the perspective of the observer, but at the moment the criteria that matter are public and explicit, and Sutton Centre knows this. Here we have a school that has clearly been successful in its relationships with students and in helping them to build a positive attitude towards schooling. It has had a reputation for being distinctively different: for example, it was committed from the start to a single system of assessment at sixteen plus; it had introduced its own profiling system, its own community service scheme, its own evening teaching sessions – all features that are now familiar across schools. It can now justifiably claim that it is a school 'in the mainstream': it works to the same curricular framework as other schools and, like them, it is making a concerted effort to raise achievement levels. What is interesting about Sutton Centre is that it is holding on to the values and principles that have guided its practices for many years and is intent on incorporating the new goal into its existing values system without compromising on what the school stands for. It looks at the moment as though 'the vision seriously intends to stay', but, as Auden says, 'time only knows the price we have to pay'.

There will be many schools in the current climate which recognise that they are at some level caught between the pressure to serve the competitive demands of a stratified society and their own concern to take a less divisive and more democratic position and respect the right of all children to develop their full potential. Sutton Centre's ambition is to fuse the two pressures but in a way that allows its existing values to remain in place. The strategies it is using are our main concern in this final section of the study.

The school improvement/school effectiveness field is burgeoning with lists of key conditions for success and key indicators of success. All of them offer common-sense reminders of what contributes to the well-being of a school. The National Commission's own list of key features makes very good sense, especially in the context of Sutton Centre. None of these items lies outside the school's current practices or plans.

Faced with an abundance of such lists, some researchers have to find common ground across lists and reduce the array to a few key factors. If we were to select one such overview for comment in relation to Sutton Centre it would be that of Gray and Wilcox, partly because of its brevity (it has only three items), but also because the items demand interpretation. The three common factors that they identify from research on school improvement are focus, ownership and time.

In relation to 'focus' and 'ownership', Louis and Miles (*Improving the Urban High School*) remind us that 'the hard work of improvement comes in negotiating the difficult path of getting new practices and ideas into the real life of the school' (1990). The task may be eased, they suggest, if a school is clear about the relationship between its goals and its targets of change. This is a simple distinction but none the less an important one. Goals tend to be abstract and distant and, in the present climate, to represent other people's priorities; targets of change, however, offer something recognisable and close at hand and their definition can reflect the context of schools at particular stages in their development. We would want to add, between 'goals' and 'targets of change', an intermediate level, 'arenas for change'.

For Sutton Centre, the goal is changing expectations and raising levels of academic achievement. The arenas for change are the attitudes of parents, students and teachers, who must be persuaded that it is important in the present climate for young people to work with commitment towards qualifications and to believe that they can achieve. In the language of national monitoring systems, targets are numerical, but what Louis and Miles are indicating is that targets of change need to be defined in terms of the 'real life' of the school, taking into account, where appropriate, the legacies of its past. One target of change is students' and parents' understanding of and capacity to manage the relatively remote reality, compared with coursework, of examinations. Ensuring that students become familiar with the conditions and nature of examining through more regular, small-scale testing and through the introduction of end-of-year examinations in Year 10, the strengthening of students' sense of individual purpose and responsibility through counselling in Year 9 and through redesigned study journals in Years 10 and 11, more opportunities for students to discuss the meaning of their patterns of progress with their tutors, the regularity and manner of the reporting system to parents – these things constitute the backbone of the strategy. Another target of change is departmental examination policy and levels of achievement; the strategy here focuses on a department-by-department analysis of examination data, regular planning and review meetings with the senior management team, and a full-scale review of the KS4 curriculum (following the Dearing review) in terms of its power to engage students in learning. A third target of change is students' knowledge and understanding of career possibilities and requirements; the strategy includes a closer liaison with the careers service in Years 9, 10 and 11, and the setting up of career monitoring groups, with each teacher working with a group of students over a period of time.

We believe that the school's fundamental commitment to doing well for all its students is strong enough to allow it to incorporate the new goal without compromising on its central values. The key is the school's determination to protect students from formal and informal 'labelling' systems that can, for some, undermine confidence. The school has many students who see, within their homes, the effects of exclusion from the labour market – the self-doubt and uncertainty that long-term unemployment can generate – and teachers feel that it is important to counter such experiences during secondary schooling and to build a strong sense of individual purpose and possibility. The school knows its students and understands the condition of their achievement. The key is 'the timing of the challenge' and the recognition that 'the longer the students are with us the better they do', as one of the deputies made clear:

> 'There is a need when they come to the new school – and they are coming from all sorts of disadvantaged social as well as educational backgrounds – of not challenging in such a way that their confidence is dented in those early years. We are doing all sorts of things to build self-esteem and confidence . . . the gradient of challenge increases quite dramatically at key stage 4 – and success there is carrying on into A level.'

Teachers recognise the need for students to achieve academically. Indeed, there was evidence of considerable excitement about the strategies for meeting the targets of change and a remarkable optimism. As one teacher said:

> 'I'm confident. I feel excited by the future . . . things are looking much better. We can offer more choice to the students and then they feel more autonomous, they feel they're in charge of their own learning and I think that helps a great deal. I think there's a lot to look forward to.'

This mood is sustained by the senior management team as well as by the key stage managers. As the headteacher said, taking on the new goal is about continuities, it is 'a channelling of the strengths of the school into a new area'. In situations where the requirement for change has come on to the school agenda as a result of pressures from outside the school, the danger is that the change effort may fail to engage the existing culture of the school and that it may remain superficial. Here, however, there is every sign that the new concerns are being carefully grafted on to existing values, and on to procedures which have evolved in the school because they

are known to be effective. In short, we would say that teachers are genuinely involved in the improvement efforts and that there is a strong sense of the common ownership of change.

In terms, then, of focus and ownership, the school knows what it is doing and where it is going and what it has to do to get there. What is more, the new goal has been well integrated with the existing system of values; teachers can accept it as their own and it is therefore unlikely to be a source of friction and division. On the third item, time, we have only one brief observation. Time is the most ambiguous of the three items but looked at in context it makes sense. Our experience of the complexity of school change would lead us to be highly sceptical of what a headteacher referred to as 'squeaky clean projects reporting and recommending overnight transformations'. The staff of Sutton Centre know that they have to continue to move forward slowly and steadily; there are no short cuts, no quick fixes.

SUTTON CENTRE

An LEA-maintained mixed school for 11–19-year-olds

The school

Headteacher appointed	1992
Number of pupils	765
Number of teachers (full-time equivalent)	52
Pupil/teacher ratio	14.7:1
Average class size	19.5
Annual school budget	£1.63 million

Pupils in the school

Registered for free school meals (%)	30
With statements of special educational needs (no.)	1
Ethnic background (%)	
White	99.6
Afro-Caribbean	0
Asian	0.4
Other	0
With home/community language other than English (%)	0.2

School outcomes

% of 15-year-olds in 1994
achieving GCSE passes

5+ A*–C grades	21.7
5+ A*–G grades	77.6
1+ A*–C grades	46.7
1+ A*–G grades	89.5

% of Year 11 (1993–94) students
who are now

In full-time education and training	43.3
In employment with training	28
In employment without training	10.2
Other	18.5

% of 16-year-olds entered for 'A'/'AS'
level (or equivalent) in 1994   14

Average points score for
'A'/'AS' results (1994)   14

11

SELLY PARK GIRLS' SCHOOL
Birmingham

Tim Brighouse, Shirley Woolley and Les Milner

Selly Park School might well have closed in 1986: the condition of its buildings, its poor record of leadership and management and its appalling academic record would have been good grounds for such a decision. The newly appointed headteacher resisted its closure and the case for the continuance of a secondary girls' school for a predominantly Muslim intake was difficult for the local education authority to resist. Supported by an excellent staff, the headteacher succeeded in making this school a place of learning where pupils are encouraged to succeed.

THE SCHOOL

Selly Park Girls' School describes itself as 'keeping pace with changes in education while promoting the traditional values of self-discipline and self-respect, caring and consideration'. It has four forms of entry (120 pupils), but teaches the year groups in five forms.

Buildings

The accommodation is a hotchpotch of an old secondary school opened in 1903 with additions in 1930, and a former primary school built on the site with the original elementary school. In the mid-1990s a new science and technology block was built by the LEA, while the school, using funds from its delegated budget, has created a new entrance foyer and administrative suite. It has plans to create a new pupils' entrance and to complete its rolling programme of refurbishment of all the old accommodation. Most teaching spaces are now benefiting from refurbishing, redecoration, carpets and an impressive whole-school colour-coded approach, including blue doors for unrestricted pupil access, red for staff and grey for 'entry by negotiation'. One small corner of the 1930 building is retained as a reminder of the former appearance of the school: it has peeling paint, crumbling plaster and a stained and gloomy appearance. It is easy to see from this reminder why the school was seen in 1986 as ripe for closure.

Curriculum

The curriculum complies with the National Curriculum with the core and foundation subjects, including a choice of French, Spanish, Russian and Urdu as a first foreign language at Year 7 and a second language in Years 8 and 9. In Key Stage 4 the core subjects, technology and one modern foreign language with either history or geography, are supplemented by options for art, business studies, child development, French, geography, history, information technology, RE, Russian, Spanish, textiles and Urdu. In addition, all pupils work towards the City and Guilds Foundation Programme through involvement in life skills, community service and general RE and leisure activities.

Staffing

As one teacher said, 'this is a good place to work', so turnover has been low: there have been changes in staff as people have retired, pupil numbers have increased and therefore new appointments have been made. The headteacher is now expecting some more recent key appointments to gain promotions elsewhere, 'which they deserve'. There are thirty-five full-time teachers, thirteen part-time teachers, including a number of visiting music teachers, five full-time and four part-time support staff: in addition, there are the usual complement of midday supervisors, meals staff and cleaners. There are two deputies and five staff carrying five points of responsibility. They comprise a 'senior team', but it is a school where responsibility and leadership are widely shared. One deputy who was at the school when the headteacher arrived in 1986 carries responsibility for pastoral matters and is retiring this summer: a second deputy post was established two years ago to oversee curriculum development and to 'act in an entrepreneurial way'. As the headteacher said, 'we had worked with Mel Tennant through TVEI (Technical and Vocational Education Initiative): we did not know he would get the job, but we were pleased when he did. He also has Technology, but that was a bonus: it was not a requirement of the job.'

As we shall see, staffing and staff development are crucial to interpreting the accelerating improvement of this school.

Odds against

It was to a set of buildings uniformly drab and inadequate to their purpose that the present headteacher, Wendy Davis, was appointed. A mere 2 per cent of pupils aged sixteen achieved A*–C grades in GCE or Grade 1 in CSE. There was no suitable curriculum for what were then called Year 4 and Year 5, now Years 10 and 11. Stories were rife of girls who in such an atmosphere had been too disruptive to be taught and so were excluded and put with senior members of staff who supervised them 'copying' and doing essays, all fully aware that they were part of a group who would take no examinations.

The headteacher was informed that the school would be closed. She refused to bow to what seemed to be inevitable.

The school is located in Selly Park off the Pershore Road in apparently pleasant surroundings, although it is on a cramped site in a sea of tar macadam and has a detached playing field five minutes' walk away. Birmingham, however, has a complex and variegated secondary schooling system. There are five King Edward's Foundation Schools and other grammar schools, as well as an array of aided, mainly Catholic, schools. The pecking order of schools is well known. Selly Park was close to the bottom of the pecking order on the arrival of the headteacher.

The school, however, was attractive to Asian families because it was single-sex. Unsurprisingly it recruited, and continues to recruit, its intake not from its immediate surroundings but principally from Balsall Heath, Highgate and the edges of Sparkbrook and Sparkhill. More than half its pupils come from this inner city area, about a fifth from Bournbrook and the rest from a wide range of housing across the city. Over 60 per cent of the pupils are in receipt of free school meals. The social mix of pupils attending the school has not changed in the last seven or eight years.

Achieving success

The school, like others which have made remarkable progress, did so at first unspectacularly. By 1989, no more than 5 per cent only were still achieving grades A*–C at GCSE. But the atmosphere had changed. On arrival the headteacher had enlisted the support of two members of staff, one of whom had taken up her appointment at the same time as Wendy Davis. This member of staff was charged with finding something more effective for the two non-examination groups in Years 10 and 11. These two – the headteacher and the member of staff – had visited other schools together and, as the headteacher generously put it, 'Miss Magrs created a spectacularly successful vocationally oriented BTec course'. Using available funds to back the change in teaching and learning style implicit in the introduction of the course, it now became possible to focus staff debate on pedagogic skills.

The headteacher's other agent of change was a softly spoken Irishman, Mike Miskella, who had been redeployed when his previous Catholic inner city school had closed four years earlier. The new headteacher recognised someone of remarkable generosity with total commitment and a self-effacing approach to work with colleagues. It was he who accompanied the headteacher in an endless round of visits to local primary schools, many of whose children, boys and girls alike, came to observe specially prepared plays and other sessions at which Mike Miskella and the headteacher supervised the audience of up to 300 youngsters while the visiting teachers had coffee with Selly Park staff and were persuaded that the school would be a good place for their pupils to attend following secondary transfer.

What the school had to offer at that stage was promise. Now it is achievement. In 1990, 5 per cent gained five or more A*–C grades; in each of the next three years that percentage had risen to 10 or 11 per cent; and, in 1994, it leapt to 29 per cent. By this time, the habits of all youngsters aiming at achievement were well established, and only four pupils left with no GCSE success. There is a growing awareness among all pupils that they *are valued*. Yet the school is not satisfied. In declaring its collective mission 'to be a learning institution for all members of our community', it recognises its achievements, but affirms that 'we are not at the level we would wish to be; but we are committed to continual improvement against our previous best in all areas of school life'. Its school aims are to

- 'provide for the development of intellectual curiosity, creativity, self-confidence and self-respect';

- 'create an educational culture which is technological, scientific, vocational and industrial';
- 'provide for the acquisition of appropriate knowledge, skills and sound judgment in line with the national curriculum'; and
- 'establish good relationships and discipline based on mutual respect'.

THE LIFE AND WORK OF THE SCHOOL

Strong, positive leadership by the headteacher and senior staff

Leadership is extensively shared in Selly Park. One of the headteacher's first acts was to create a senior management team. The headteacher herself was recognised by members of staff as someone with drive, with energy and an incredibly positive attitude. She is, however, not a high-profile leader – she has an under-stated style. Sometimes she has difficulty articulating the clear vision she has for the school, preferring to share it with senior staff by encouraging direct action around the vision. As one put it, 'I have been on the street with her putting leaflets through doors.' Another declared: 'I have lots of autonomy. . . . Mrs Davis allows me to make decisions: it is based on trust.'

Of the two deputies, Mel Tennant complements rather than supplements the headteacher. He is a whirlwind of action and energy who has quickly learned to temper his own wish to see things done yesterday by celebrating others' achievements. An increasing number of staff have exercised key leadership roles. Indeed, all the staff have been encouraged to take the lead in some aspect of school life as the headteacher is keen to promote collegiality, and this is made evident in their job descriptions. 'In a sense all should be chiefs and all Indians' might be the motto of the way in which in practice staff self-esteem is honoured by conferring status on post-holders.

The headteacher's personal vision has grown throughout her career's experience, and in a real sense eight years after her arrival it now permeates Selly Park Girls' School. She would identify five strands as follows:

- 'girls should have equal opportunity so they should always be given the best possible resources and support';
- 'staff are the most valuable resource and they should be enabled to develop in those areas where they can excel. Good teachers are encouraged to stay at Selly Park or join the staff';
- 'management is team work: again using people's strengths to the full';
- 'successful science and technology enable barriers to girls' progress to be reduced';
- 'information technology is an enabling tool which can provide opportunities for pupils, and extend the teaching and learning styles available'.

Leadership in Selly Park is not confined to staff: pupils, too, lead. Their participation in the various national events in which the school has taken part has ensured that they also have exceptional opportunities for taking initiatives and in confidence-building events.

A good atmosphere and spirit

The remarkable spirit of the school has its roots in the threat to close it in 1986–87 because of falling rolls. Adversity brought staff together. A good spirit was forged at that time, enabled because of the headteacher's refusal to accept the 'inevitable', even though rolls were low and the received wisdom was that the school would close, just as Selly Oak Boys' School had done earlier.

A contributory factor to the present-day success is the transfor- ation of the physical environment over the last few years. This ed morale at a time when many teachers were suffering from externally imposed stress. The senior managers and governors were keen to ensure that part of the refurbishment programme demonstrated to staff that they themselves were valued. All staff feel they have benefited in some way; for example, there was a new staffroom and staff toilets, and the classrooms create a better learning environment. Apart from a rolling programme of carpeting areas and providing new classroom furniture, the new science and technology block (which cost over £600,000) has given an impetus to these aspects of the curriculum and enabled classroom allocation to be replanned in departmental suites throughout the school.

This reconsideration of the physical layout of the accommodation has been a significant change agent. 'We have had ten staff days with an external consultant directly debating teaching and learning styles and the possibilities for classroom layout, the organisation of resources and the need for shared planning.' The main funding has come from the LEA, although much has been raised from industry. Indeed, promises of £100,000 in cash or in kind have been arranged to support the school's recent Technology College DfE bid. The school decided early on to regard the extra money generated from entitlements to free school meals in the LMS formula as an earmarked 'set-aside' aimed at continuing to multiply technology in the school.

It has already been noted that the headteacher's first actions were in the area of the curriculum and in particular the creation of a new and more motivating course for Years 10 and 11 pupils, at that time excluded from certificated success. The school now sets targets for pupils as a matter of routine. It has a set of both academic and pastoral tutors for groups of five or six pupils with a system to ensure that progress is monitored: their efforts are supplemented by 'compact' tutors drawn from industry, the university and the community. There is a homework diary which is monitored. 'There is an expectation here that girls will perform. Everyone is at the school on the day when the examination results are published to see how the pupils have done. No-one wants to let them down.'

The same staff members referred to 'the most important thing' being to 'improve results. We have still got a long way to go, but the girls know that.'

Teaching and learning

As we have seen, the school is obsessed by teaching and learning. The TRIST initiative of 1987 was used to get teachers to think about different styles of teaching and the frequent use both of LEA staff and of consultants – Ruth Sutton and Rob Powell, both nationally known, were mentioned – has kept the focus on the centrality of teaching and learning. Tables rather than desks were introduced to encourage teaching 'fit for purpose'. Most impressively, all the school enjoyed an exciting use of IT. A pioneer of global maths and English, the school sees the distinction between four computer uses: as a tool; as an extension of the library; as a means of communication; and in computer-assisted learning as a 'tutor'. The whole is beginning to be organised into an open, integrated learning system. The school seems to be poised to take advantage of the imminent breakthrough in pedagogy implied by IT. One computer program was described as follows:

> 'It can make a significant contribution to a teacher's effective-ness. It diagnoses, assesses levels, patiently marks and records pupil progress, releasing teachers to work with groups and individuals. We have teachers, however, who know how much to use computer-assisted learning and when to bring the class together as a whole.'

Significantly, the staffroom has a network of computers ready to take imminent advantage in staff development terms of conferencing through the Internet and the worldwide web.

Well-developed assessment procedures

The use of personal academic tutors, allied with 'compact' tutors, has ensured that pupils in Years 10 and 11 are well aware of how they are performing. There is a whole-school monitoring, evaluation and assessment policy and this has recently developed into work specifically supporting pupils with special educational needs (SEN). The school makes use, through an arrangement promoted by the LEA, of the YELLIS surveys pioneered by the University of Newcastle-upon-Tyne. This encourages clearer reflection on individual pupils' attitudes, aspirations and achievements.

There was a commitment by staff to give the National Curriculum assessment models a fair try, and these are now being reviewed. The Records of Achievement are also used well, particularly the pupil self-assessment forms.

From the point of view of the staff, each faculty area has developed an approach to assessment within a whole-school frame of reference. Because the senior management team takes the opportunity to 'cover', they can see the consistency of application and have a low-key approach to fine-tuning it with individuals and departments.

Responsibility for learning shared by pupils

The use of IT within the ambitious integrated learning system has created circumstances in which it is routine for pupils to self-monitor their progress in learning. Homework is monitored through a diary system with academic tutors and time managers issued to Years 10 and 11 to support their own programmes. These were linked to the National Curriculum, and all pupils have their own 'pupil versions' of the curriculum with coursework deadlines clearly defined and linked to their 'compact' goals.

The school provides the opportunity for pupils to carry out homework in time set aside after the normal school day. This is encouraged in Years 7 to 9, three age groups where the school intends to focus its next drive for improved achievement.

Perhaps a significant indication both of the responsibility for learning being shared by the pupils and evidence of their participation in school life is the way in which substantial parts of the school are available to them at break and lunch-time, where self-discipline is expected and achieved. One illustration of the way in which pupil views are taken into account is in the serious consideration given to their opinions on the siting of lockers.

Participation by pupils in the life of the school

The school has a system of prefects, with Year 11 pupils given responsibility to help staff with certain duties: they are given a high profile in the school. Year 9 pupils work in the library and help with the computer system. There is a house system which is over-laid on other pastoral measures and encourages participation in the life of the school and also in the school council. There are many and varied activities, which include:

- self-help groups in music;
- an annual school production;
- many different school sports with school teams, where success is celebrated by the whole community;
- a youth panel led by the local police;
- pupils allocated as mentors to new pupils, to ease their transition into secondary school;
- use at lunch-time of library and computer rooms and specified departmental areas;
- organisation by pupils themselves, supported by teachers, of charity events; and
- visits to outside groups to talk about the school.

The school has also developed a high profile through a number of activities and now uses this to the full to the advantage and development of the pupils. Thus, recently, pupils have represented the school at:

- the British Education Training and Technology show in London on a commercial stand;
- the Houses of Parliament launch of the Technology Enhancement Programme;
- the school's own stand at the Design and Technology show;
- radio and TV presentations; and
- the Education Show at the National Exhibition Centre in Birmingham.

Together with showing many industrialists and other visitors around the school, this involvement has helped to raise the self-esteem of all girls, not only those who took part.

Rewards and incentives to encourage pupils to succeed

House systems cross all other areas: there is the reward of house points either for good academic work, consistent effort or helping the school in any field. In using the house system, the school believes that team work is encouraged along with inter-generation support and continuity.

Different levels of certificate are available and merit awards are given each term for attendance and punctuality. The annual award evening rewards every aspect of school life and not just the academic.

The headteacher has established a tradition of giving certificates out publicly at assembly in order to recognise achievement. Parents are involved at an early stage, and receive letters to point out when pupils have received awards. There is a positive marking policy rewarding both effort and attainment.

Parental involvement

The headteacher has always operated an open-door policy for all parents. Someone will always see them whenever they might turn up at school. The headteacher leads on this and encourages parents to look at pupils' work through the homework diary system. Parents can request a report on a child's academic achievement and behaviour at any time: this is in addition to parents' meetings each term and the formal report then. At these termly meetings they can meet the senior management team, academic tutors or subject teachers.

Parents are part of a three-way partnership in the learning process, and their supporting role is emphasised as far as possible, couched in positive, not critical, terms. The school ensures that encouraging, as well as negative, letters go home.

There is a 'Friends' Association' which is being transformed into a full Parent–Teacher Association. Recently the school appointed a home/school liaison person who has been very successful in improving attendance and punctuality.

Extra-curricular activities

Friday is a differentiated day. The early finish at 2.15 p.m. enables a range of activities to take place; and opportunities to participate in a wide range of sports are also available every lunch-time or after school. The majority of girls take advantage of these opportunities.

The school is also keen to extend pupils' horizons and take advantage of

- visits away;
- work experience;
- day trips to France;
- form trips every year, seen as more than just socialisation;
- visits to old people;
- theatre trips, and so on.

SCHOOL POLICY

It would be easy to say that development planning had been the key to the success of the school, but that would be misleading. The encouragement of planning and review at departmental level has been crucial, but at a whole-school level the pace of change has been sensed intuitively by a headteacher whose judgement of people and situations has been enviably pitched at just the right point.

In the academic year 1993–94 the school embarked on what, at the time, seemed a seismic shift of gear. This was the year in which room allocations were radically reorganised, the use of IT in curriculum areas was accelerated, and science and technology teachers had to adapt to the open-plan design of their new block. In addition, the school was pioneering post-sixteen GNVQ

(General National Vocational Qualifications) courses through a franchise arrangement with further education colleges. All this change was undoubtedly stressful for staff; but by the end of the year, encouraged no doubt by the quantum leap in examination results, teachers were reconciled to this rate of change. It was, however, as Wendy Davis puts it, 'touch and go'. The school's involvement with the community and business in particular was expanding at the same time as the new second deputy, Mel Tennant, brought his exceptional energy to make successful bids for external resources and to capitalise on links through governors and elsewhere with those who were thought to be generously disposed towards Selly Park.

There was a clear policy decision for this thrust. It was understood by all as a means of going 'beyond the walls of Selly Park'.

The school had become hungry for external contact. For example, there are now links for a variety of purposes with no fewer than nine universities: a few of these are connected with student access, but all are linked to increasing the sum of intellectual curiosity among the school community either through research projects, curriculum development or extending the horizons of girls into areas which are non-stereotypical – for example, in science, maths, engineering and business.

The school is insistent on pointing up the contributions of local education authority advisers, three or four of whom are seen by the school as 'collaborators' in the school's growth. Unlike universities, these links are pro-active in both directions and, as we shall see below, contextualised by a common drive for school improvement.

Policies

As might be expected, the school has simple and well-understood policies – which are always being developed and given new and improved directions – for most aspects of school life. To suggest that the school in consequence has no problems in respect of truancy and bullying, for example, would be misleading. As one staff member said,

> 'Any school that claims that is dangerously complacent. What we know is that we have some simple principles and policies and that these are translated into practices which we constantly adjust in the light of the evidence.'

Among the small details which appear currently significant are the early identification of likely truants shared by all staff at daily briefings, telephone calls on the unnotified absence of girls in Years 7, 8 and 9 – 'We are just 'phoning to see how Begum is and whether she needs any work sent home' – and an involvement of the school's youth panel and other agencies on an annual basis to review 'bullying'.

There is a sense in Selly Park that notwithstanding the intuition and the reliance on tunes rather than words, very little is left to chance.

ACCOUNTABILITY

The school will be inspected by OFSTED for the first time in 1995–96. So far, therefore, the remarkable progress of the school owes nothing to external processes of inspection. There is a trusted 'critical friend' relationship with the school adviser and other advisory colleagues. Governors, too – 'especially those appointed by the LEA', as one staff member put it – now want to be sufficiently informed and knowledgeable about the workings of the school, both to be its advocates and to act as active participants in the continuing debate about the school's next steps. Several governor training sessions have therefore been used to focus on school improvement. The chair, a former headteacher and colleague of Wendy Davis, starts each governors' meeting with a five-minute item on some aspect of governor responsibility. Governors visit specific departments and receive reports from subject departments on a regular basis as well as analysing annual examination performance. By judicious use of cooptions the body now includes people in significant positions in business, commerce, the university and the city.

There is a very strong professional accountability. As more than one member of the teaching staff has expressed it: 'It is what the girls deserve: you cannot sell them short. It is not fair.' One long-standing member of staff perhaps encapsulated the shift in attitude in the comment that 'girls at this school are not as awful as they used to be – in fact, they are really nice now'. All staff are informed about the direction of the school and are empowered through delegated decision-making on financial and curriculum decisions. As one member of staff put it: 'Our department has not yet received the treatment – furnishings, equipment, carpets – but we know it is coming and when it will happen. And we know it will happen.'

The school's external professional accountability, moreover, extends to reinforcing links with primary schools as well as with colleges of further education.

It is fair to say that parents trust the school and this is reinforced by the cultural traditions of the families. It does not mean, though, that the parental community is not involved or critical, especially if the changes – as was the case with the change in the time of the school day – are perceived to be potentially in conflict with the needs of the mosque. The careful monitoring of the changes in practice, however, coupled with an expressed willingness subsequently to review, means that all change in Selly Park is contingent on subsequent evidence of effectiveness, and parental opposition is turned into energetic support.

THE BIRMINGHAM CONTEXT – A MAP FOR SCHOOL IMPROVEMENT

It is perhaps important to note the particular context of school improvement in Birmingham. The city has set out its stall not merely to use the features or characteristics of school success outlined in *Learning to Succeed*, but also to try to create a shared map of processes within which actions can be taken which are likely to lead to school improvement. In effect, the city is creating a shared language, among the headteacher, deputies and, progressively, governors and other staff in school. The seven processes involved are:

- the exercise of leadership at all levels within the school and with due regard to the different stages and plans of leadership;
- the practice of management, with particular regard to adjusting methods according to size of school or units within the school;
- the creation of an environment optimally fit for learning visually, aurally and behaviourally;

- the practice of collective self-review, which might or might not involve development planning;
- a focus on teaching and learning;
- staff development; and
- the encouragement of parental and community involvement.

It is within that context that the final section of this report is written.

REFLECTIONS ON THE PROCESSES OF SCHOOL IMPROVEMENT AND THE KEY FACTORS IN ITS SUCCESS

At face value, Selly Park is a puzzle in so far as school improvement is concerned. Probably the key processes are staff development and teaching and learning. It is surely also significant, however, that the overriding impression of the headteacher is one of irresistible cheerfulness in a low-key and unobtrusive way. Her intuitions are reliable and she trusts them: she is a person who knows the tune better than the words.

That intuition and those characteristics, coupled with an overwhelming commitment to the school, has led her to make a succession of inspired appointments. With each appointment she extended the energy of the staff. In her conversation she returns time and again to people. It worries her that there was such difficulty initially in appointing someone for IT. Her instincts told her that it was going to be an important area for her pupils and for transforming learning in the late 1980s. But she waited for the right person. It is surely no accident that, with the advent of LMS in 1989, the headteacher casually describes how she appoints a 'good' Section 11 teacher to the main staff of the school who, in the fullness of time, becomes the head of English. In effect, what the headteacher demonstrates is what football managers would recognise as an exceptional scouting system. In this way, the language department is enhanced by the appointment of an LEA advisory teacher who had earlier been a regular visitor to the school. The head of technology, similarly, is an ex-advisory teacher recommended by the school adviser.

This judicious and highly effective method of staff selection has cumulatively tipped the balance of the staffroom to a point where there is exceptional energy. If it is the case that there are two kinds of teachers in staffrooms – on the one hand those who create energy, for whom a glass tends to be half full, and on the other those who consume energy and for whom the same glass is half empty – then Selly Park has tilted the ratio heavily towards the former. Moreover, the staff display high-quality intellectual energy which is continually re-created by the habits of the school. Questioning staff and the headteacher reveals that it is the senior management team which provides cover in order to release teachers for visits, teacher observation or explorations to industry. In this way the senior management team reveals practical interest in teaching and learning to the staff, samples standards of achievement in the departments they cover, compares marking practices – in short, demonstrates how to engage simultaneously in three or four key processes towards school improvement. What starts as a matter of routine and of economy with the supply budget becomes an appreciation of the centrality of teaching and learning, generous release for professional development and a sophisticated but non-threatening monitoring system.

The school is perpetually engaged in the evaluation of teaching and learning. This goes far beyond curriculum debate, though that is present too. The links with the advisory service are continually referred to by senior staff in reviewing the curricular growth of the school. On arrival at the school, for example, the headteacher perceived the RE teacher as being the only person apparently prepared to declare publicly an interest in the curriculum. The discussion, through IT and in particular the integrated learning system, will have increasingly explored pedagogy in a general sense. The school knows itself to be on a voyage of discovery in the use of the computer and IT. A substantial proportion of the staff are aware of the benefits arising from increased pupil motivation, concentration and achievement: moreover, that is within the context of being a package – global maths – which elsewhere was yet to produce impressive results.

In short, Selly Park closely resembles – indeed, conforms with – the four characteristics relating to staff habits listed by the American researcher Judith Little. First, teachers often talk about teaching practice. There have been frequent in-service days devoted to the issues since the headteacher's appointment in 1986, and the arrival of the second deputy in 1992 gave added impetus to that. Senior staff refer to 'agreements about practice' devised in departmental meetings – meetings, incidentally, which are voluntarily attended and well beyond those timetabled. Second, teachers plan, design, research and prepare teaching materials together. An early example was the joint visits of the headteacher and the RE teacher to write a Theatre Arts course for BTec work. Two years later, using a local authority advisory input, the RE and maths departments collectively debated and rewrote work materials with an eye to differentiation after extensive debate about teaching method. Third, in the course of collecting evidence teachers have the privilege of observing one another's practice. Finally, through the non-threatening collective adventure in IT, staff are frequently teaching one another new facets of the pedagogy of IT. Their talk is of curriculum, pupil achievement, teaching and professional development.

In a very real sense, through the intuitive identification and overt support for certain key members of staff who would never claim anything for themselves but are acknowledged as committed, generous and highly professional, the school has allowed pockets of irresistible optimism to be created – in maths, in English, in art, in technology, in languages, in the upper and lower schools – so that now they meet and touch so frequently that the tide of improvement becomes greater and almost inevitable.

It has already been pointed out that the environment has been transformed, visually, aurally and behaviourally: 'the girls are very nice now'. That transformation will have reinforced the focus on teaching and learning and, indeed, it has been used for that purpose. And there is more to come. But it is a process being subordinated to the promotion of staff development and teaching and learning. Similarly, the process of community involvement with a number of major firms, universities and parents is all within a clear objective of improved teaching and learning.

The process map of school improvement is being used at Selly Park, but there is a differential value on the processes, with the highest value being placed on teaching and learning and staff development. It was unsurprising to discover that the school intends to take on 'Investors in People' not as a panacea, but as another device to strengthen yet further the development of all staff.

To the observation by one member of the research team that the experience of visiting Selly Park had been really interesting, another replied: 'Yes, future perfect.' The school would not claim for itself perfection, now or in the future, because it would know that it had lost the zest and intellectual energy which has brought it so far. Subliminally, however, the phrase captures the school's contrasting past, its present achievement and the certainty of its future success.

It is of course dangerous to make predictions about where a school might be in two, three or four years' time. Nevertheless, there is sound evidence that Selly Park Girls' School may well be continuing to make astonishing progress in achieving success against the odds. That success will increasingly touch all of its pupils.

SELLY PARK GIRLS' SCHOOL

An LEA-maintained school for 11–16-year-olds

The school

Headteacher appointed	1986
Number of pupils	610
Number of teachers (full-time equivalent)	38.8
Pupil/teacher ratio	15.7:1
Average class size	21
Annual school budget	£1.25 million

Pupils in the school

Registered for free school meals (%)	53
With statements of special educational needs (no.)	4
Ethnic background (%)	
White	9.7
Afro-Caribbean	5.1
Asian	79.8
Other	5.3
With home/community language other than English (%)	79

School outcomes

% of 15-year-olds in 1994
achieving GCSE passes

5+ A*–C grades	29
5+ A*–G grades	79
1+ A*–C grades	71
1+ A*–G grades	95

% of Year 11 (1993–94) students
who are now

In full-time education and training	62
In employment with training	6
In employment without training	5
Other	27

LESSONS IN SUCCESS

Margaret Maden and Josh Hillman

VISIONS OF SUCCESS

What do these eleven studies of successful schools in different parts of the United Kingdom tell us? Of particular importance must be the meaning of 'success' in situations where it is difficult, and may even seem unrealistic, to think in terms of challenges and opportunities rather than of dense and ostensibly insoluble problems. But in each of these schools there is a powerful experience of moving forward, of achievement, and of 'irresistible optimism'. There are, quite clearly, strong visions of *further* success at work, possessed by many key players and based on an amalgam of potent feeling and cool calculation. In this concluding chapter we try to identify the nature of this amalgam of heart and mind and, in doing so, provide some further insights into *how* such schools get better.

It would be wrong to try and create a sub-species of school improvement studies for schools serving disadvantaged areas. It is clear that most of the improvement processes described here apply to all types of school and area. None the less, from these case studies emerge characteristics of an improvement process which benefit from separate description and analysis. Whether the resulting distinctiveness is a matter of degree and emphasis, rather than of kind and substance, is arguable.

These schools collectively face a plethora of difficulties and challenges. In the past, these prevented the schools from moving forward. Many had been stuck in a cycle of low expectations, lack of direction and external perception of failure. Most had experienced inertia or had neglected to focus on, or even recognise, the need to improve on a continuous basis. The schools now look ahead with confidence and optimism: the 'future perfect' coined by one of the researchers at Selly Park. A teacher at Sutton Centre said: 'I'm confident. I feel excited by the future. . . . I think there's a lot to look forward to.' Each school sets itself standards that were previously inconceivable, and in addition each has developed an in-built culture of continuous improvement. Furthermore, mention of the possibility of failure, whether in the present or in the future, is notably absent from all of the case-study accounts. 'This is a school that does not understand failure,' said a parent at Lochgelly North.

Pride in the school, not just within its walls but beyond them into the community, forms an intrinsic part of the virtuous spiral of improvement. The 'turning round' of Lochgelly North had involved the replacement of the 'special school stigma' by a positive self-identity. As one parent put it:

> 'Parents are proud of their children and proud of the school. They used to be embarrassed about saying where their children went to school. Now they are proud to say "My child goes to Lochgelly North".'

When such perceptions extend to those unconnected with the school, the effects can be even more positive. A local resident in Bristol said of Fair Furlong: 'Families on the estate are proud of the school – some walk a long way to get here.'

The researchers in Stoke-on-Trent emphasise that the 'can-do' culture of Haywood High is more important to the success of the school than its more concrete systems or policies. Perhaps, though, this is a false dichotomy: it is more a matter of confidence and optimism being needed so that systems and policies can be made to work. How is such a philosophy instilled in a school where the odds appear to be stacked against success or even the hope of it? First of all, it has to be understood that the atmosphere of a school will be greatly influenced by the degree to which it functions as a cohesive unit. For the school as a body to be working towards improvement, all those involved in the school must have reached some sort of consensus as to its aims, and such a consensus needs to be reached as early as possible.

The vision a school has of itself and its possibilities seems to be shaped by a number of influences from both inside and outside the school. In some of the case-study schools, it is at least partly derived from their particular histories or long-standing foundational aims: the Roman Catholic creed in St Michael's; the community schooling ideal at Sutton Centre; the evolution from a 'dumping ground' in the case of Lochgelly North. In Hazelwood College, the principles set out by the parents and the educational trust when the school was established remain, including those relating to the contribution to social change and the reconciliation of religious strife. In other cases, aspects of the vision emerged in response to the specific circumstances of the locality: the relative isolation of the community in West Glamorgan; racism in Tower Hamlets; and intensification of social problems such as drugs, crime, unemployment, family breakdown, poor parenting skills and low aspirations in Bristol, Stoke and Manchester. In several cases, overt threats to the school's very survival and stability have had a dramatic, consolidating effect. Such instances include the threat of closure at St Michael's and Selly Park, the challenge of actual amalgamation with another school at Haywood High and Burntwood and, later, a significant change of character at Burntwood again. At Crowcroft Park, the Parental Alliance for Choice in Education had a similarly galvanising effect, and at Fair Furlong there was a serious fire which, elsewhere, could so easily have resulted in total despondency.

Obviously, such threats cannot be engineered as an instrument of policy, but it is noteworthy that in these schools the will to succeed was strengthened, rather than weakened, by calamities. More generally, it may be safely observed that the schools are directly and intimately engaged with their own particular localities and histories. They do not try to operate as remote offshore islands or as closed systems but, rather, strengthen and hone their vision in relation to whatever vicissitudes are thrown up by their environment. Many of these challenges have been turned into opportunities by the schools.

Such examples tell only part of the story of the way that a shared vision has emerged in the eleven schools. Just as important are the people in the school; especially the headteacher, but also the rest of the staff and the governors, and in many cases the pupils and parents. Changes in personnel, particularly at the senior management level, had been seen in several of the schools as a concomitant to the establishment of an ethos conducive to success. There is little doubt that 'new brooms' can have a part to play in fostering a common purpose and in raising aspirations, as we shall discuss later. But wholesale changes in staff were by no means necessary for a change in direction.

The process of change generally originated with a single individual (usually the headteacher) engaging in hard-edged analysis, identifying and getting to grips with the critical issues of the school and its community and defining strategic priorities, all as a matter of urgency. The resulting aims and associated policies were then reshaped and refined by as many people in the school as possible, before new or amended policies could take root. In Lochgelly North this took place through the formal procedures of staff working groups and resulted in a shared vision described by the researchers as 'tangible'. Even such a strong-willed headteacher as that at Blaengwrach ensured that his own powerful vision would be associated with the school as a whole. As one teacher in his school put it:

'There is a collective expression, a collective commitment here. What goes on in this school isn't just down to personalities. There is a central ethos, a central driving force in us all – it isn't just down to one person.'

The gradual emergence of ideas through participatory processes allows greater opportunity for the collective development of vision. In many of the case-study schools, visions became consensual through genuine opportunities to contribute personally, and a spirit of active commitment and enrolment rather than passive compliance. Schools varied in the degree to which different stakeholders were involved. In all of the schools teachers were involved; in some, non-teaching staff as well; and sometimes governors, parents and pupils.

Most of the schools had gone to considerable trouble to make sure that the school's vision was widely disseminated and understood, both formally and informally. Hazelwood College was particularly vigorous in formally presenting and explaining its vision: internally, through a manual for new teachers; and externally, through speeches, presentation evenings and public assemblies. In other schools the attitudes and behaviour of the headteacher were felt to personalise and make manifest the school's vision, inspiring and helping others to subscribe to it.

The resulting unity of purpose is a condition of achieving consistency of educational practice across all staff in the school. As we discuss later, most of the schools needed to develop common and agreed approaches to teaching methods, assessment, discipline and behaviour. More generally, they articulated common philosophies of education, often geared to the circumstances of disadvantaged areas: for example, 'all children can succeed' at Crowcroft Park; 'educability of all children' at Blaengwrach; not blaming falling standards on the children at Columbia; equity at Sutton Centre and other schools; and care for the emotional welfare of children at a number of schools, including Fair Furlong and Blaengwrach. In general, the schools aimed to tap the immense potential for growth and learning in every child. As a pupil at St Michael's said:

> 'The school is excellent because it sets high standards for pupils to follow whatever their ability is. Pupils with less ability get the same attention as normal pupils so everyone is equal. Respect for all is taught at St Michael's.'

The impression that emerges from the case studies is that, while vision must be dynamic and responsive to changes both within and outside the school, it takes effect when it becomes an integral part of the identity and daily life of the school. Possession of a shared vision provides both a sense of higher purpose beyond the everyday routines of school life, and ballast against the turbulent waves of excessive change. The notion of the school's vision as being an arbiter to which to appeal is an important one. For example, the ethos of Columbia is described as creating 'a moral high ground that is empowering for those who are usually the most disempowered'. More often than not such a vision is expressed in a succinct aim statement for the school; one which could be used as a guide for exercising a multitude of judgements during the course of day-to-day working life.

All of the case-study schools have a 'can-do' philosophy, but, crucially, they combine this with a constant belief that they 'can do better'. This is enshrined, for example, in the following extract from the mission statement of Selly Park:

> 'We are not at the level we would wish to be; but we are committed to continual improvement against our previous best in all areas of school life.'

In a couple of schools such an ethos was expressed in the school's explicit wariness at being categorised as a 'success'. The schools are continuously striving to reach standards higher than those being achieved, using a shared vision as a spur for improvement. As the headteacher of Fair Furlong School put it: 'The minute I feel the school has gone as far as it can, I should go.' The ambitions expressed both by her and others in the school make this seem unlikely in the near future.

WHOLE-SCHOOL POLICIES AND PRACTICE

The vision, values and goals of the school provide a rhetoric which not only informs and gives shape to staff, pupil and parent attitudes, but also underpins organisational processes. How does this happen? As was said in relation to Selly Park: 'very little is left to chance'. Each of the successful schools endeavours to have a unified approach to the aims of the school. This often requires an explicit agreement among teachers about their aims and the implementation of policies and systems in many aspects of the life of the school.

The deputy head of Blaengwrach put it thus:

'We have developed together a similar philosophy about children and how they learn. We all have essentially the same values and beliefs, and those values and beliefs are communicated in our teaching: in how we assess, how we teach, how we praise, how we relate to the children, how we relate to the parents – and it has evolved [over the last five years].'

This sense of tight articulation between broad aims and operational procedures is evoked in the chapter about Burntwood School, whose ethos is described as a 'self-reinforcing system'. It is pointed out that the name of the school has now acquired the status of an adjective. This is partly the result of a conscious effort to build a 'strong corporate identity', both through the public face of the school (for example, its uniform, newsletter and logo) and also its internal policies and systems (for instance, for discipline and rewards).

In a number of the schools, the school development planning

process has been instrumental in providing a cohesive whole-school approach. It is most effective when it is used to establish priorities for the school and to set targets which can be monitored. This is an ongoing process involving as many people as possible: for example, at Columbia where 'every year the development plan is evaluated, reviewed and developed for the next year by the whole staff'. At Lochgelly North, the school development plan was highly commended by a senior adviser:

> 'The documentation is clear and sophisticated, a good example of what a development plan should be, but it was the richness of the discussion which led up to it which will be the real long-term benefit to the school.'

Here, again, our attention is drawn to the importance of the quality of human interactions and learning as an essential corollary to any formal statement of school policy or procedures. A genuinely whole-school approach to policies and systems must also be dynamic and responsive. This point was put well by a member of staff at Selly Park.

> 'What we know is that we have some simple principles and policies and that these are translated into practices which we constantly adjust in the light of the evidence.'

Crowcroft Park develops its policies on a cooperative basis involving all staff and, in many cases, parents. Its new anti-bullying policy has been drawn up in consultation with pupils as well. Reading, attendance, punctuality and parental involvement are also the subjects of consistent and clear school policies and are regularly reviewed.

Perhaps the three most important aspects of the school which require a whole-school approach are its physical environment, the behaviour and industriousness of the pupils, and the assessment and reporting of pupil progress. These are now dealt with in some detail.

Physical environment

The physical fabric of a school conveys messages to both pupils and staff which affect their self-esteem and the way in which they approach their work. All the accounts of successful schools in this study give a clear impression that the working environment is seen to be important in promoting positive achievements and attitudes. Selly Park, where extensive work had transformed the buildings into 'an environment optimally fit for learning', had left a small corner untouched to highlight the improvements. In some of the other schools, particularly the secondary schools, the direction of resources and energy into the fabric of the school had been seen as an important investment. Building work at Haywood High, for example, had been 'an important contribution to raising morale'. St Michael's had raised extra funds from a range of sources to ensure that the school had 'well-designed and well-maintained buildings'. Similarly, Burntwood had benefited from the favourable capital funding enjoyed by grant-maintained schools to 'improve and extend the facilities'. HMI commented on the 'freshness of appearance' at Sutton Centre, also remarking that

> 'The unobtrusive way in which all users have contributed to a well kept building deserves high praise.'

However, it is certainly not the case that all of the schools were in good physical condition. In many, all resources allocated for buildings were eaten up by non-structural maintenance and repair, rather than being used to improve the learning environment. Some of the accounts are punctuated by descriptions of draughty classrooms, leaking roofs and failing heating, electricity and water systems. These are the legacies of poor design, inadequate structural repair and short-term attempts at improvement. The most striking example of this was Hazelwood College, whose premises were described as 'dilapidated' and 'woefully inadequate'. At both that school and at Crowcroft Park, temporary Portakabin classrooms had practically acquired the status of permanent school buildings.

While it is difficult to gauge the extent to which the educational experience of the pupils may have been marred by these conditions, there are certain important observations that can be made. The first is that those schools in need of physical improvement compensated for these shortcomings by making the best of the buildings, encouraging an ethos of care for their appearance by everyone in the school, and keeping all areas clean, bright and tidy.

Second, imaginative use of space has created exciting possibilities in some schools. For example, the 'large glass panel . . . arches and mezzanines and unexpected comfortable nooks and crannies' of Columbia have defied the limitations of the school's Victorian design. Most strikingly, Sutton Centre had adapted its large, open-plan spaces both to meet the needs of the pupils and to provide the scope for continuous two-way community involvement.

Third, schools found ways of carefully targeting limited resources on buildings and equipment to have as much of an impact on morale and achievement as possible. Excellent examples of this are the 'beautiful and interesting things' distributed around Fair Furlong and the school's policy of repairing broken windows immediately; the new staffroom and toilets, and imminent access to the information superhighway at Selly Park; and the collection of art books at Blaengwrach. The latter school was also channelling money raised from industry into a new computer laboratory. Burntwood spent its capital windfalls on teaching facilities for science, technology and modern languages. With local authority help, Haywood High had built a drama studio and Sutton Centre, through its full integration in the local community, had managed to exploit a wide range of joint facilities, including a sports hall, a theatre, information technology suites and an ice rink. Sometimes the priorities identified by the headteacher or the senior management team were surprising to others in the school. The deputy head of Fair Furlong tells us:

'When the head wanted to improve the staffroom, by painting the walls and recovering the chairs, I couldn't believe it – I thought we should spend the money on books. Now I see why she was doing it – it wasn't obvious then.'

Fourth, some schools, both primary and secondary, emphasised the display of pupils' work as an important feature of the learning environment. In each case, the displays were plentiful, well laid out and changed on a regular basis. At Fair Furlong the particularly high quality of displays was the result of a whole-school policy driven by high expectations of the work to be displayed, and the allocation to named members of staff of well-understood responsibilities and procedures for different parts of the school.

Fifth, it might be speculated that in some schools the physical environment may not be a necessary condition of effective learning. The authors of the chapter on Hazelwood College suggest that the effectiveness of the school despite its physical state shows that 'human resources provide the bedrock for a successful school'. While the truth of that statement cannot be disputed, it is still clear from these studies that a key component in the strategy for improvement has been the close attention paid to the physical environment.

Pupil behaviour

A key aspect of the ethos of the successful schools, and much more important than might previously have been thought, is the creation of an orderly and industrious climate in which effective learning can take place. Good pupil behaviour was seen to be an important precondition for staff motivation for improvement, and early identification of this was a critical issue. At Fair Furlong, the headteacher's initial assessment of the school included the observation that 'the most obvious and immediate problem was that the children's behaviour was very poor and this made teaching a difficult and stressful experience for the staff'. Similarly, at Haywood High, the researchers noted that 'poor behaviour and attendance threatened to overwhelm the school around the time of amalgamation', but that now conditions of 'calm purposefulness' were activating the intellectual energy and innovation of teachers.

A teacher at Selly Park said: 'Girls are not as awful as they used to be at this school – in fact, they are really nice now.' How is this apparent change in human nature achieved?

The first point that needs to be made is that there are few common features among the schools in terms of the strictness of teachers, or in terms of the degree of formality of pupil–teacher relations. The schools have very different means of encouraging positive attitudes to learning among their pupils. Looking through the case studies we can see a wide variety of approaches to disciplinary rules and regimes and to the sanctions associated with them, to school uniform, and to the forms of address between teachers and pupils. It is safe to say that no particular combination of these characteristics is associated with success in our case studies.

The essential feature seems to be the *clarity* of the school's policies on behaviour and discipline. Later, the issue of praise for good work will be discussed. Just as important are clear policies for praising good behaviour, and public acknowledgement when pupils are working well. The extent to which these policies are understood (and in some cases formulated) by teachers, support staff and pupils is a key factor; as is the degree to which they are applied *consistently* throughout the school. At Haywood High it is pointed out that 'the behaviour policy was arrived at through widespread consultation among staff. . . . The key to successful behaviour policy is consistent application.'

Fair Furlong, as with the display of pupils' work, also has a formal whole-school policy on pupil behaviour, developed by the staff. The policy is based on a minimal number of rules linked clearly to systems of rewards and sanctions. As with a number of the other schools, an industrious atmosphere is supported by the visibility and accessibility of the headteacher and the senior management team:

> 'The headteacher and the staff strive to create a calm and orderly atmosphere in which the children behave well because they are learning self-discipline rather than because they are constantly chided.'

Columbia has moved even further away from the model where the headteacher or senior management team set school policies from on high. Here, the pupils themselves are actively involved in the formulation of the school's behaviour policy. This is defined by a booklet setting out everyone's responsibilities, and behaviour to be avoided, again clearly tied to sanctions. This booklet was compiled by *all* children and adults in the school.

Another key feature of school behaviour policy which emerges from the case studies is the early identification of difficulties and immediate intervention to sort them out. A teacher at Hazelwood College said that the school

> 'tries to identify and target pupils who are having problems as quickly as possible, and, by keeping a close eye on them for a time, tries to sort the problem out as quickly as possible'.

This approach is echoed in a number of the other schools, which in some cases bring parents in to discuss the situation at quite an early stage. The best example of this is provided in the chapter on Lochgelly North in the case study of one particular boy, where the school found success 'less by focusing on his behaviour than by addressing the factors which set the context for that behaviour'.

In the next sections, important issues which are closely related to good pupil behaviour are discussed, especially the maintenance of close links with parents and the praising of children's efforts.

Pupil progress

The powerful relationship between high expectations and effective learning has long been recognised. Of course, the causal process runs in both directions: positive attitudes among teachers are communicated to pupils, boosting their self-esteem; in turn, high achievement enhances optimism among teachers.

How are expectations raised in a practical and realistic way? Curriculum planning and the assessment and reporting of pupils' work have been recognised as instrumental in raising expectations and helping staff to gear their teaching to the needs of individual pupils. These are partly down to individual teachers, but the idea of the teacher as lone practitioner behind closed doors is not applicable to the case-study schools. By encouraging a whole-staff approach, the headteachers had been able to bring 'out of the closet' a strategy for consistent judgements about quality and standards.

In each of the schools, senior staff are involved at a practical level in monitoring all aspects of teachers' work, and in ensuring that targets are set for pupils, and in some cases departments and the whole school. Positive feedback such as praise and rewards is given not just for good academic performance but also for improvement, attendance, behaviour and extra-curricular activities. In Sutton Centre and other schools there are plenty of 'opportunities for students to discuss the meaning of their patterns of progress with their tutors'.

There are particular lessons for all schools from Lochgelly North's policies on pupil progress: measuring, monitoring, setting targets and discussing. The following extracts from the relevant chapter illustrate each of these four:

> 'Measurement of progress is an ongoing part of school life and an integral part of staff consciousness. A high level of alertness and interest in progress means that every gain is noticed. Because even the smallest gain is significant it is celebrated, shared and recorded.'

'I can look back at where Alice was last year and see the progress she has made. When I see how much progress she has made in that time it makes me more optimistic in what she might be in the year to come.'

(Parent)

'The experience of failure is minimised by setting appropriate and realistic targets, with every small incremental gain recognised and rewarded.'

'The pupil has got a valid opinion. A lot of people don't appreciate how much they can contribute to their own learning. Self-assessment gives them the opportunity to say how they are feeling . . . they can identify strengths and it gives them a sense of self-worth. They get a lot out of it.'

(Teacher)

Many of the schools integrate these activities through mechanisms such as portfolios of each pupil's work in primary schools, day-books and homework diaries in secondary schools, and videos in the special school. These serve a number of purposes:

- giving pupils more responsibility for their own learning;
- helping teachers to assess, moderate, record and report on pupil progress;
- providing a basis for discussions between pupils and teachers, including feedback and target-setting;
- keeping parents in touch with and, at best, directly involved in their child's learning.

Many of the schools are keen that positive reinforcement should be given to pupils as often as possible, either immediately in the form of praise, or delayed in the form of rewards and prizes. At Fair Furlong, for example, praise and rewards are given for work, effort and behaviour:

'The school assembly every Friday morning is used as an opportunity to publicly praise pupils who have been identified by their teachers for good work and behaviour – they come to the front of the hall and receive a certificate from the headteacher which they can take home and keep.'

Sutton Centre had introduced a system of interim reports which are 'as far as possible "praise" reports'. As well as certificates and school assemblies, several schools had created opportunities for more public recognition of success, such as awards evenings. The Presentation Evening at Hazelwood, for example, 'reflected a diverse interpretation of achievement', with awards given not only for academic work, but also for sporting achievement, vocational work, community service, attendance and commitment.

INCLUSIVE SCHOOLS

The schools are quite clearly inclusive organisations where staff share ownership, involvement and responsibility with pupils, parents and the wider community:

'What was impressive . . . was the clear sense that the pupils felt that this was their school.'

(Researchers at Haywood High)

'There is . . . a powerful alliance of teachers and parents working for common objectives in the education of the pupils of St Michael's.'

'The school is demonstrating that there is a life beyond [the estate] and is providing examples of things that you can achieve.'

(Bristol community worker on Fair Furlong)

Pupils

The eleven accounts are full of examples of schools encouraging pupils to take greater control over their work, listening to and responding to their views, and giving them responsibilities in the life of the school. It has evidently been recognised that these are all crucial ways of enhancing the self-esteem of pupils and raising their levels of competence as learners. This type of approach works best when it starts as early as possible in the pupils' time at the school and is bolstered through extra-curricular and out-of-school activities. At Sutton Centre, all new pupils go with their teachers to a residential centre for three days. This not only allows the teachers to get to know the pupils on an informal and personal basis early on, but also enables pupils to feel part of a supportive team right from the start.

Out-of-school activities are an important way of enabling pupils to join in, and of breaking down the boundaries of the school. This is epitomised at St Michael's, where pupils help children at feeder primary schools with reading, writing and football. Lochgelly North is more self-critical than other schools about its extra-curricular activities, but in fact there are regular opportunities for after-hours participation for all the pupils. A number of the schools recognise that important learning experiences often take place outside the school rather than in its classrooms. This is well illustrated by the simulation of the Victorian classroom at the Welsh folk museum, and the project on the local war hero in collaboration with a pottery firm by the group of pupils at Haywood High. In these examples, and others, the potential for cross-curricular symbiosis had been exploited thoroughly.

It is particularly important that pupils feel that responsibilities are not simply delegated but that they can be defined and then exercised to some extent by themselves. At Crowcroft Park:

'Children take an active part in the running of the school, not only by being asked to undertake jobs, but also, very often, by using their own initiative.'

Pupil involvement in the running of the school is an ambitious objective, but many of the schools found that giving pupils positions of responsibility is an extremely effective way of conveying trust in their abilities and setting standards of mature behaviour. In the case-study schools there are a number of ways in which pupils have active roles in the life of the school. At Lochgelly North, Fair Furlong and, in particular, Columbia the introduction of systems which involve older children helping and supporting younger children is impressive.

A couple of the schools have prefect systems. At Haywood High, prefects represent quite a significant proportion of Year 11 pupils (around one-third). There is no formal limit to numbers, and any pupil who wishes to become a prefect has a good chance of doing so at some time unless there is a problem of behaviour or commitment. It therefore could not be said that the prefects constitute some sort of an elite in the school. Moreover, the fact that prospective prefects have formally to apply and be interviewed according to objective criteria for selection develops skills that will be useful in later life.

School councils, even in primary schools, are another good mechanism for including pupils in the decision-making process and allowing them to shape both the day-to-day life and the culture of the school. Columbia has a council with representatives elected each term from all classes from Year 3 upwards, with formal meetings chaired by a pupil and the production of minutes for the whole school. Judy Porter from BP sets out the merits of this system:

> 'It is evident that this is teaching the young people both communication and meeting management techniques normally not experienced at this age, giving young people a sense of responsibility, and a feeling of ownership of both the issues and solutions relating to school life. The type of issues raised and discussed at this meeting demonstrates the strong ethos of the school: the emphasis on caring and consideration for others.'

In some schools pupils are involved in decision-making at other levels; for example, in the formulation of particular school policies.

As with school councils, roles of this type help to sustain a whole-school approach underwritten by clear rights and responsibilities. At Columbia, in the production of the booklet on behaviour, the collaboration among pupils and staff itself had great value; the outcome was clarity as to acceptable and unacceptable behaviour on the part of both children and adults. At Haywood High the pupils had played a role in drawing up the school policies on behaviour and bullying. The expectations policy at Burntwood, which is reproduced in full, clearly benefited from the involvement of the pupils.

These types of roles for pupils are often stepping-stones to even greater responsibilities. At Burntwood pupils now even have a system through which they can comment on staff behaviour, raising expectations of staff in a similar way to the experience of Columbia just described. Schools may also create opportunities for these responsibilities to be taken outside of the school walls:

> 'Leadership in Selly Park is not confined to staff: pupils, too, lead. Their participation in the various national events in which the school has taken part has ensured that they too have exceptional opportunities for taking initiative and participation in confidence-building events.'

Parents

All of the schools recognise the key role that parents play in enhancing pupil achievement. Parents are potential co-educators, in that children spend more time at home than at school. They are also co-learners, and addressing their own needs can have a tremendously positive impact on the progress of their children. Where teachers and parents have similar objectives and expectations for children, it is a powerful force for improvement.

Securing more active participation by parents both in children's own progress and in the life of the school can be more difficult in disadvantaged areas, especially where larger proportions of parents have not had much formal education. Parental involvement was described at Haywood High as 'a demanding uphill struggle in which success was at best limited'. The headteacher referred to the decline of parenting and the failure of many to provide 'the secure, supportive upbringing that young people need in areas where drug-related crime has steadily increased over the last few years'.

What lessons are there from the case studies, in terms of the role that a school can play in enabling parents actively to enhance its work in fostering pupil progress? The first step would appear to be engaging positive interest, cooperation and supportive relations between home and school. In many of the schools, parents had previously felt threatened by the school, or their interest had tended to be expressed negatively. Parents' reasons for coming in now were that they wanted to support school activities, look at pupils' work, attend school events, or simply to keep in touch. The headteacher of Haywood High 'no longer has to deal with a stream of angry and sometimes aggressive parents as she did in the late 1980s' but instead receives complimentary letters on a regular basis. Similarly, a teacher at Fair Furlong said:

> 'When I first came here parents were only coming in to complain, often in a very aggressive way; most parents now are very positive, very appreciative, they are not afraid to come in for a chat.'

The headteacher at Crowcroft Park distinguished parental support from parental involvement. When she arrived at the school the former was present, but she saw boosting the latter as a top priority. A number of strategies can be identified across the eleven schools which have contributed to engaging parents as partners in the learning process.

First, initiatives often need to be started up by the staff themselves, the governing body or an agency outside the school. They can later be taken over by the parents themselves. A good example of this is the parents' room at Crowcroft Park, with its coffee mornings, toddler group, book and uniform sales, library service and information leaflets.

Second, the school may have to take steps to help parents exercise their role more effectively. This may be done formally as with the Parental Involvement Project at Crowcroft Park, funded by the LEA, which runs training courses for parents; or it may be informal, as with the discussions between staff and parents at Fair Furlong dealing with discipline problems.

Third, parents should be encouraged to get involved as early as possible. Those primary schools with nursery classes found the early years the easiest during which to get parents involved. An alternative was the practice of staff meeting parents in their homes before the children start school.

Fourth, the importance of what two research teams call an 'open door policy' for all parents cannot be stressed enough. Many of the parents whose support is most needed are the least likely to be involved. Most of the schools put great effort into breaking down barriers to parents' access to the school. For example, at Crowcroft Park, a noticeboard displays photographs of all of the staff, and training courses for parents are available.

Fifth, there needs to be a free flow of information to and from parents. The school must keep parents informed both about the school itself and about the progress of their own children. St Michael's and Burntwood have newsletters about the school. At Hazelwood College, parents receive monthly progress reports covering not just academic achievement but also attendance, behaviour and punctuality, with parts of the reports completed by the pupils themselves. A number of schools have schoolwork or homework diaries, including a video version at Lochgelly North. At Lochgelly North, the diaries, as well as keeping parents informed, improve communication between pupils and their parents about school. Parents at Selly Park have the right to request a report on their child's academic achievement and behaviour at any time. These systems all seem to work well – with the possible exception of the pupil at Hazelwood who complained that his teacher 'was never done calling my mum and dad on the phone'.

Sixth, many of the schools consult parents regularly, and where possible involve them in decision-making. Sometimes this process is informal and *ad hoc*. In other cases, opportunities for parental input are more formal. For example, at St Michael's the Home/School Contract for Partnership must be signed by all parents of Year 7 pupils, to sustain the ethos and rules of the school.

One other point must be made about parents: a message emerges from the case studies that parental involvement – for example, helping in the classroom – also benefits the parents in ways independent of their children. At Columbia it was observed:

'The helpers find that not only do they participate in the life of the school by helping the teachers and the pupils, but that they too are learning. Their sense of self-development makes for a more enjoyable and rewarding partnership.'

Indeed at Blaengwrach, it was reported that involvement in their children's education had led some parents to undergo training to be carers or nursery nurses themselves.

Community

A school's community is a difficult notion to pin down: it embodies the local geographical area which will often contain several social and cultural groups, and it also includes the local economy. There are substantial differences among the eleven schools, not only in terms of the nature of their surroundings but also in terms of their relationships with the local communities. In West Glamorgan, 'the tightly-knit nature of this village provided both an enrichment and a challenge'. In Fife, the special school had to cope with negative attitudes from local residents. In Stoke-on-Trent and elsewhere, the school has been faced with 'historically low expectations in the community'. Nevertheless, whether urban or rural, primary or secondary, most of the schools are well rooted in their localities.

Some schools had stronger links with their communities than others. The most striking example of the beneficial effects of integration with the outside world is at Sutton Centre, where the authors of the case study point out that 'it is difficult to know whether you are on the school premises or not'. The school's status as a community school is reflected in its design, with dozens of openings, paths winding through joint facilities and a layout where 'shoppers are literally two feet away from the children doing their lessons'.

Although this is an attractive model, the central question is: in what way does it help the pupils to be more successful than otherwise? In the case of Sutton Centre, community school status is also justified by the wide range of 'opportunities for adolescents and adults to learn and work together'. The participation of adults in the evening and Saturday morning classes, whether academic or leisure, encourages pupils to opt for them as well. Similarly, Hazelwood College seems to have found ways of turning the exceptionally high number of visitors to the school to the advantage of the pupils. Meanwhile, the adults enjoy contact with the school as a focal point in the community, or benefit from its facilities. The new computer laboratory at Blaengwrach was seen by a governor as 'developing the school as a tool for the community', and also contributing to the aim that school should continue in some form after 4 p.m.

In such cases, pupils clearly benefit from the presence in school of adults who are not staff, especially when they are co-learners. With voluntary learning going on around them, pupils get a glimpse of the 'learning society': this is a powerful message, especially in areas where education may not have traditionally been seen as important. Opportunities for the stimulation of a wider range of pupil interests are also increased.

It is more difficult for schools in disadvantaged areas to involve local business in the life of the school or to attract extra financial support. Sometimes, as in the case of Lochgelly North, this is not for want of trying, and there is a certain amount of resentment of the fact that local business has done little to make the pupils feel that they have opportunities in the world outside. In other cases, such as Columbia, the school has until recently decided to keep its distance from business. However, many of the schools now see the involvement of business as a priority. At Crowcroft Park it was remarked:

> 'There is a lack of commerce and industry in the locality but, in spite of that, continued attempts are made to involve a range of people with a variety of experiences and approaches in the life of the school and membership of the governing body.'

When a school starts improving, it may in fact find it easier to raise extra funds. At Blaengwrach:

> 'local industry is beginning to note the high standards which the school is setting and is responding to an appeal for a responsible partnership between community, industry and the school.'

LEADERSHIP AND MANAGEMENT

The right sort of leadership is at the heart of effective schooling, and no evidence of effectiveness in a school with weak leadership has emerged from any of the reviews of research. Strong leadership requires both vision and clear and consistent policies, practices and systems, all discussed earlier. In schools serving disadvantaged and frequently troubled areas, an abundance of energy and commitment is needed just to tread water. From these studies, it is apparent that an unusually high level of human effort is being spent in a very focused way. A headteacher, more than anyone else, has the capacity to bring about such a release of energy and, even more importantly, a belief in the school's potential to succeed. Although we do not know nearly enough about the personal histories of the eleven headteachers to understand how they became effective leaders, it is possible to make some important observations about the features of their leadership which have benefited the schools.

Judgement

The case studies are littered with illustrations of carefully exercised professional judgement on the part of the headteachers: for example, deciding that executive action is needed, rather than more discursive consultation; and selecting from a repertoire of channels for keeping the various stakeholders fully informed about successes, problems and targets. Not surprisingly, the 'intuitive hunches' displayed by these headteachers are often remarked on. The research team at Selly Park, in describing the headteacher, comments that 'her intuitions are reliable and she trusts them'. These intuitions were probably developed and honed over the years, not least in the classroom where effective teachers regularly make detailed and vital judgements about pace, when to move on to higher levels of activity, when to have fun, when to be serious or 'tick off' the laggardly, while remembering the importance of regular encouragement and praise. Similarly, maintaining a fine balance between cool, cerebral analysis of key issues and targets, and a genuine optimism of a more affective kind characterises all these headteachers, as it does good teachers generally.

Permeating any notion of leadership, however, must be a power-ful and abiding commitment to the point of all this expenditure of effort and energy. At the heart of each school is the headteacher's vision and analysis of what constitutes good learning and teaching. The refusal to be deflected from this and its corollary – an under-standing of the difference between *means* (intensive and sensitive work with parents, for example) and *ends* (high academic and social achievement) – marks out these headteachers and their colleagues.

Omnipresence

A headteacher is clearly responsible for the administration and management of a school; as one of the accounts puts it, the headteacher is 'the managing director'. The details of these responsibilities are vital, but they must be founded on the principle that they improve teaching and learning. The most basic way in which the headteachers exercise educational leadership is by 'being about the school', as the researchers put it at St Michael's. By keeping a high profile, getting to know the pupils, following their progress and spending time observing the processes of teaching and learning, headteachers amass information to underpin feedback to both teachers and pupils. One routine of the headteacher of Fair Furlong illustrates this well:

> 'Each Monday morning, she spends a couple of hours in a different class, observing the teacher and talking to the children about their work and she follows this up with a feedback discussion with the teacher.'

The Crowcroft Park team note that 'the headteacher knows the names, home and family circumstances and progress of every child'.

In some schools headteachers get involved by themselves teaching; at St Michael's, for example, the headteacher has a regular teaching commitment. At both St Michael's and Selly Park, the senior management team provides lesson cover when there is illness or when teachers are released. This keeps them in touch with pupils, their progress and assessment. It also contributes to an ethos based on the primacy of teaching and learning, and to the blurring of the distinction between managers and teachers, integral parts of the philosophies of the schools.

Being the leading professional means taking the lead in monitoring the quality of teaching and the progress of pupils, providing feedback and setting standards. The following extracts from the case study of Crowcroft Park show the admirable approach of the school's headteacher on this front:

'The headteacher formally monitors individual teacher planning, recording and assessment and is a frequent visitor to all classrooms. Professional discussions are held with staff about the progress of individual children and where necessary targets are set with individual children.'

'The school is small enough for the headteacher to discuss frequently work with all staff directly on an individual basis.'

'Each class teacher . . . feels responsible to the headteacher for the children's progress and frequently looks to her for guidance, encouragement and commitment of resources.'

It is also important for headteachers to extend their presence beyond their own schools. In some cases headteachers had been keen to forge links with other schools. Others had concentrated on enlisting support where it was available. Crowcroft Park not only benefits directly from a good relationship with its LEA, but also indirectly through associated collaborations:

'The headteacher plays a full part through her networks, and is seen as a leader amongst her peers.'

Some activities of headteachers may not be directly connected to the school, but can take effect through the broadening of their personal perspectives. For example, the headteacher of Burntwood is associated with a number of national and local bodies, possibly contributing to perceptions of her as a 'respected leader'.

Personal style

The headteachers of the eleven schools appear to have similarities in terms of their personal styles of leadership. In each case the vision of the headteacher is a pervasive and influential force, but the individual is not necessarily a dominating character. Their drive is essentially positive, confident and pro-active, supported by clear objectives, but not imposed on staff against their will. The chapter on Selly Park gives a flavour of this: 'The overriding impression of the headteacher is one of irresistible cheerfulness in a low key and unobtrusive way.'

The word 'understated' is used in the accounts much more frequently than 'charismatic'. Headteachers use quiet encouragement to persuade everyone in the school to share ownership of the vision. The headteacher of Blaengwrach, for example, is a strong character, but it is commented:

'His quality of leadership is not one which forces itself upon the staff. Rather, he is seen as an enthuser and enabler who has convinced those he works with by his example.'

Key elements of a headteacher's leadership style are accessibility, willingness to build the expertise and experience of others into the management of the school, and a desire to get the best from every member of staff. Teachers at Lochgelly North described the headteacher as 'informal and approachable' and 'responsive'. As one parent observed: 'she doesn't carry her professionalism in front of her'. An extract from the chapter on St Michael's is also relevant here:

'The headteacher is commended for his open, approachable and consultative style of leadership. The headteacher perceives his own role to be fundamentally about enabling others to do what they are good at doing.'

There is a clear sense in which the headteachers have an impact by setting an example to the rest of the school, providing powerful role models. At Burntwood, the 'commitment, attention to detail and high expectations' of the headteacher are well appreciated by staff. In the words of the headteacher of Fair Furlong:

'My vision was to offer these children the same quality of education that I had offered in my previous school – the same as they would have in a very middle class area.'

Staff and others involved in the school welcomed these high expectations. Similarly, the 'professional risks' taken by the headteacher of Blaengwrach in promoting his own vision soon paid off, through the enhanced commitment and motivation of staff.

Shared leadership

In all eleven schools it appears that autocratic modes of decision-making are avoided, and leadership responsibilities are shared wherever possible. At Selly Park the approach to leadership is that 'all should be chiefs and all Indians'. This is shorthand for a similar comment on St Michael's:

'A particular strength of the current leadership style is that it has rejected traditional hierarchy and also more recent notions of senior line management to celebrate shared involvement in leadership and management.'

Interestingly, a number of the schools, before they started to improve, had seemed to be thwarted by an absence of senior management structures. New headteachers were quick to put senior management teams in place, as a first step towards shared leadership. But across the eleven schools, there is no common arrangement for allocating or sharing responsibility among senior personnel. At Crowcroft Park, the secondment of the deputy head has led the school to appoint two acting deputies, partly as a professional development opportunity. A common feature, however, is that the schools recognise the importance of the skills and style of deputy heads and other senior managers complementing those both of one another and the headteacher.

Making time to exercise effectively the aspects of headship relating to educational leadership and quality assurance often requires the delegation of administrative responsibilities: at the policy level, to other senior managers or bursars; and at the day-to-day level, to secretaries. At Burntwood:

> 'A senior manager with a financial background was recruited at deputy principal level and has invested his time and energy in creating good systems and sound financial policies.'

Leadership is not just shared with the senior management team and other post-holders; it can also be extended to a wider range of staff. In some of the schools, certain leadership responsibilities are delegated through the establishment of special groups. At St Michael's, any staff can contribute to school policy through 'a regular forum for consultation and staff involvement'. Staff at Haywood High praised the headteacher for her ability to delegate more specific areas:

> 'She did so not only through the formal hierarchy but also through responding to the initiatives of individuals and through asking teams of volunteers to take responsibility for drawing up school policy on important themes.'

In none of the eleven schools does it seem that decision-making has swung so far the other way as to become an end in itself. As the chapter on Burntwood points out, deciding who should be involved in decision-making across a range of larger and smaller issues requires careful judgement. There are several examples in the accounts where the headteacher had made important but autonomous decisions without involving others. The headteacher of Fair Furlong distinguishes between, for example, the development of a language policy which needs a full professional debate before a decision is reached and a basic procedural matter (such as how milk should be distributed in classrooms) where she decides but briefly checks with other staff that her decision makes sense: 'Her policy is to consult the staff as fully as possible, but to be aware of the demands consultation can make on staff time.'

Good leadership on the part of the headteacher involves recognising the high actual and opportunity costs of having all staff meeting in one room, and evaluating the benefits of doing so in different situations. Whether the aim is to exchange information or work up new ideas, it may be just as effective to send a memo or set up a small working group of staff.

Building a team

Unity of purpose and consistency of practice are the mainstay of well-defined policies and systems centred on teaching and learning, reinforced by collegiality among staff. A number of the accounts highlight the sense of team work holding staff together, often underpinned by strong belief in the vision and aims of the school and sustained by ongoing communication. The headteacher of Lochgelly North said:

> 'We have a totally committed strong team who are interested in what they do and committed to working together to achieve their goals.'

The chapter captures the sense of teamwork and collaboration among staff and, interestingly, comments that 'visitors to the school do have difficulty in knowing who are teachers, instructors, auxiliaries or who is the headteacher'.

What can a headteacher do to build a team with such admirable features? In some of the schools, it seems that team work and collaboration have been made possible by the team itself being chosen and organised with this in mind. At Blaengwrach, it was noted that:

'The staff's strength as a team has been further reinforced by the very careful consideration given to the new appointments that have been made.'

Headteachers show great skill in judging the quality of job applicants and spotting professional potential, whether among existing staff or outside applicants. Associated with 'a succession of inspired appointments', this practice was compared to talent-scouting by football managers, in the chapter on Selly Park.

In the early days of the headteacher's incumbency, some changes of staff may be thought to be necessary. Perhaps surprisingly, this was a feature in only a minority of these schools although the high turnover of teachers in Tower Hamlets has been turned to the advantage of Columbia, where the headteacher was able to select a completely fresh team.

Developing the team

Most of the accounts suggest that it is not essential to have new staff in order to create a new ethos in the staffroom, and vigorous staff development had been used in preference to the replacement of teachers. Successful approaches involved knowing how to develop or 'grow' staff capabilities, and acknowledging, in effective operational terms, the importance of non-hierarchical team work, which includes non-teaching support staff. The ways in which these staff are fully involved in promoting and sharing the school's vision, as well as in their daily work as team members, are well described at Lochgelly North, Crowcroft Park and Columbia. A participative approach, such as the 'cohesive and broad-based strategy' adopted by the headteacher of Columbia, is not just about management structures and formal consultation. It is also about establishing a collaborative culture, through the encouragement of collegiality and high staff morale. What is essential here is the development of cohesive and professional relationships among staff.

At Fair Furlong, the new headteacher had, on arrival at the school, particularly identified the lack of team work and collaboration among staff as inhibiting improvement. She accordingly instigated a number of changes which have very quickly transformed the staffroom culture. These included weekly formal staff meetings, publicising the agenda and minutes of staff meetings and those of the new senior management team; the creation of a resource and preparation room; and the establishment of a mentoring system for new teachers. In larger schools, it may become necessary to be even more systematic in promoting collegiality among staff. Burntwood had established 'clusters' of departments in the school with regular meetings and opportunities for two-way channels of communication with senior management. The headteacher also used special consultation exercises to inform herself regularly of the views of staff.

In some of the schools – for example, Selly Park, Hazelwood College, Haywood High and Columbia – staff have short briefing sessions every day, as a means of continuous exchange of information, as an opportunity for the headteacher to focus staff, and as a way of reinforcing team work and an inclusive staff culture. The authors of the case study of Haywood High note that the headteacher in early days at the school did not under-estimate the impact of these sessions:

> 'She spent a great deal of time every evening planning that brief ten minutes, seeing it as a vital opportunity to shift the culture.'

Here, also, the building of a 'sense of team work' and focusing on 'the positive' are identified by the headteacher as key purposes of such briefings. Thus, she will 'congratulate colleagues publicly for recent achievements' and 'share a joke' (and why not, indeed!). At Selly Park, the same importance is attached to these briefings, which are seen as part of the school's 'tunes' and rhythms as much as a further example of its attention to detail (in this case, the early identification of likely truants).

As mentioned earlier, good management practice requires knowing when and in which forum different issues should be discussed. Judy Porter, from BP Oil, commended Columbia for its matching of purpose to the allocation of time in bringing together the whole staff:

> 'The staff have a daily fifteen-minute staff meeting which all teaching staff attend to discuss immediate matters of the day and take the opportunity to share each other's plans. Points are also raised for discussion at greater length at the full staff meeting. This is proven good practice. It enables matters to be dealt with as they arise and ensures that everyone knows what is going on.'

Apart from sharing such collaborative experiences, staff also learn to develop through involvement in their professional review and appraisal. A high priority for most of these headteachers seems to have been the establishment of one-to-one discussions with colleagues, through which the school's development can be aligned with the individual teacher's professional development. For these to work, there has to be a genuine dialogue and sufficient time available, without the usual distractions of a busy school. At Columbia and at Fair Furlong, there is an acknowledged relationship between the distinctive processes of informal review and formal appraisal. The opportunity for staff, as individuals, to discuss their aspirations, priorities and development needs with the headteacher or other senior colleagues is a key component of continuous improvement in these schools. In Columbia, reference is also made to a weekly review meeting held with the non-teaching support staff by the deputy head, where it is clear that professional development is an important part of the 'hidden agenda', at least. It is probably significant that, at Selly Park, the researchers' conclusions highlight the 'promotion of staff development and teaching and learning' as the major, pre-eminent focus of the school's improvement strategy.

Of course, important as formal systems and pre-arranged meetings are in providing the foundations for staff collegiality, it is the ongoing, informal and personal relations among staff which provide the cement. The interaction may relate to educational practice; for example, the collaborative work, observation of one another's teaching, and teaching of one another at Selly Park. Similarly, it may give the teachers a breather from the school, such as the water-sports outings of the teachers at Blaengwrach.

Headteachers are also attentive in taking opportunities to raise morale among both pupils and staff. At Burntwood, the headteacher's 'habit of thanking and congratulating staff for particular achievements is highly reinforcing'. Similar comments are made at Haywood High, where it is also pointed out that the headteacher attends to 'those critical personal details which matter so much'.

THE IMPACT OF EDUCATION REFORMS

It would be surprising if the successes achieved by the schools presented here were not, in some way, linked to an unprecedented range and depth of government-led reform. Indeed, the typical period during which these schools moved forward and secured real improvement coincided with the early years of major educational reforms; the local management of schools (LMS), a national curriculum with its associated assessment systems, including standard assessment tasks (SATs), the opportunity for schools to 'opt out' of their local education authority (LEA) and acquire grant-maintained status, and the abolition of the Inner London Education Authority (ILEA). These major components of the government's programme of educational reform during the period 1988–95 were underpinned by several reforming principles and beliefs, including the idea of an 'educational marketplace'. In this, schools would compete for customers (parents) who would exercise informed choice partly, at least, on the basis of published performance data about their local schools. The funding of schools would be primarily determined by the number of pupils enrolled, with marginal variations allowed for age, special educational need and socio-economic disadvantage. The incentive to improve school performance, especially examination results and SAT scores, was embedded in these funding rules because, unless a school maintained or increased the number of pupils on roll, its budget would be cut and staff numbers likewise. Within such a 'marketplace', the autonomy of schools was implicitly valued and closely associated with the drive towards higher standards of achievement.

A related 'hub-and-rim' concept saw the school system as comprising a central government 'hub' with a 'rim' composed of some 25,000 schools in England and Wales, the spokes of the wheel being a basic set of statutory requirements, especially those associated with the National Curriculum and later OFSTED inspections of all schools every four years. Otherwise, a light steer was all that was envisaged as necessary, and crucially, if never fully debated, a much diminished role for local education authorities. In other words, no intermediary level of authority or governance was believed to be either necessary or desirable. Such a model also presupposed a more active and powerful role for school governing bodies, which would both represent and respond to increased parental choice and 'voice'.

The authors of these case studies were asked to consider how, if at all, such a significant programme of educational reform had influenced the development of the schools. Although this was not a major line of our enquiry, it none the less gave rise to a range of important and interesting issues concerning the linkages between macro policy and institutional response and behaviour.

At institutional level it is perhaps understandable if the significance of remotely prescribed policies is resisted or, at the very least, barely acknowledged as a major determinant of success. Thus, the research team in Stoke-on-Trent note that in discussions with the headteacher and her colleagues at Haywood High, the government's reforms were 'barely referred to' and that, by inference, the school had 'simply taken [these] in their stride', while, meanwhile, 'they focus on the *higher goals* [our emphasis] of school improvement'. At Columbia School, we are told that the otherwise 'progressively' inclined staff 'appear to have embraced the reform of the last ten years, yet in reality they are antipathetic to much of its thrust'. Interestingly, and not uniquely, we are told that the aims of an older 'progressive platform: child-centred primary education, comprehensive secondary education, anti-racism, a heavy emphasis on equal opportunities' still apply, but that the headteacher's strategy is 'to colonise whatever structures present themselves in pursuit of these aims'.

A similar pragmatism exists at Sutton Centre, where there is a conscious attempt to fuse the 'competitive demands of a stratified society' with the desire that the school should 'play a socially integrative and democratic role, serving the right of all children to develop to their fullest potential'.

In other schools also, there is evidence of a refusal to deny or jettison so-called 'progressive' principles relating, for instance, to equal opportunities, Plowden primary practice or mixed-ability teaching. Equally, however, there is a refusal to be diverted into displays of *Angst* by less welcome elements of government reform, but rather, a readiness to make use of those which are more likely to underpin improvements in pupil performance. Additionally, when so much reform is enshrined in statute, it is part of good management practice to ensure that what is thus a mandatory requirement is clearly understood and, as the Tower Hamlets team put it, 'colonised'.

However, much of the spirit and intention of government reform since 1988 remains contentious and open to mediation and interpretation at the level of the individual school. The notion of an 'educational marketplace' could be characterised *in extremis* by intense competition between schools, with parents treated simply as 'customers' and headteachers acting as 'chief executives'. Such a model does not emerge in these case studies.

What is clear is that parents are most often recruited as partners rather than as customers. In any case, choice of school often does not exist in practice, either because the school is the only one available in the area or because the social and economic pressures and problems experienced are such that exercising school choice is low on the parental agenda. More importantly, many of the schools have identified a pressing need to involve parents both as co-educators and co-learners. Achieving success with pupils *depends* on such a strategy. Lochgelly North, Crowcroft Park, Fair Furlong, Blaengwrach, Sutton Centre and Haywood High all demonstrate this most markedly.

At Fair Furlong, for example, a local community worker observes that the school's success combines high expectations with 'no competitive snobbery . . . a sensitivity to children who don't or can't – no sense of writing children off and a genuine concern for families who can't perform well'. At the same school we are perceptively told about parents who are 'frightened of their kids and have no control over them' or who 'collude with the child's behaviour and don't back up the school'. Working with such parents is clearly vital and necessary; regarding them simply as 'customers' would be both insufficient and inappropriate.

However, the researcher tells us that at Haywood High 'market accountability has been a powerful influence' even though he later observes that 'more powerful accountabilities are at work' in relation to the local community, to the students themselves and within the staff collegium. In Burntwood and St Michael's there is perhaps evidence of a stronger allegiance to the new marketplace. In Burntwood, we are told about the school's attempts to remodel the sixth form so as to retain a larger number of students in competition with local colleges. There is an element of similar thinking in the school's decision to select, by ability, 30 per cent of the intake at age eleven. The reason claimed for doing this is to maintain a balanced, comprehensive intake, but it could also be viewed as a means of reducing the odds against which the school is so admirably succeeding. We need to know who, if anyone, will be denied a place at Burntwood as a result of such change. Interestingly, 'healthy competition' among staff at Burntwood is evinced as a means of promoting good teaching, but reference is also made to a potential or feared growth of a 'staffroom culture' characterised by 'rivalries and cliques'.

At St Michael's, favourable comments from local employers refer to the school's 'visible market success' in being oversubscribed and the effectiveness of the headteacher as a 'charismatic entrepreneurial manager'. Overall, however, there is little evidence that behaviours and processes associated with the idea of an educational marketplace have strongly or overtly contributed to the successes described in the eleven schools. In particular, there is little sense in which competitiveness has played a significant part in the dynamics of change and improvement.

The importance of whole-school policies in how pupils' work is assessed, however, is certainly evident. Other components of the government's reform programme also arise in the analyses of how these schools improved themselves. The National Curriculum and its associated assessment systems appear to have been taken on board without much evidence of anger or resistance. At Sutton Centre, there is a plaintive *cri de coeur* at the deleterious effect on pupil motivation and performance of a government restriction on the coursework element in GCSE syllabuses. However, the critical issue throughout is the intellectual and professional energy deployed in both curricular and pedagogic matters. These teachers do not passively wait to be told what their pupils can or should learn. At Selly Park, the 'high-quality intellectual energy' displayed by the staff is spent equally on the 'what' and the 'how' of teaching and learning. The conventional wisdom that the National Curriculum has now determined the 'what' (curricular content) and that it is for teachers, within the constraints of a national assessment system, to decide the 'how' (teaching methods and pedagogy) is not borne out in these schools. Such a false and undesirable dichotomy is exposed in the strong curricular developments described in all cases. Perhaps the relationship between teachers as innovators and a National Curriculum framework is best stated at Lochgelly North:

> 'The process of constant invention does not mean that there is no repository of expertise or a curricular framework. In fact, there are clear and specific learning targets in line with the national 5–14 guidelines, but geared to addressing each individual need. The translation of these targets into learning and teaching strategies comes about by trying out and sharing good ideas.'

Neither does OFSTED's mission statement, 'improvement through inspection', appear to feature strongly in the development of any of these schools. Perhaps because the schools are now moving in a self-propelled 'virtuous circle' of improvement and development, they will not benefit particularly from OFSTED's national framework for inspection. For what is clear is that particular performance targets and priorities have emerged which are related to each school's previous best and which are relevant to *that*, not just any, school.

While only two schools had experienced an OFSTED inspection and report, they had all (except in Scotland) experienced the publication, locally and nationally, of some performance data about them, through the national league tables. A reasonable assumption is that because most of these schools serve severely disadvantaged communities – and do not appear at the top end of such tables – the impact of publication must be a key issue for teachers, pupils, parents and governors. Thus, one might expect the existence and increasing prominence of 'league tables' and other published data to take up a central position in the schools' improvement strategies. There is little evidence, however, that these assumptions are borne out in practice. The Stoke-on-Trent researchers comment that the data (on examination results, pupil attendance and published student destinations at sixteen) 'probably help to galvanise the staff in its determination to improve', but then express the opinion that of greater importance are the targets defined within the Two Towns Project, mainly because these are set so as to check improvement in relation to the school's 'previous best'.

It is equally surprising that the much greater financial and management responsibility and opportunity accorded through LMS in recent years are not put forward as major factors in school improvement. Having control of at least 85 per cent of the total school budget (and 100 per cent in the case of the two grant-maintained schools) must surely have strengthened and facilitated the schools' sense of a 'can-do' determination to succeed. The improvements to the physical environment are one obvious example of how LMS has enabled priorities and needs identified by the school to be addressed. For instance, we are told that for the development of technology in Selly Park, there is the earmarking of that part of the school budget allocated by the LEA based on entitlements to free school meals.

In other cases, the capacity now to switch resources between different kinds of staffing, books, equipment, small improvements to the building and professional consultancies, including in-service training, must be included as a positive gain from recent government reforms. Of course, such flexibility is necessarily circumscribed by the amount of money available to each school and this in turn depends on policies at both central and local government levels.

A ghost at this particular feast is the governing body. In law, it is the governors who are 'the school' and who now have formal responsibility for a range of important decisions made under their local authority's scheme of delegation (LMS). Broadly similar powers exist in grant-maintained schools where the governing body, not the LEA, is the legal employer. In practice, none of these schools reflect this intended change of emphasis or substance.

Rather, it looks as though the headteachers and their colleagues are firmly in charge of the leadership of and direction taken by the schools. Much support is provided by governors and there is often a tacit sense of governors acting as intermediaries between the internal world of the school and the local community. This 'conduit' function is important but, perhaps, not quite what was foreseen in the original legislation. At Selly Park, however, governors are described as 'active participants in the continuing debate about the school's next steps', and at Hazelwood, the unique way in which the school was established is closely linked to an active board of governors who are 'motivated by a sense of being pioneers'.

The diminished role of the local education authority is a further feature of recent government policy which fails to be clearly enunciated in these studies. Where the school has opted out of its LEA altogether (Burntwood) or opened independently of it (Hazelwood), there is little love lost and a decidedly chill relationship is evident. In other cases, there is no consistent view presented about how, if at all, the local education authority helps or hinders. At Selly Park there is a strong and structured affinity between school and LEA perceptions of school improvement processes. We are also told about the 'critical friend' role of the school's LEA advisers (who are interestingly listed in the staff handbook alongside staff and governors), and two former LEA advisory teachers have been appointed to the staff. Similar but less clear associations between school and LEA are mentioned at Haywood High, Crowcroft Park, Sutton Centre and Columbia. In different ways, the encouragement and climate of improvement provided by the LEA are significant elements of a favourable context for change in such cases. A linked feature is the role played by a 'third party', sometimes recommended by, or in association with, the LEA. At Columbia School, the use of a Grubb Institute consultant is an example of this, as is the Two Towns Project at Haywood High, the employment of independent consultants at Selly Park, and the collaborative inter-school reading programme at Crowcroft Park.

The government's decision to introduce teacher appraisal schemes, starting with headteachers, is another example of a significant national reform having a highly beneficial effect on these schools, but without any indication of the source of funding for such an important development. In this case, the schools' 'colonisation' of the underlying principles has resulted in carefully considered and very effective, but time-consuming, professional development interviews for all staff.

Perhaps the important lesson to be learned is that the energy released in these schools is generated primarily by what the school itself believes it can and must do. Sometimes, beyond this, is a useful LEA or independent consultant, either or both of whom provide an added stimulus as a 'critical friend', a benchmarking device or an additional source of expertise. Similarly, government policy and ensuing statutory requirements are part of the larger context within which the school operates and moves forward. Exploiting and managing these, including those which might be viewed as irritants, is part of the successful school's improvement strategy. Whether the school's leading protagonists *acknowledge* the significance of such external forces is a separate and less important issue.

WHERE NEXT?

From these descriptions of schools which are successful in circumstances which are decidedly unpromising, there are plenty of practical ideas which schools and LEAs can immediately take on board and adapt to their own circumstances. Equally, however, there remain several questions which need to be answered. Further enquiry and research would provide a more secure basis upon which policy could be built and good practice emulated, appropriated and further developed.

For schools serving disadvantaged communities (and for other schools where there is a need to work more positively towards greater success) the many lessons contained in these case studies can be used straight away. The question 'where next?' for a particular school's governing body, headteacher and staff will be answered by means of the kind of hard-edged analysis of the school's current strengths and weaknesses which, in these eleven schools, took place at an early stage in the improvement process. The combining of 'heart and mind' is evidently important in this process – that is to say, the vision, optimism and rhetoric supporting and informing a thoroughgoing review and development of whole-school policies and procedures. These are invariably centred on clarifying what is expected of pupils and staff, and what each has the right to expect of the other and of the headteacher and senior colleagues.

A recurring theme related to this is that everyone in the school needs to be clear about his or her own *role*, whether pupil, teacher, classroom assistant or governor. Equally important is the role of parent and how that role as co-educator, and often co-learner, may be best defined and supported. Systems of communication, of consultation, of debate, and of assessment and reporting of pupils' work to the pupils themselves and to their parents, are also needed. These are significant elements of the improvement strategies described here and are open to adaptation and further development in any school. Again, however, they need to be informed and underwritten by a thoroughgoing commitment, among both teachers and support staff, to the infinite potential for learning and growth in all pupils, as well as in their parents.

Perhaps the best single example of how philosophy and vision combine with a clear enunciation of procedure is found in these schools' approach to praising pupils' efforts and progress. When anxious about an organisation's conditions, it is all too easy to forget the importance of this and its relevance, also, to staff motivation.

Apart from the immediate applicability of the approaches and strategies contained in these case studies, especially for schools and local authorities, there remain at least four areas of further enquiry which should be pursued. These are policy issues which emerge from the case studies and which need to be addressed if schools generally, but especially those in disadvantaged areas, are further to strengthen their position.

A first-order question must address what is meant by 'success'. Although continuous improvement (sometimes steady and some-times in stops and starts) is one kind of success, it is not enough. Indeed, because there is reason to believe that the whole school system needs to perform at a higher level than currently in terms of some key international indicators, and that the gap between our highest and lowest performers is too great, it follows that a special effort is needed in schools serving disadvantaged areas. The reason for this is that low educational performance remains closely linked to social and economic disadvantage in Britain, as elsewhere. The intelligence and talents of children who experience problems of disadvantage are no different from those of any other children, and it is a matter of both justice and equity, as well as of expedience, that we enable them to grow and flourish. Throughout these descriptions, there are tantalising glimpses of how much difference is made to the self-image and optimism of whole communities when a school gets itself on to an upward-moving escalator. Without doubt, the social and cultural impact of children's success, in terms of their increased capabilities, skills and knowledge, should not be under-estimated or viewed sentimentally. The longer-term reconstruction of damaged and frequently distressed communities depends, to a significant degree, on advancements in the human capital available to an area.

However, the schools that work under such circumstances need to decide what pupil outcomes they are aiming for, beyond year-on-year improvements. For instance, how applicable are the revised National Targets for Education and Training? By the start of the next millennium at least 85 per cent of nineteen-year-olds should have acquired five GCSE subjects, grades A*–C, or their GNVQ or

NVQ equivalent. For students at age sixteen, the three most disadvantaged secondary schools in our studies currently perform on this criterion at below 30 per cent.

A further national target is for 60 per cent of young people, by age twenty-one, to have achieved two GCE 'A' level passes, or their vocational equivalent. Such national targets need actively to be taken on board and pursued by schools and other education and training agencies in areas of disadvantage. Primary and nursery schools, as well as schools and colleges, will want to think hard about the relevance and achievability of such targets and how they should be included in their own development plans. What, for instance, do such national assessment targets mean at Key Stages 1 and 2, in a school where most children do not speak English at home or whose earliest years may have been spent with a non-communicative child-minder? Would such national targets be consigned to a distant horizon in a secondary school whose basic priority is to achieve better attendance, punctuality and homework completion among pupils in order that a lower GCSE target, at least, may be secured? These and other questions are the concern of schools serving disadvantaged areas, but in order that the multiple handicaps experienced by children and their families are lessened, strategies are also needed which extend beyond the remit and capacity of schools.

This leads to a second set of issues which relate to the 'odds' side of our equation. While it is nothing less than heroic that the schools whose stories are told here make such a difference to so many children and their families, it is also unreasonable to leave it at that. Do the odds against which schools succeed need to be so great? If it is true – as at least three of our schools suggest – that parenting skills are woefully lacking, should it be for the schools, alone, to take action? Schools are probably in the best position to work with parents so that, in partnership, home and school can be at their most effective in stimulating children's learning. However, identifying best practice and funding such developments should not be left to schools alone. Further enrichment of learning needs to be community based, and, while frequently connected with schools and colleges, other agencies also need to be involved. For children who live in areas of multiple disadvantage, these studies suggest that their learning can go so far, and no further, *unless* parents (especially) are actively involved as co-learners and co-educators. Some local framework of support and facilitation is needed for this to happen. If the idea of a 'learning society' is to be realised, then its true value and purpose will be tested in the disadvantaged communities described here. An alliance of schools, colleges, churches, voluntary groups and business is required if any kind of serious educational attack is to be launched on behalf of, and with, such communities.

In the Lochgelly North study, the portrait of Mark is not simply an isolated, extreme example of why we need alliances which extend beyond the period of statutory schooling. We are reminded that

> 'success for the individual is measured by what the community and the wider society can do to sustain and promote growth, to maintain the quality of relationships and opportunities for achievement and fulfilment. The danger is that these particularly vulnerable young people who have enjoyed such a high quality of care in childhood and adolescence will, as adults, find their expectations sadly deceived.'

The accountability of the community to its schools is thus as important as the accountability of the school to its community. The roles and tasks of each need to be clearly understood and carried out on the basis that they are complementary but distinct.

The large-scale research project on local governance, funded and commissioned by the Economic and Social Research Council, will have reported by 1997 and should further illuminate the nature of this crucial relationship (for more information see reference to Ranson *et al.*, page 12, at note 9). Among the twenty-seven distinct projects within the research programme, there is one which examines new forms of education management in seventeen disadvantaged areas, covering over 350 schools. Already it is clear from early transcripts that there are findings and observations that will reinforce much of the work presented here. We are reminded, for example, of the different forms educational success can take in such areas as the Easterhouse housing development in Glasgow, or Moss Side in Manchester, where regular school attendance is, for some young people, a huge achievement.

> 'The scale of unemployment means that many young people on these estates never become acquainted with the disciplines and routines which go with work – of getting up in the morning and leaving the house on time. Children are often the only people in the family who have to get up and get out of the house in the morning. There is a prevailing sense of a lost tradition of work which once provided people's lives with a sense of orderliness.'

Such 'odds' need to be thoroughly understood if educational success is to be properly calibrated and seized. In line with our own conclusions, one of the principal researchers, Professor Stuart Ranson, comments:

> 'The conditions for young people taking themselves and thus their learning seriously depend upon the school establishing a vision of achievement and practices of learning which are shared by teachers, the different parent communities and the young themselves. Schools can transform the way in which young people think of themselves and what they are capable of achieving when shared values – of the highest expectations of potential, belief in capacity, and value of cultural difference – are invested in agreed practices of learning and teaching.'

Beyond these two issues of what exactly constitutes educational success in disadvantaged areas and the policy implications of the school in its community, a third focus for further enquiry relates to headteachers. In these case studies, we learn very little about how these key agents of change came to acquire their present level of skill, empathy and 'intuitive' judgements. Only at Burntwood and, less fully, at Fair Furlong are we given some clues about the previous career experiences of the headteachers. Perhaps it is significant that both had worked in more advantaged, middle-class areas in their earlier careers, but without much more detailed and systematic data across all eleven schools it is not possible to build up the kind of career (or personality) profile that is needed. In hindsight, it would also have been helpful and probably instructive if the business representative in each of the visiting teams had been more precisely asked to comment on management and leadership processes. In the case of Columbia School, the BP commentator shows us what could have been more fully achieved through such an exercise. It may well be the case that what is happening in these schools is, quite simply, good management in a generic sense. This does not mean that effective headteachers can manage without a powerful and well-articulated educational philosophy, probably centred on what amounts to an obsession with the nature of successful teaching and learning. However, there is presumably a body of skills and knowledge concerning good management which is general rather than professionally specific or, indeed, specific to schools in disadvantaged areas.

The way in which headteachers and other leading professionals in schools are nurtured and developed has been identified by the National Commission as a matter of real concern. Allied to their professional development is the selection and appointment system for headteachers, currently a random and pot-luck affair at best. Quite apart from the high level of public investment involved, it is clear from all studies of school effectiveness that top of the list of required characteristics is the quality of school leadership and management. However, from these case studies it is far from obvious that there exists a sufficiently robust or analytical template of characteristics, skills and experience which could provide an agreed context within which the professional development or selection of headteachers might safely proceed.

The staff profile more generally might also be a matter for further investigation in these schools. Again, the authors were not asked to provide any detail about this, and it is interesting that the gender, age and ethnic composition of staff were not advanced by any of the schools as a key issue, and neither was the composition of the governing body. Given that several of the schools subscribe to and support policies which seek to promote equal opportunities and equity, these data omissions are slightly perplexing.

A fourth and final area of analysis which would benefit from further work relates to the pace of school improvement. In particular, some of the evidence presented here concerning outcomes suggests that it cannot be assumed that a steadily upward curve of improvement is to be expected. At Sutton Centre, Haywood High and Selly Park, in particular, it is often a matter of 'two steps forward, one step back'. At Selly Park, the 'gold standard' of five GCSE subjects at grades A*–C stubbornly held at between 5 and 11 per cent until the headteacher's 'touch and go' year, when the figure rose to 29 per cent. More needs to be understood about these data and about what, in these circumstances, is meant by the term 'trend'.

Related to this, there appear to be distinct stages in a school's improvement process. Initially, morale and self-esteem are raised, often aided and abetted by clearer expectations concerning pupil behaviour and study habits. The earlier improvements in *outcomes* are probably those associated with pupil attendance and behaviour while, at a later stage, better academic results show through. If there is any truth to this model then more needs to be understood about it and more recent, hurried strategies concerning 'failing schools' rethought. The public spotlight, if focused too strongly and too quickly on better academic outcomes (SATs or GCSE results), could well be an unreasonable, unrealistic expectation. Equally, the extent to which such schools are not fully 'inclusive', by virtue of selecting their intake (or by excluding pupils more than very rarely for unacceptable behaviour), must be considered before too many conclusions are drawn about 'success'.

Thus, the nature of school improvement, especially in areas where the odds are stacked against smooth or rapid changes, has yet to be thoroughly understood and measured in a sensible and sensitive way. As these studies show, the application of comparable indicators of disadvantage (such as poverty, unemployment, English as a second language) conceals many degrees of challenge and difficulty. The upward curve of improvement at Burntwood or St Michael's is hard won and impressive, but differently pitched and timed from that at Selly Park, Fair Furlong or Crowcroft Park. We need to be clear about why this is so and what, if anything, could be done to maintain and accelerate that upward rate of improvement.

It is clear, then, that there is plenty to be gained by further enquiry into how schools succeed. But the major lesson of this study is already plain for all to see. It is that *every* school has the opportunity to succeed against the odds. None of the schools studied holds itself out as exceptional or puts success down to any particularly gifted individual. Nor does the possibility of success arise as a once-for-all, 'gift-wrapped' opportunity. On the contrary, it arises every day in a hundred different ways, large and small, and what matters is that the school should form a consistent habit of creating or taking advantage of these fleeting opportunities. It is the steady accumulation day on day, and week on week, of positive progress which emerges so clearly.

Moreover, it is clear too that the will-power of one strong leader, such as the headteacher, or even of a determined management team, is important but not in itself enough. Improvement is achieved by the whole school: by the teachers, but also by the pupils; by all the staff, not only the teachers; and by the parents and the wider community. The whole process, moreover, in time generates a momentum of its own that itself catches up and involves all concerned, imparting back to them an enthusiasm and commitment that perhaps many of those involved did not know that they possessed.

At the very heart of the professionalism of the headteacher and all other teachers lies that sense of the need to set in motion processes which lead to achievement of a goal: the learning of pupils, and hence their growth towards the fulfilment of their true capabilities. The fascination of these studies lies in the way they demonstrate how the goal can be achieved, no matter what the obstacles.

APPENDIX A
Guidelines for authors

THE PROJECT

Success Against the Odds involves teams from all four countries of the United Kingdom examining schools in disadvantaged areas which are believed to be particularly effective. Every team consists of an educationist, someone from the business world, and someone involved in local regeneration outside education.

All three members of each team will have important contributions to make. The educationist will provide in-depth knowledge of effective teaching and learning and school improvement. The business person will provide insight into the successful management of an organisation and the relationship between schools and the world of work. The person involved in regeneration will provide a perspective that recognises that education takes place in a multi-agency context where schools operate within and interact with a local community.

RESEARCH METHODS

Each team will evaluate why its chosen school is successful and investigate how it has become so. Prior to visiting the school, it will be helpful for the teams to examine statistics relating to the school, inspectorate reports, school development plans and other background documents.

Visits to the school will need to include both interviews and observations.

Any or all of the following might be included in the round of interviews: the headteacher, the teaching staff, the pupils, parents and governors (including parent governors and business representatives). Interviews with senior staff and governors should be open, wide-ranging and in-depth. Care should be taken to ensure that retrospective accounts of actions that led to school improvement are fair and accurate. Sensitive information – for example, relating to difficult decisions that may have been made in relation to staffing – can be included in our general report on the project without reference to the individual school. This should be put across to interviewees who may in some cases be encouraged to speak off the record.

Observations might, where possible, include lessons, extracurricular activities, assemblies and, where possible, staff meetings.

FOCUS FOR INVESTIGATION

It is expected that the investigation and its report will cover the five areas (A to E) set out below.

A Background information about the school, its achievements, its environment and the community it serves

To limit the burden placed upon the schools we are enclosing a form on which for you to obtain basic data about the school (either from the LEA or from the school itself). Most of the information is required by OFSTED for pre-inspection reports. Other background information will be needed as appropriate, relating to, for example:

- staff (e.g., responsibilities, turnover over recent years, gender- and age-profile);

- school buildings (age, condition, repairs outstanding);
- admissions procedures, the school's catchment area, and, if relevant, the extent of competition for pupils with other schools;
- the area in which the school is located.

B A description of the life and work of the school

We ask that as a guide to your investigation of the attitudes and procedures of the school, you make particular reference to the ten postulated features of success in *Learning to Succeed* which formed the basis for the proposals for raising achievement in the chapter on 'Successful Schools for All':

1 Strong, positive leadership by the head and senior staff.
2 A good atmosphere or spirit, generated both by shared aims and values and by a physical environment that is as attractive and stimulating as possible.
3 High and consistent expectations of all pupils.
4 A clear and continuing focus on teaching and learning.
5 Well-developed procedures for assessing how pupils are progressing.
6 Responsibility for learning shared by the pupils themselves.
7 Participation by pupils in the life of the school.
8 Rewards and incentives to encourage pupils to succeed.
9 Parental involvement in children's education and in supporting the aims of the school.
10 Extra-curricular activities which broaden pupils' interests and experiences, expand their opportunities to succeed, and help to build good relationships within the school.

Of course, there are bound to be other features of success in the school which you will wish to investigate and draw attention to.

C School policy

Aspects of school policy and resource allocation may need to be considered in some depth, for example:

- development planning, the process of school management, staffing practices, staff development;
- teaching methods, classroom organisation, curriculum and assessment policy, guidance and learning support, special needs strategies;
- community and business links, extent to which the school motivates pupils for the world of work;
- educational technology and other innovation;
- school policy towards truancy and bullying;
- external intervention and/or support (e.g., from LEA, inspection bodies or higher education institutions).

D Accountability in the school

An important question to address is what accountability means to different people in the school and whether they think it matters, in order to relate the success of the school to people's perceptions of it. The various ways in which the school is accountable (both formal and informal) should be examined. For what is the school accountable and to whom? How is this accountability made manifest, how is this perceived by different people and to what extent are motivation and performance affected? Issues might include:

- the degree of openness of financial decisions;
- publication of school outcomes and the repercussions of this on the school's approach;
- the processes of monitoring, target-setting, review and evaluation;
- the effect of the inspection system;
- the extent to which the school responds to the demands of

parents, governors, community, business, other schools and colleges (including those in other phases), the LEA and central government;
• the ways in which teachers relate to pupils and parents in terms of 'first-line' professional accountability.

E School improvement

What characterises the improvement that has taken place, and who were the key people in this process?

• This might include descriptions of particular initiatives taken by the school; what their precise objectives were, how they related to the problems recognised, what they aimed for in concrete terms and what their results have been.
• Reference to previous actions will be necessary, as will an indication of actions necessary to maintain and improve present achievements.
• It may be the case that off-the-record discussions will be necessary to elicit information about decisions relating to staff who were under-performing or who were resistant to change.
• The role of the governing body in the life of the school and its contribution to the improvement process should be explicitly addressed.
• Accounts of how success has been achieved must get beyond the descriptive approach and analyse the *process* of change.
• It would also be useful if key small but symbolic events or characteristics that have reinforced the school's mission and expectations could be picked out.

REPORTS

Each team is asked to write an account of between 5,000 and 8,000 words of how the school has become successful and why they think that it has become so.

These accounts will be edited and collected in a book which will also include an introductory chapter on the difficulties faced by education in disadvantaged areas and conclude with a section drawing out key themes and lessons from the case studies.

APPENDIX B

Terminology used in case studies

It is hoped that this section may, in the light of the many radical changes in education since the passing of the 1988 Education Reform Act (ERA), be of value to readers both in the United Kingdom and overseas.

- The **National Curriculum** has had an extended period of gestation. It consists of four **Key Stages (KS)**, each appropriate to an age group: KS1 applies to pupils aged five to seven (Years 1 and 2) with an expectation that, of the ten attainment levels, the great majority of pupils will achieve levels in the core subjects (English, mathematics and science) in the range 1–3 by the end of the Key Stage; KS2 ends with Year 6 (age eleven) and expects a range of 2–5; and so on. Although there are attainment levels for KS4 for Years 10 and 11, external examinations at sixteen are currently of greater significance. For each of the ten subjects there is a precise programme of study and at the end of each Key Stage there are **standard attainment tasks (SATs)** taken by all pupils.

- In 1992 the **Office for Standards in Education (OFSTED)** was created, largely replacing **Her Majesty's Inspectorate (HMI)**, a body that both inspected schools and colleges and gave independent advice to the Department of Education and Science (DES), later called the **Department for Education (DfE)** and now named the **Department For Education and Employment (DFEE)**. Under OFSTED, schools are inspected every four years by private teams selected by registered inspectors who have undergone rigorous selection and training, and who may include head-teachers and teachers in service. All parents receive a summary of the team's report, and governors must draw up a timed action plan to remedy failings indicated in the report.

- The **examination system** has experienced the successful amalgamation into the 16+ **General Certificate of Secondary Education (GCSE)** of the post-war General Certificate of Education (GCE 'O' level) and the Certificate of Secondary Education (CSE) instituted in the mid-1960s for those pupils for whom the GCE syllabuses were considered unsuitable. There is now a substantial swing from the GCSE at 16+ and from Advanced Level at 18+ towards a wide range of vocationally orientated subjects. The entry for the foundation level of the **General National Vocational Qualifications (GNVQs)** is growing rapidly for school pupils aged fourteen to sixteen who wish for a technical and vocational bias to their learning. The vocational qualifications can be pursued currently at three levels (Foundation, Intermediate, Advanced), and pilots for a Part One GNVQ (worth two GCSEs and taken at age fourteen) are being introduced into selected schools.

- ERA introduced far-reaching changes in the **governance of schools**. Governing bodies now have extensive responsibilities for and powers over the deployment of the school budget through **local management of schools (LMS)**. The powers of the **local education authority (LEA)** are now largely restricted to the provision of central services.

- In the past fifteen years **in-service education and training (INSET)** for serving teachers has become increasingly important. First, the growing concern about the need for secondary schools to introduce the **Technical and Vocational Education Initiative (TVEI)** into the curriculum for older pupils led to extensive funding for **TVEI-related INSET (TRIST)** to reskill teachers and curriculum managers. Second, following an increased awareness of the needs created by the rate of the introduction of organisational and managerial change, funding under specific heads was made available to LEAs through DES circulars. Third, there was built into teacher contracts a requirement to take part in a specified number of school-based training days each year. Fourth, following ERA, schools received as part of their consolidated budget a **Grant for Education Support and Training (GEST)**, that they could use at their discretion.

• When LEAs determined the staffing of schools, partly on a formula basis and partly by recognising particular needs, there was a growth in the numbers of non-teaching classroom assistants. In nursery schools, and in nursery and reception classes in primary schools, assistants to the teacher qualified through the **Nursery Nurses Examinations Board (NNEB)** training were employed, and still are though their continued employment is now dependent on the school's consolidated budget. Second, as children with physical handicaps and statements of special educational needs (**SENs**) were increasingly being accommodated in mainstream schools, general assistants were appointed. Third, the need for education support in small groups for children of immigrant families where the mother tongue was not English was, albeit tardily, recognised by the employment of what are known as **Section 11** teachers, who help children to bridge from their home language to the medium of instruction in their schools. These teachers often also perform a valuable role in home–school liaison with, in particular, Asian families.

• Schools in the public sector are described as **maintained** unless they have religious affiliations, when they are known as

voluntary aided. ERA gave parents of children in state schools the opportunity to ballot in order to opt out of local government control. These schools are known as **grant-maintained** and are funded indirectly from central government. The financial advantages of grant-maintained status have become less attractive and parents are increasingly voting to remain in local control.

INDEX